# Government Regulation of Accounting and Information

Edited by

A. Rashad Abdel-khalik

Proceedings of a Conference
sponsored by
The Accounting Research Center
of
The College of Business Administration
University of Florida

(under a grant from the Peat,
Marwick, Mitchell Foundation)

University of Florida
Accounting Series Number 11

[Round Table Conference on Government Regulation of accounting and Information]

UNIVERSITY PRESSES OF FLORIDA
FAMU/FAU/FIU/FSU/UCF/UF/UNF/USF/UWF
Gainesville

University of Florida Accounting Series No. 11
A. Rashad Abdel-khalik, Series Editor

School of Accounting, University of Florida
Robert F. Lanzillotti, Dean
John K. Simmons, Director



University Presses of Florida is the central agency for scholarly publishing of the State of Florida's university system. Its offices are located at 15 NW 15th Street, Gainesville, FL 32603. Works published by University Presses of Florida are evaluated and selected for publication by a faculty editorial committee of any one of Florida's nine public universities: Florida A&M University (Tallahassee), Florida Atlantic University (Boca Raton), Florida International University (Miami), Florida State University (Tallahassee), University of Central Florida (Orlando), University of Florida (Gainesville), University of North Florida (Jacksonville), University of South Florida (Tampa), University of West Florida (Pensacola).

**Library of Congress Cataloging in Publication Data**

Round Table Conference on Government Regulation of Accounting and Information, University of Florida, 1979.

Regulation of accounting.
(University of Florida accounting series ; no. 11)
Conference was held in 1979 at the University of Florida.
Includes bibliographical references.
1. Accounting – United States – Congresses. 2. Accounting – Law and legislation – United States – Congresses. 3. Government paperwork – United States – Costs – Congresses. I. Abdel-khalik, A. Rashad. II. Florida. University, Gainesville. Accounting Research Center. III. Title. IV. Series: Florida. University, Gainesville. School of Accounting. University of Florida accounting series ; no. 11.
HF6501.F55 no.11 [HF5616.U5] 657'.08s [657]
ISBN 0-8130-0663-5 79–26555

PRINTED IN THE U. S. A.

# Contents

Preface v

Participants vii

Session 1

Corporate Cost for Compliance with Government Regulation of Information, by Rogene A. Buchholz 1

Comment by Yuji Ijiri 56

Comment by Raymond E. Perry 63

Session 2

The SEC and Financial Reporting: The Sand in the Oyster, by John C. Burton 74

Comment by George R. Catlett 91

Comment by Ross L. Watts 96

Session 3

Regulation of Accounting: Practitioner's Viewpoint, by Robert K. Elliott and Walter Schuetze 104

Comment by Raymond C. Lauver 133

Comment by Douglas H. Thompson, Jr. 140

Comment by Stephen A. Zeff 165

Reply by Robert D. Elliott and Walter Schuetze 199

Session 4

Would Market Forces Cause Adequate Securities Disclosure without SEC Mandate? by Homer Kripke 202

Comment by Russell M. Barefield 225

Comment by Felix Pomeranz 231

Session 5

The Effect of State Accounting and Auditing Regulations on Municipal Borrowing Costs and Bond Ratings, by Wanda A. Wallace 241

Comment by Paul Rosenfield 289

Comment by Katherine Schipper 295
Reply by Wanda A. Wallace 304

Session 6
Synthesis, by Nicholas Dopuch 307

## Preface

This eleventh volume of the University of Florida's Accounting Series contains the proceedings of the Round-Table Conference held at the University of Florida on March 30-31, 1979. The theme of the conference, "Government Regulation of Accounting and Information," is a timely topic in view of the intense involvement of regulators characteristic of the environment of the past few years.

To illustrate, the Securities and Exchange Commission has issued more disclosure regulations in the form of Accounting Series Releases since 1972 than in its entire history. In addition, the hearings held by subcommittees of the Senate and House of Representatives about the so-called accounting establishment have clearly heightened the interest in debating government regulation versus self-regulation of professions (*Accounting and Auditing Practices and Procedures*, Hearings before the Subcommittee on Reports, Accounting, and Management of the Committee on Governmental Affairs, U.S. Senate [Washington, 1977]; *Reform and Self-Regulation Efforts of the Accounting Profession*, Hearings before the Subcommittee on Oversight and Investigations of the Committee on Interstate and Foreign Commerce, House of Representatives [Washington, 1978]). Other federal regulations of paperwork added fuel to the debate.

The objective of the conference was to provide a forum that would facilitate the exchange of ideas and the understanding of alternative views. For this reason each session was organized in such a way that its participants espoused different points of view on the subject. This arrangement encouraged a free and constructive exchange of ideas and enhanced the achievement of the conference objectives.

In addition to the papers in this volume, Arlene Hershman and Patricia Pride presented thoughtful ideas which were not formally prepared for inclusion.

On behalf of the School of Accounting, I would like to express deep appreciation to the authors and the participants who have generously contributed their thoughts and time. I would also like to acknowledge the financial support of the Peat, Marwick, Mitchell Foundation, the assistance of Sylvia Wrobel in preparing the manuscript, and the staff of the University Presses of Florida.

A. Rashad Abdel-khalik
Director
Accounting Research Center

## Participants

| Name | Affiliation |
|---|---|
| A. Rashad Abdel-khalik | University of Florida (Conference Director) |
| Russell Barefield | University of Arizona |
| Rogene Buchholz | Washington University |
| John C. Burton | Columbia University |
| George Catlett | Arthur Andersen & Co. |
| Eugene Comiskey | Purdue University |
| Daniel S. Dhaliwal | University of Iowa |
| Nicholas Dopuch | University of Chicago |
| Robert Elliott | Peat, Marwick, Mitchell & Co. |
| Marvin Feller | Ernst & Ernst |
| Natwar Gandhi | U.S. General Accounting Office |
| Arlene Hershman | Dun's Review |
| Gary L. Holstrum | Deloitte, Haskins & Sells |
| Yuji Ijiri | Carnegie-Mellon University |
| Robert Jensen | Florida State University |
| Orace Johnson | University of Illinois/V.P.I. |
| Homer Kripke | New York University |
| Harold Langenderfer | University of North Carolina |
| Robert Lanzillotti | University of Florida |
| Raymond Lauver | Price Waterhouse & Co. |
| Wesley Magat | Duke University |
| Benjamin Makela | Financial Executives Research Foundation |
| Robert K. Mautz | University of Michigan |
| S.D. McElyea | U.S. General Accounting Office |
| James L. Nelligan | (Staff) U.S. House of Representatives |
| Raymond Perry | Touche Ross & Co. |
| Felix Pomeranz | Coopers & Lybrand |
| Patricia Pride | Financial Accounting Standards Board |
| Joshua Ronen | New York University |
| Paul Rosenfield | American Institute of Certified Public Accountants |
| Clarence Sampson | Securities and Exchange Commission |
| Katherine Schipper | Carnegie-Mellon University |
| Walter Schuetze | Peat, Marwick, Mitchell & Co. |
| John K. Shank | Ohio State University |
| Barbara J. Shildneck | Journal of Accountancy |
| John K. Simmons | University of Florida |
| David Solomons | University of Pennsylvania |
| Gary Sundem | University of Washington |
| Douglas Thompson, Jr. | Florida State Board of Accountancy |
| Wanda Wallace | University of Rochester |
| Ross Watts | University of Rochester |
| Thomas H. Williams | University of Wisconsin |
| Stephen A. Zeff | Rice University |

Also in attendance were members of the Steering Committee and of the faculty of the School of Accounting.

UNIVERSITY OF FLORIDA ACCOUNTING SERIES

No. 1 Financial and Managerial Reporting by Certified Public Accountants
62 pp., 1963

No. 2 Annotated Bibliography of Electronic Data Processing
52 pp., 1968

No. 3 The American Accounting Association--Sponsored Statements of Standards for Corporate Reports, A Perspective
by Harvey T. Deinzer
52 pp., 1964

No. 4 Aspects of Contemporary Accounting
83 pp., 1968

No. 5 Methodological Presuppositions in Financial Accounting Models
by Harvey T. Deinzer
99 pp., 1968

No. 6 Theory Formulations
edited by Williard E. Stone
97 pp., 1970

No. 7 Foundations of Accounting Theory
edited by Williard E. Stone
163 pp., 1971

No. 8 The Accountant in a Changing Business Environment
edited by Williard E. Stone
82 pp., 1973

No. 9 Financial Reporting Techniques in 20 Industrial Companies Since 1861
by Richard Vangermeersch
100 pp., 1979

No. 10 Disclosure Criteria and Segment Reporting
edited by Russell M. Barefield and Gary L. Holstrum
176 pp., 1979

No. 11 Government Regulation of Accounting and Information
edited by A. Rashad Abdel-khalik
320 pp., 1979

# Corporate Cost For Compliance With Government Regulation Of Information

Rogene A. Buchholz

Washington University

## Introduction

The corporate cost for compliance with government regulation of information, particularly on the federal level, is a matter of concern to many people. The most visible aspect of this cost is paperwork. Recently the private sector has become concerned about the growth of paperwork, as some corporations study its impact on their organization.[1]

The first part of this paper focuses on the paperwork cost during the 1977 calendar year for a large multinational corporation headquartered in the United States. Such a case study can show in detail what paperwork consists of, categorize it in some meaningful fashion, and assign cost figures. This study deals with the paperwork cost of complying with federal government regulation of information only, exclusive of corporate tax reports which are related more to the revenue raising function of government than to the regulatory function.

The second part of the paper deals with other costs that the company faces because of government regulation of information. These include such costs as the effect of regulation on innovation, those involved in avoiding information disclosure, organization changes caused by regulation of information, and the impact of regulation on management decision-making. While these costs cannot be measured in any systematic fashion, their importance can be examined and pointed out.

## Paperwork Costs

### Background

The Federal Paperwork Commission, formed to study the cost of paperwork to society and to make recommendations for the elimination of needless paperwork, estimated that the cost of federal paperwork for the entire country was in the neighborhood of $100 billion a year, about $500 for each person in the country. The costs imposed on private industry alone were estimated to be approximately $25-$32 billion per year. The 10,000 largest firms were estimated to spend $10-$12 billion on paperwork, or an average of over $1 million each.[2]

Other figures also demonstrate the overall impact of federal paperwork. Estimates given the Federal Paperwork Commission at public hearings held throughout the country indicated that some 10 billion sheets of paper a year are filled out by business organizations, enough to fill more than 4 million cubic feet of file space.[3] The file space used by the federal government for fiscal year 1976 totaled 12.8 million cubic feet to store the annual average of over 320,000 tons of paper the government accumulates in a typical year.[4]

The government's regulation of business information is, of course, related to its involvement in the economy. Prior to 1930, the government imposed minimal paperwork burdens on business organizations. Before the New Deal, the federal government was not, for the most part, directly involved in social and economic matters affecting the country, and the regulation of information reflected this situation.

In the period of the New Deal, foundations were laid for increased government participation in the economy. This trend continued through World War II as government's role in the economy increased because of its financing the war effort and regulation of the economy by price controls and rationing. An increased paperwork burden accompanied this increased government intervention. Business organizations supplied the nation with needed goods and services, but they also filled out more and more forms required by government bureaucracies.

Figure 1.1 shows the increase in the cost of paperwork to the federal government from 1950 to the present.[5] The data for this chart come from various attempts to control paperwork made by the federal government, in addition to those of the Paperwork Commission.[6] The big jump in the early 1970s set off the current concern about paperwork costs. This jump is explained by looking at the new agencies and programs established by the federal government in 1970-74, most of which still function in some form. These are shown in table 1.1.[7]

In theory, the Office of Management and Budget is supposed to control federal paperwork. The Federal Reports Act of 1942 set up a review process within government. As it currently operates, any government agency that wants to collect data from ten or more person (persons are defined to include individuals, corporations, associations, and so on), on either a repetitive or a one-time basis, must obtain approval from the Regulatory Policy and Reports Management Division of the OMB. A form called "Clearance Request and Notification of Action" specifies the nature of the data to be collected and the estimated respondent burden, that is, the number of responses and man-hours required to complete the form. Theoretically, a form may not be used at all if OMB does not review and approve it and must not be used past an OMB specified expiration date.[8]

There is no evidence that this review process has decreased federal paperwork. During fiscal year 1972, for example, a total of 2,193 repetitive-use forms were submittend to the OMB for review. Only 22 were disapproved--a bare 1 percent of the total. In the same year, 724 single-use forms were submitted for review and all but 30 (4.1 percent) were given OMB approval.[9]

## Categories of Information Disclosure

The paperwork burden is, of course, a result of requests for information from the federal government. An information request has been defined as "any request from the federal government which requires the respondent to respond, organize, or maintain information for use by a federal government initiator."[10] This study is concerned with the standard forms, usually repetitive-use, that have to be filled out by a company. These forms can be categorized according to the type of information requested.

Much of the information requested is simply *statistical information* such as a summary of yearly plant operations, turnover, and so forth, that goes, for example, to the Bureau of Census or Bureau of Labor Statistics. This statistical information is not used for purposes of control, but most likely is aggregated with the same type of information from other companies and reported by the government in this fashion.

*Financial information* can take the form of reports filed with the Federal Trade Commission or the annual report general form, better known as the 10K, filed with the Securities and Exchange Commission. Information related to the *personnel and benefits* area of a company concerns those aspects of pension plans that companies now have to disclose, affirmative action plans required of government contractors, and equal employment reports disclosing the number of minorities and women employed in various occupational categories.

The type of *environmental information* requested will, of course, vary by kind of industry. If the company is discharging pollutants into the air or water, it may be required to report this aspect of its operations. If it manufactures chemicals which government agencies consider to be toxic, it is currently required to inventory its current production and report this to the federal government. Once this inventory is finished, it will then be required to report periodically on detailed scientific data for all new chemicals that are developed.

*Safety and health* information related to occupational injuries and illnesses, while not sent directly to a federal government agency, is required to be maintained at each plant or workplace of a company. These records are subject to review by government inspectors.

The disclosure of *energy information* is a growing area because of the energy problem facing the United States and the creation of a new federal Department of Energy. Energy information can take the form of disclosure of domestic natural gas reserves, domestic crude oil purchases, and so on. Information related to *agricultural chemicals* is required for the purpose of regulating the use, testing, and sale of pesticides. Finally there is *miscellaneous information*, any that does not fit into one of the other categories. The reports presented in this study will be organized into these categories of information disclosure.

## Types of Paperwork Costs

The Paperwork costs associated with information disclosure can be divided roughly into start-up costs and reporting costs (see table 1.2). Start-up costs are involved when there has to be some effort to determine exactly what is required by a federal agency. The explanation accompanying the information request may be vague and require discussion and interpretation. Extreme cases involve travel to government offices to discuss the requirements. When new types of information are involved, other starting-up costs arise. The information requested may not be readily available in existing reports or computer files if it is different from what the company normally requires for its own operations. Thus a new system may have to be installed to supply the information to the federal government, which can mean new computer programs or the creation of new computer files. In addition, people may have to be trained to fill out the forms and supply the right information.

Reporting costs refer to employee time involved in filling out reports, computer expense, hiring of consultants, lawyers, accountants, or other professionals to prepare reports, miscellaneous costs if applicable, and some indirect costs. Most of these are variable and depend in part on the frequency with which the report has to be completed and sent to a federal agency. Ideally the one-time start-up costs associated with any given report should not be completely charged to the year incurred. An estimate could be made regarding the life of the report and then some straight-line or accelerated method used to allocate and spread the start-up cost over the life of the report.

## Methodology of Costing Paperwork

In practice, it is impossible to recover or systematically deal with start-up costs for reports that have been filled out on a routine basis for some years. Most companies have not had any reason to keep account of these costs in a fashion that would be useful for purposes of costing paperwork.

The company under study here, however, was involved in complying with the new Toxic Substances Control Act, which requires inventory reporting. This one-time effort is a start-up cost because the inventory has to be completed before routine reporting of toxic substances can begin. Estimates of inventory reporting costs, which were entirely related to paperwork, will be presented in a separate section of the report.

Reporting costs are thus the only category of costs that can be reported in a systematic fashion. In most instances only direct labor costs and indirect costs were calculated. Any computer costs were included in the indirect costs for practical reasons, and there were few contractual or miscellaneous costs. The first step in calculating direct labor costs is to determine the type of employee who usually completes the reports. Despite the fact that the information the government wants already may exist on some report, this does not mean that numbers from a company report can simply be copied onto the federal forms. Information from many different company reports may have to be gathered in order to fill out completely a single federal form. Then the information may have to be aggregated or disaggregated. Finally, there may be some necessity for interpreting exactly what information is needed.

Thus it was determined in discussion with company managers that whoever was to fill out federal forms needed knowledge of accounting at the level of a B.S. or B.A. degree. This person would also have to have had at least five years experience with the company to know the accounting system and to be aware of existing company reports. The monthly salary of this type of employee was taken as a base figure. A 30 percent salary overhead charge was added for such items as health benefits, social security tax contributed by the employer, pension expenses, and unemployment insurance. This net monthly figure was divided by the average working hours in a month to get an hourly direct labor cost rate.

Indirect costs were than factored in by simply doubling this hourly rate. This was the standard method for calculating the overhead recharge rate, which is defined as the dollars per person-hour charge that a company must apply to compensate for person-hours spent on any office project executed primarily by exempt personnel. It is generally used as a charge-back rate by the corporate office for work done for divisions or subsidiaries. In this case it includes secretarial support costs.

The final result of these calculations is an hourly rate that represents the total reporting cost for complying with an information request from the federal government. This rate can be multiplied by the total time it takes to complete a report to get a total cost per report. The calculation of this rate is summarized in table 1.3.

To find out how many employee hours are involved in filling out forms for the federal government, a questionnaire was sent to the controllers and other personnel in the operating companies or divisions of the organization studied. (The study was limited to the parent company and did not include the subsidiaries.) This questionnaire asked which federal reports the divisions submitted, the reporting interval (monthly, yearly), and the hours involved in filling out each report. These figures were put on an annual basis when necessary (figures for a monthly report were multiplied by 12) and multiplied by the total reporting cost hourly rate to calculate the total annual cost of filling out a federal form. The results of these calculations by report are shown in the appendixes and summarized in the following sections. Calculation of costs other than reporting costs are described in the appropriate sections.

## Reporting Costs By Category By Information Disclosure

### *Statistical Reports*

For the firm studied the total cost of supplying the

federal government with statistical information is $99,270 a year (see table 1.4 and appendix). The bulk of this cost is involved in reporting to the Bureau of the Census: $47,250 or 47.6 percent of the total cost of all statistical reports. Other agencies with a significant percentage of the total cost are the International Trade Commission (20.5 percent), the Bureau of Labor Statistics (12.4 percent), and the Bureau of Economic Analysis (10.0 percent). The most costly report is a summary of yearly plant operations called "Annual Survey of Manufacturers" and filed yearly with the Bureau of the Census. For years ending in 2 or 7 the report is expanded to include details of the items reported, which increases the usual cost fivefold. Although this was true of 1977, the $26,550 figure shown represents a more typical year. Other costly reports are the annual and monthly "Synthetic Organic Chemicals Report," filed with the International Trade Commission at a cost of $10,500 and $9,750, respectively. Finally, a "Monthly Report of Employment, Payroll, and Hours" is sent to the Bureau of Labor Statistics at an annual cost of $7,600. In total, there are 59 statistical reports at an average cost of $1,682 per report.

*Financial Reports*

Financial reports required by the federal government are fewer in number but greater in cost than statistical reports. The 18 reports have a total cost of $136,960 and an average cost of $7,609 a report.

The most expensive report in the financial area is the "Line of Business Report," prepared for the Federal Trade Commission. There has been much controversy about this report, and a decision about it will be made by the Supreme Court in the near future. In the meantime the company prepared the report at a cost of $35,100 for the year. Another costly report is the "Annual Report General Form," better known as the 10K, filed annually with the

Securities and Exchange Commission, at an estimated cost of $22,200 a year.

The main part of the expense in the financial area is in reporting to the Securities and Exchange Commission (52.9 percent of the total cost); the Federal Trade Commission is responsible for 32 percent and the Internal Revenue Service for 12.5 percent. The reports listed for the Internal Revenue Service are those more regulatory in nature than directed to raising revenue--for example, a report on money paid to individuals other than employees. The amount listed also includes a contractual charge of $4,300 as noted in table 1.5.

### *Personnel and Benefits*

The reports in this area go to two agencies, the Department of Labor and the Equal Employment Opportunity Commission. The Department of Labor is responsible for 83.8 percent of the total cost and the Equal Employment Opportunity Commission for the remaining 16.2 percent (see table 1.6).

The most expensive report is the "Annual Report 5500" for salaried and hourly pension plans, filed annually with the Department of Labor as required under the Employee Retirement Income Security Act. This report cost $81,450 to complete and involved 2,715 employee hours. The "Affirmative Action Plans" filed annually with the Office of Federal Contract Compliance Programs of the Department of Labor were also very costly. Lengthy documents which must be prepared and filed for each location of the company, they totaled $45,000 for calendar year 1977. Finally, there is the EEO-1 form, filed annually with the Equal Employment Opportunity Commission. To complete this report, statistics on the employment of minorities and women are gathered at each company location by personnel officials and forwarded to corporate headquarters to be compiled on the appropriate forms, at a cost of $25,650 a year. In total, there are only 13 reports in the personnel and benefits area, but these average $12,159 each.

*Environmental Reports*

The environmental area presents a special problem as far as costing of paperwork is concerned. The reporting in this area is done, by and large, at the plant level because many states are involved in implementing federal laws with respect to air and water pollution control and waste disposal. Since each state's forms and requirements differ, each of the company's 25-30 plants affected by environmental legislation would have to be individually contacted in order to obtain an accurate estimate of paperwork. This proved prohibitive.

However, some data were available at the headquarters level on the types of reports that have to be filed for state and federal agencies and on the overall frequency of reporting (see table 1.7). The highest frequency of reporting concerns waste disposal. Some 105 reports are filed each year at the plant level and an additional 30 reports at the company level. These figures on frequency, however, often bear no relationship to cost. Air and water pollution control information may be much more complex and difficult to obtain and thus more costly. Additional information on these reports is contained in the appendix.

Using these data, an estimate of the cost of environmental reports can be made on the basis of the average time it takes to fill out a report of any type. There are a total of 3,680 environmental reports filed each year, assuming that there are 25 plants involved. The average time spent in filling out a report, using most of the reports for which direct estimates were obtained, is 10 hours. In arriving at this figure, all large reports of over $10,000 were omitted from calculating the average because they would tend to distort the average upward. The single daily report was also omitted because it would tend to distort in the other direction. Thus the average of 10 hours was calculated using 117 of the 137 reports in all the other areas where estimates were obtained. Ten hours times a rate of $30 per hour times the 3,680 reports totals $1,104,000 for the environmental area. This cost will be used in the summary tables.

*Safety and Health*

The regulation of information in the safety and health area takes a different form from the other areas discussed in this paper. There are no forms that have to be filled out on a periodic basis and sent to a federal government agency. The record-keeping or paperwork requirements are for internal purposes only, but deficiencies are subject to monetary penalties.

Two types of safety and health records have to be maintained. The OSHA 200 form is a log and summary of recordable injuries or illnesses occurring in each plant or workplace. This log provides a means for classifying cases of injury and illness and for noting the extent and outcome of each case. A supplementary record (OSHA 101) also has to be maintained for additional information about each injury or illness reported on the 200 form.

These records must be retained in the establishment for five years after the year to which they relate. They can be inspected and copied at any reasonable time by authorized federal or state government representatives. At the time of writing, OSHA was also considering a provision for employee access to the Log and Summary of Occupational Injuries and Illnesses (OSHA 200).

Since these records are kept on a more or less continuous basis, it was not possible to determine the number of hours per year spent filling out each one. It was determined, however, that one person at each "large" plant of the company spent about 10 percent of his or her time maintaining these safety and health records. Since there were about 80 such plants, this amounted to the equivalent of eight full-time people. Two more full-time equivalents were added to this, one to cover the smaller plants and one at headquarters, bringing the estimated total to the equivalent of 10 full-time people involved in maintaining safety and health records throughout the company. This amounted to a cost of \$564,000 (1,880 hrs. x 10 x \$30) in the safety and health area.

*Energy Reports*

Supplying the government with energy information has become a growing area since the creation of the Department of Energy (DOE). All reports that went to the Federal Energy Administration and Federal Power Commission now go to this agency. Fully 91.4 percent of the cost in this area is due to supplying the DOE with energy information; 8.5 percent is accounted for by reports filed with the U.S. Geological Survey in the Department of the Interior, and one very small report goes to the Bureau of Mines (see table 1.8).

Included in the Department of Energy figures are two direct labor costs that cannot be broken down by report. Information requests from the DOE are so complex that they require the services of a manager and a lawyer to interpret the requests and to inform those who complete the forms what is required. These costs were estimated at \$56,400 (1,880 hours x \$40/hour) for calendar year 1977. The company also had to provide an employee to aid two full-time government auditors who reviewed the records of the company, at an estimated cost of \$43,200 (1,440 hours x \$30/hour) for calendar year 1977.

The most costly report (\$73,200 a year) is an "Energy Conservation Report" filed semi-annually with the Department of Energy. Other costly reports include the "Refiner's Monthly Cost Allocation Report," filed with the Department of Energy ($27,600), and the "Monthly Report of Sales and Royalty" to the U.S. Geological Survey ($20,160). The total cost of the 40 energy reports is $344,760 or $8,619 per report.

*Agricultural Chemicals*

Agricultural chemicals are regulated by the Federal Insecticide, Fungicide, and Rodenticide Act of 1972 (FIFRA), which deals with the use, testing, and sale of pesticides. This act is administered by the Office of Pesticide Programs which is now part of the Toxic Substances Control Administration within the Environmental Protection Agency.

Numerous reports have to be filed with the EPA for each product of this type the company makes. Perhaps the most important is a request for a label, because until a label is approved the product simply cannot be sold on the market. Other reports are experimental use permits, requests for tolerances or extensions, request for new uses of an old chemical, and reports pertaining to plant shipments of a product.

As in the safety and health area, it was not possible to determine the number of hours per year spent filling out each report. The reports are product-related, and the volume can be quite heavy. It was estimated that 11 people are involved on a full-time basis filling out these reports and another 10 people on a part-time basis; 25 more people become involved in paperwork when the workload is heavy. Thus in the neighborhood of 20 to 25 person-years are involved in paperwork related to agricultural chemicals. Using the lower figure as a conservative estimate, costs amount to $1,128,000 (1,880 hrs. x 20 x $30).

*Miscellaneous Reports*

Miscellaneous reports are those that do not fit into

any of the other categories. Such reports are sent to the Bureau of Alcohol, Tobacco, and Firearms, the General Services Administration, and the Renegotiation Board (see table 1.9). The latter is a holdover from World War II, and its existence was recently extended. One costly report is the "Users Report of Denatured Alcohol and Rum," filed monthly with the Bureau of Alcohol, Tobacco, and Firearms. The total cost of the seven reports in this area is $54,330, at an average cost of $7,761 per report.

## Summary of Paperwork Costs

For the company studied, the total cost of paperwork imposed by the federal government is $3,589,390 for calendar year 1977 except as noted. The breakdown of these costs by type of information shows that the most costly are the environmental and agricultural chemicals areas, accounting for 30.9 percent and 31.4 percent, respectively, of the total cost (see table 1.10).

Table 1.11 presents the breakdown of compliance costs involved in reporting to federal government agencies. The safety and health area is included even though no direct reporting is required. As shown, 62.2 percent of the total cost is due to reporting to the Environmental Protection Agency, another 15.7 percent due to the requirements of the Occupational Safety and Health Administration, and 8.8 percent due to reporting to the newly formed Department of Energy.

The time required to fill out federal forms came to 119,503 employee hours. On the basis of a year, consisting of 1,880 employee hours, this total represented the equivalent of 64 full-time employees at the salary level indicated earlier, all involved in complying with regulation of information by the federal government.

It must be pointed out that the total figure of $3,589,390 does not represent the total paperwork cost the company faces resulting from government. Paperwork costs imposed by state and local government regulation of information were omitted as beyond the scope of this study.

There may also be something of an upward bias to the figures reported. Some portion of the indirect costs are fixed costs--rent, heat, light, and so on. It could be argued that these costs should not be allocated to paperwork and that all of these costs are variable. Presumably the company did not build any new buildings or hire any new employees simply to fill out federal forms. On the other hand, if there were no federal forms to fill out, and alternative use could not be found for the physical and human resources now put to that effort, these resources would be gotten rid of somehow. As a practical matter, some fixed costs become variable over time.

## Start-Up Costs

The company used as the subject for this paperwork study was faced with complying with the Toxic Substances Control Act (TSCA). This effort will be used as an example of start-up costs. The initial impact of TSCA has been in the area of inventory reporting. The act requires the Environmental Protection Agency (EPA) to compile and publish an inventory of chemical substances manufactured, imported, or processed in the United States for commercial purposes. This inventory will be compiled from reports which manufacturers, importers, processors, or users of chemical substances are required to prepare and submit to the agency.[11]

There are two reporting periods relative to this inventory. During the first, which ended May 1, 1978, most manufacturers and importers were required to report. From this information, the EPA will compile an initial inventory of chemical substances, which is expected to be published toward the end of calendar year 1978.

A second 210-day reporting period will begin when

the EPA publishes the initial inventory. During this period, importers of chemical substances, as part of mixtures or articles, and companies who have only processed or used (since January 1, 1975) a reportable chemical substance that did not appear on the initial inventory, may report such substances for inclusion on a revised inventory. This revised inventory will be published as soon as possible after the end of the second reporting period. After that, the EPA will add new chemical substances to the inventory after these substances have satisfied the premanufacture notification provisions of the act. These premanufacture notification provisions will become effective 30 days after publication of the initial inventory and will require companies to notify the EPA at least 90 days in advance of the manufacture or importation in bulk form, for a commercial purpose, of a chemical substance not identified in the initial inventory.

Thus the costs covered by and reported in this study relate to information supplied to the EPA for preparation of the initial inventory. There are four different forms for reporting this information. Different forms will be provided by the EPA at a later date for the revised inventory.

Form A is to be used only to report chemical substances which appear in the "Toxic Substance Control Act Candidate List of Chemical Substances," published by the EPA, or any addendum to that list for which a notice of availability is published in the Federal Register. All chemical substances appearing on the Candidate List and addenda have Chemical Abstracts Service (CAS) Registry Numbers and valid EPA code designations.

Form B is to be used to report chemical substances with known CAS Registry Numbers that do not appear in the TSCA Candidate List of Chemical Substances. Form C must be used to report chemical substances with no known CAS Registry Numbers, and to report chemical substances whose identities for purposes of the inventory are claimed confidential. Importers who are assisted in reporting by foreign suppliers must also use Form C for each chemical substance they jointly report.

Finally, Form D can be used by manufacturers or importers to ensure commercial users of their products that all reportable chemical substances contained in these products have been reported for the inventory. Its purpose is to assure processors and others who use their products during the 210-day second reporting period that they may continue to do so without notifying the EPA. Product trademarks may be reported if all reportable chemical substances which are part of the trademarked product have been reported for the inventory. Use of Form D is voluntary.

In complying with TSCA, which at present is entirely paperwork compliance, there are both start-up and reporting costs. The start-up costs involve determining what the EPA requires in the way of information,[12] developing and installing a system to gather this information, and training employees to gather the proper kinds of information.

The reporting costs for the company in this cost study are divided into three major categories, which differ somewhat from the general categories mentioned earlier as a result of the particular way the company kept its cost records.

The first category includes the functions of accumulation, review, and approval. The information for the inventory has to be accumulated, first of all, from manufacturing cost sheets and sales statistics of each operating division of the company. Then it has to be reviewed by a Toxic Substance Control Act Committee, set up by the company for this purpose, and by the Purchasing and Medical Departments. Finally, the information has to be approved by the TSCA Administrator, who actually signs the forms and thus ultimately is responsible for their proper completion.

The second category consists of computer and contractual costs. Some of the information supplied the EPA can be prepared on computer tapes according to a specified format. In addition to these computer costs, however, a form which contains the same information has to accompany each tape.

Finally, there are costs related to the actual preparation of the forms. Approximately 350 forms had to be filled out and sent to the EPA. These different cost categories are summarized in table 1.12.

The total cost of this effort for fiscal year 1977-78 (April 1, 1977, to March 31, 1978) is estimated to be \$598,000.[13] Another \$40,000 of reporting costs should be added for April to bring the period involved up to the May 1 reporting date, making a total start-up cost of \$638,000 to comply with the initial inventory requirement. Even though there are start-up and reporting costs related to this effort, the whole effort is a start-up cost when viewed in its entirety. It will never have to be done again, but it is a prelude to the premanufacture notification provisions, which will eventually be done on a routine basis for new chemicals or significant new uses of existing chemicals.

## Other Costs

### Avoidance Costs

Avoidance costs are expenses that may be incurred in attempting to avoid disclosing information to the federal government.[14] This could involve lobbying efforts to support or oppose legislation with reporting implications when it is introduced in Congress, attempting to change the ruling of an agency to avoid having to disclose certain types of information, testifying at a court hearing to obtain a favorable decision on some disclosure requirement, or research into the implications and feasibility of an information request. These avoidance costs are probably not applicable in the majority of information requests, but where new areas of regulation are being considered with potentially severe implications for reporting to the federal government, these kinds of costs may be significant. Some possible costs of this type are determining avoidance possibilities, additional legal and clerical staff, advertising and public relations, bargaining, lobbying, litigation, and research. It was not possible to measure these avoidance costs in any systematic fashion. In fact, because of confidentiality problems, it was not possible to get any costs of this type related to a particular report that could have been presented as an example, The Line of Business Report would have been a good candidate, as it is generally known that many large corporations fought hard against this requirement in every way possible. However, no figures related to this report were made available.

## Effects on Innovation

Regulation of information also has costs related to the dampening effect it may have on innovation--the development of new products for the market. Bureaucratic interference in this process may increase the length of time it takes to get a new product to market, or discourage a company from introducing new products, or reduce incentives to invest in basic research where the effects of any new development are unknown.

This can be a cost to the company in lost sales and profits--an opportunity cost that results through loss of a market opportunity that may not be exploited. As with any opportunity cost, it is impossible to quantify or determine on a systematic basis. However, the process whereby new products are introduced can be examined, looking for bureaucratic interferences that might indicate where such dampening effects on innovation are likely to happen.

In the case of the company examined in this study, the toxic substances area proved to be a good place to look. After the publication of the initial inventory described previously, the premanufacture provisions of TSCA go into effect. These provisions require a manufacturer who has developed a new chemical not on the inventory list to submit a notice to the EPA at least 90 days before beginning manufacture or importation of a new chemical substance for commercial purposes other than in small quantities solely for research and development. The exact information that has to be given the EPA is still being determined, but in general it will probably include the following:

> a description of the new chemical substance, including the chemical identity, molecular structure, and the common or trade name;
>
> the estimated total amount to be manufactured and processed;
>
> the proposed categories of use;
>
> the estimated amount to be manufactured and processed for each proposed category of use;
>
> the manner and methods of distribution in commerce and disposal;
>
> the estimated amount of the substance for each manner and method of distribution in commerce and disposal;
>
> direct and indirect exposure of humans and of ecological populations, including exposure levels, as a result of manufacture, processing distribution in commerce, use, and disposal

of the chemical substance;

releases to the air, land, and water (including emmissions, effluents, and other discharges), whether intentional or unintentional;

assessments of risks to health and the environment resulting from the manufacture, processing, distribution in commerce, use, and disposal of the chemical substance;

safeguards, controls, and other measures to be used to limit exposure;

descriptions and other information concerning related chemical substances and mixtures, including by-products, coproducts, impurities, and degredation products;

descriptions of mixtures and articles which contain or may contain the new chemical substance.[15]

In addition to this information, the submitter must append any test data in his possession or control and descriptions of other data concerning the health and environmental effects of the substance. The EPA encourages, but does not require, the submitter to follow the premanufacture testing guidelines the EPA has published. In any event, all test data of the above sort are to be submitted regardless of their age, quality, or results.[16]

The administrator of the EPA has a number of options available to him after receipt of this information. He may extend the 90-day premanufacture review period for an additional 90 days for good cause. He may choose to initiate no action within the 90-day period because the chemical is deemed not to present a hazard to health or the environment.

In the event such a hazard is believed to exist, however, the administrator may issue a proposed order to take effect on the expiration of the notification period to prohibit or limit the manufacture, processing, distribution in commerce, use, or disposal of such substance, or to prohibit or limit any combination of such activities. This action can be taken for either of the following two reasons:

> The information available to the Administration is insufficient to permit a reasoned evaluation of the health and environmental effects of a chemical substance and in the absence of sufficient information to permit such an evaluation, the manufacture, processing, distribution in commerce, use, or disposal of such substance, or any combination of such activities, may present an unreasonable risk of injury to health or the environment.
>
> Such substance is or will be produced in substantial quantities, and such substance either enters or may reasonably be anticipated to enter the environment in substantial quantities or there is or may be significant or substantial human exposure to the substance.[17]

If a total ban on the substance is not necessary, the administrator can issue further directives regarding regulation of the substance. He may set concentration levels, limit the use of the chemical, require warnings or instructions with respect to its use, require public notice of risk or potential injury, or regulate methods of disposal. If the administrator has reason to believe the method of manufacture rather than the chemical itself is at fault, he may order the manufacturer to revise quality control procedures to the extent necessary to remedy whatever inadequacies are believed to exist.[18]

In addition to these premanufacture notification provisions, there is another section of TSCA that may affect innovation. The act empowers the EPA administrator to require manufacturers or processors of potentially harmful chemicals to conduct tests on these chemicals. The need for such testing must be based on the following criteria:

> The chemical may present an unreasonable risk to health or the environment, or there may be substantial human or environmental exposure to the chemical.
>
> There are insufficient data and experiences for determining or predicting the health and environmental effects of the chemical.
>
> Testing of the chemical is necessary to develop such data.[19]

This section applies to all chemical substances already in existence. An interagency committee has been established by the act to assist the administrator concerning chemicals that should be tested, but his actions are not limited to these recommendations by the committee. This committee may designate, at any one time, up to 50 chemicals from its list of recommended substances for testing. Within one year, the administrator must either initiate testing requirements for these designated chemicals or publish in the Federal Register his reasons for not initiating such requirements.[20]

The reason for going into such detail on these provisions of TSCA is to show the impact this will make on management decision-making and innovation regarding the introduction of new chemicals. This act creates a bureaucratic layer of information requirements that have to be met before a new chemical can be marketed. It gives the administrator of the EPA a great deal of decision-making authority relative to innovation without having the responsibility of a corporate manager for bottom-line performance. While the effects on innovation have not yet been felt, the potential is there. Because of the testing requirements, there will undoubtedly be more money spent on defensive research rather than research devoted to the development of new products. The effects of regulation on innovation in the drug industry have been researched and found to be substantial.[21] The same effect may happen in the area of chemicals, which indeed may represent quite a cost to the companies affected.

## Organizational Impacts

Government regulation of information has an impact on the business organization directly in that it may entail changes in organizational structure by causing the formation of new positions or departments. In most cases, it is impossible to separate the impact of regulation of information per se from that of regulation in general. But at least something can be said to indicate the kinds of organizational change that regulation may entail.

In the safety and health area, for example, every large plant in the company, about 80, has a full-time safety director with a staff of three or four people. In addition, there is a headquarters staff in the safety and health area to coordinate plant programs and provide centralized services. These changes have come about partly because of government regulation in the safety and health area. As mentioned, about 10 percent of the time of one person in each of the large plants is spent meeting paperwork requirements to comply with regulations.

Toxic substances regulation has necessitated the new position of TSCA administrator at the headquarters level.

Thus far, there have been no permanent staff in addition to this position, but about 30 people throughout the company have been involved on a part-time basis complying with the information requirements issued thus far. Further organizational changes are expected when the premanufacture provisions of TSCA are put into effect.

Other environmental regulation has had a significant impact on organizational structure and personnel requirements. From 1973 to 1977, the number of people involved in meeting environment regulations increased 220 percent. Projections through 1987 show that there will be a 415 percent increase in people. Part of the time of these people is, of course, involved in meeting the information requirements associated with environmental regulation.

## Conclusions

One of the most interesting questions to emerge from this study is related to possible usage of all this information. What happens to the reports once they are sent to the federal government? Do they end up in some agency's files never to be looked at again? Or is the information from this one company's reports actually used, along with that from thousands of other corporations, to make important policy decisions? A study attempting to follow up some of this information and see what happens to it would be interesting. Perhaps such a study would also give some indication of possible benefits to society from such information-gathering.

There are many proposals to control the growth of paperwork or at least to reduce its cost. Many in business feel that the experience and expertise of business is seldom if ever tapped, either in the process of framing legislation or in working out the details of legislative requirements. These are some typical comments from businessmen:[22]

> Representatives of government agencies should consult with industry prior to the requesting of new reports or the revisions of existing reports. Such meetings would greatly reduce misunderstandings or misinterpretations and also provide an opportunity to learn in advance of any problems anticipated in gathering the data. A positive example is the current effort being made by the Bureau of the Census in discussing changes to the MA-100.
>
> In one of our recommendations, we urged the use of an advisory committee drawn from industry to establish better control of forms, systems, and paperwork.
>
> The federal government should look at their requests through the eyes of the reporting firms and become more reasonable in their approach.

The approach of the Commission on Federal Paperwork to reducing paperwork is the adoption by government of a philosophy called service management. This concept is, "first, a shift in perspective--one which compels public officials to examine critically the consequences of legislative and administrative decisions for those directly affected. Second, service management is the set of analytic tools and techniques needed for this critical examination."[23]

Service management involves two new management disciplines according to the Commission on Federal Paperwork. First, information must be managed as a resource--just as money, personnel, and property are managed as resources. Second, public officials must analyze alternative ways of operating programs for which they are responsible to distribute appropriately the costs of the program among the parties involved: "Fundamentally, service management requires attitudes and actions by people at all levels in and out of government to work in a partnership toward more effective programs free of unnecessary paperwork. A willingness to discuss and resolve problems in the operation of Federal programs can and must be based on a mutual sense of trust and respect. Most people wish to obey the law and help achieve our national goals; they are frustrated by the waste and ineffectiveness caused by unnecessary paperwork."[24]

While the Federal Paperwork Commission must be praised for its intentions to reduce paperwork, it must also be criticized for a very weak approach toward its achievement. Service management is an empty concept. It contains no incentives for a federal bureaucrat to reduce paperwork, and without incentives the whole concept is reduced to a set of meaningless platitudes. Thus another effort of the federal government to reduce paperwork is likely to have no positive effect.

A way to implement the intent of the concept of service management is to require that an economic impact statement be filed along with the request for approval of a new form to collect data from corporations. This statement could deal with not only the more visible aspects of paperwork costs but also the effects of a whole series of regulations on innovation, decision-making, and organizational change. These are costs that also should be taken into account when considering whether additional regulation of information is warranted.

Figure 1.1

Growth trend of paperwork costs of federal government

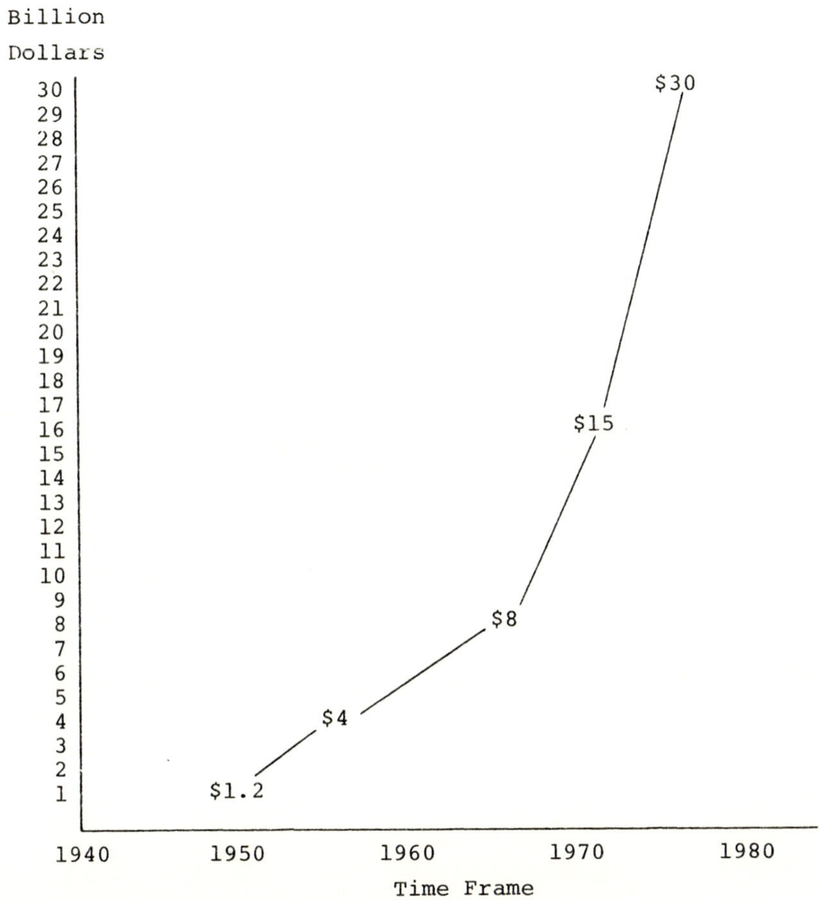


Sources:

First Hoover Commission - 1949
Second Hoover Commission - 1955
House Committee on Post Office and
  Civil Service - 1965
General Accounting Office - 1972
Commission on Federal Paperwork - 1975

Table 1.1

Examples of new programs established 1970-74

| | Year Established |
|---|---|
| Clean Air Amendments | 1970 |
| Occupational Safety and Health Act | |
| Poison Prevention Packaging Act | |
| Securities Investor Protection Act | |
| Economic Stabilization Act Amendments | 1971 |
| Federal Boat Safety Act | |
| Lead-Based Paint Elimination Act | |
| Consumer Product Safety Act | 1972 |
| Equal Employment Opportunity Act | |
| Federal Election Campaign Act | |
| Federal Environmental Pesticide Control Act | |
| Federal Water Pollution Control Act Amendments | |
| Noise Control Act | |
| Ports and Waterways Safety Act | |
| Agriculture and Consumer Protection Act | 1973 |
| Economic Stabilization Act Amendments | |
| Emergency Petroleum Allocation Act | |
| Flood Disaster Protection Act | |
| Atomic Energy Act | 1974 |
| Commodity Futures Trading Commission Act | |
| Council on Wage and Price Stability Act | |
| Employee Retirement Income Security Act | |
| Federal Energy Administration Act | |
| Hazardous Materials Transportation Act | |
| Housing and Community Development Act | |
| Magnuson-Moss Warranty-Federal Trade Commission Improvement Act | |
| Pension Reform Act | |
| Privacy Act | |
| Safe Drinking Water Act | |

Table 1.2
Types of paperwork costs

A. Start-Up Costs

1. Determining what is required
2. Installing an information system
3. Training of employees

B. Reporting Costs

1. Direct Labor Costs--the cost of gross salary and normal fringe benefits of professional and clerical personnel employed in complying with a given information request.
2. Computer Cost--the cost of using an EDP system to comply with a particular information request.
3. Contractual Cost--any external costs required to comply, such as costs for legal services, consulting services, accounting services, and time sharing.
4. Miscellaneous Costs--"unusual" costs such as photocopying, supplies, storage, etc., that cannot be fully accounted for in using the standard overhead recharge rate.
5. Indirect Costs--the overhead rate associated with hours of labor time used in complying with an information request. These indirect costs are usually estimated by utilizing standard overhead recharge rates. These rates often include secretarial support costs associated with an hour of professional time, postage, supplies, rent, heat, light, and occasionally even computer expenses.

Table 1.3

Reporting cost hourly rate calculation

| | |
|---|---|
| Monthly base salary | $2,000 |
| Add 30 percent salary overhead | $ 600 |
| | $2,600 |
| Divide by average working hours in a month (174) | $ 14.94 |
| Double for indirect costs | $ 29.88 |
| Rounded figure | $ 30.00 |

Table 1.4

Annual cost of statistical reports filed with federal government agencies

| | | |
|---|---|---|
| Department of Agriculture | $ 720 | 0.7% |
| Department of Commerce | | |
| Bureau of the Census | 47,250 | 47.6 |
| Bureau of Economic Analysis | 9,960 | 10.0 |
| Office of Export Administration | 1,140 | 1.1 |
| Department of the Interior | | |
| Bureau of Mines | 4,860 | 4.9 |
| Geological Survey | 1,500 | 1.5 |
| Other | 1,320 | 1.3 |
| Department of Labor | | |
| Bureau of Labor Statistics | 12,270 | 12.4 |
| International Trade Commission | 20,250 | 20.5 |
| Total | $99,270 | 100% |

Table 1.5

Annual cost of financial reports filed with federal government agencies

| | | |
|---|---|---|
| Department of the Treasury | | |
| Federal Reserve Bank | $ 1,410 | 1.0% |
| Internal Revenue Service | 17,100 | 12.5 |
| Other | 1,200 | 1.0 |
| Cost Accounting Standards Board | 750 | 0.6 |
| Federal Trade Commission[a] | 44,050 | 32.0 |
| Securities and Exchange Commission | 72,450 | 52.9 |
| Total | $136,960 | 100% |

[a]Included is a contractual charge of $4,300 from Haskins and Sells for reviewing the "Corporate Patterns Report."

Table 1.6

Annual cost of personnel and benefit reports filed with federal government agencies

| | | |
|---|---|---|
| Department of Labor | $132,420 | 83.8% |
| Equal Employment Opportunity Commission | 25,650 | 16.2 |
| Total | $158,070 | 100% |

Table 1.7

Environmental reports filed with state and federal government agencies

| Name of Report | Frequency[a] |
|---|---|
| Air pollution | |
| Source construction permits | 3/yr. |
| Source operating permits | 10/yr. |
| Emission reporting | 12/yr. |
| Water pollution | |
| NPDES application forms | 1/5 yrs. |
| Monthly discharge reporting | 12/yr. |
| 308 questionnaires | 1/yr. |
| Dredge and fill permits | 1/6 yrs. |
| Waste disposal | |
| Notification of hazardous waste | 5/yr. |
| Manifest for each waste shipment | 100/yr. |
| Disposal site permit application | 30/company |
| Drinking water | |
| Deep well permits | 6/company |
| Injection rates reporting | - |
| Well water supply permits | 1/plant |
| Withdrawal rates reporting | 1/quarter |
| Other | |
| Pesticide annual reports | 1/yr. |

[a]Figures refer to the plant level and are on a yearly basis unless otherwise noted. There are 25-30 plants on average that are involved in reporting this information.

Table 1.8

Annual cost of energy reports filed with federal government agencies

| | | |
|---|---|---|
| Department of Energy | $315,120 | 91.4% |
| Department of the Interior | | |
| U.S. Geological Survey | 29,460 | 8.5 |
| Bureau of Mines | 180 | 0.1 |
| Total | $344,760 | 100% |

Table 1.9

Annual cost of miscellaneous reports filed with federal government agencies

| | | |
|---|---|---|
| Bureau of Alcohol, Tobacco, and Firearms | $42,180 | 77.6% |
| General Services Administration | 450 | 0.9 |
| Renegotiation Board | 11,700 | 21.5 |
| | $54,330 | 100% |

Table 1.10

Annual paperwork cost by type of information for a large corporation

| Type of Report | Employee Hours | Annual Cost | Number of Reports | Cost Per Report[a] | Percent of Total |
|---|---|---|---|---|---|
| Statistical | 3,309 | $ 99,270 | 59 | $ 1,682 | 2.7% |
| Financial | 4,422 | 136,960 | 18 | 7,609 | 3.8 |
| Personnel and benefits | 5,269 | 158,070 | 13 | 12,159 | 4.4 |
| Environmental | 36,800 | 1,104,000 | 15 | 73,600 | 30.9 |
| Safety and Health | 18,800 | 564,000 | - | - | 15.7 |
| Energy | 11,492 | 344,760 | 40 | 8,619 | 9.6 |
| Agricultural chemicals | 37,600 | 1,128,000 | - | - | 31.4 |
| Miscellaneous | 1,811 | 54,330 | 7 | 7,761 | 1.5 |
| Totals | 119,503 | $3,589,390 | 152 | $12,482 | 100.0 |

[a]This cost is determined per individual report irrespective of the frequency with which it is filed.

Table 1.11

Annual cost of reports filed with federal government agencies

| | Cost ($) | Percent of total |
|---|---|---|
| Department of Agriculture | 720 | - |
| Department of Commerce | | |
| Bureau of the Census | 47,250 | 1.3 |
| Bureau of Economic Analysis | 9,960 | 0.3 |
| Office of Export Administration | 1,140 | - |
| Department of the Interior | | |
| Bureau of Mines | 5,040 | 0.2 |
| Geological Survey | 30,960 | 0.9 |
| Other | 1,320 | - |
| Department of Labor | | |
| Bureau of Labor Statistics | 12,270 | 0.4 |
| Occupational Safety and Health Administration[a] | 564,000 | 15.7 |
| Other | 132,420 | 3.7 |
| Department of Energy | 315,120 | 8.8 |
| Department of the Treasury | | |
| Bureau of Alcohol, Tobacco and Firearms | 42,180 | 1.2 |
| Federal Reserve Bank | 1.410 | - |
| Internal Revenue Service | 17,100 | 0.5 |
| Other | 1,200 | - |
| Cost Accounting Standards Board | 750 | - |
| Environmental Protection Agency | 2,232,000 | 62.2 |
| Equal Employment Opportunity Commission | 25,650 | 0.7 |
| Federal Trade Commission | 44,050 | 1.2 |
| General Services Administration | 450 | - |
| International Trade Commission | 20,250 | 0.6 |
| Renegotiation Board | 11,700 | 0.3 |
| Securities and Exchange Commission | 72,450 | 2.0 |
| Total | 3,589,390 | 100. |

[a]Reports are not actually filed with this agency as explained above. It is included to present a complete picture of the cost of compliance.

Table 1.12

Cost of complying with TSCA initial inventory

| |
|---|
| Start-up costs |
| Reporting costs |
| Accumulation-review-approval |
| Computer-contractual costs |
| Preparation of forms |

# APPENDIX I

## STATISTICAL REPORTS

| NAME OF REPORT | REPORT NUMBER | SUBJECT MATTER | AGENCY | REPORTING INTERVAL | EMPLOYEE HOURS/YR | ANNUAL COST |
|---|---|---|---|---|---|---|
| Naval Stores Consumers Report | CE-13-001C | Consumption and stock of turpentine and resins | Dept. of Agriculture | Annual | 6 | $ 180 |
| Fertilizer Survey | CE-6-78 | Fertilizer survey by state | | Annual | 12 | 360 |
| Situation 1975 and Outlook 1976 | 40-R-3995 | Survey of pesticide | | Annual | 6 | 180 |
| Economic Censuses - Pretest | CB-150-W | Miscellaneous nondurable goods | Bureau of Census | Upon Request | 6 | 180 |
| Inorganic Chemicals | M-28-A-1 | Production and Stock | | Monthly | 12 | 360 |
| Production of Industrial Gas | M-28-A-2 | Same as name of report | | Monthly | 12 | 360 |
| Inorganic Fertilizer Chemicals | M-28-A-3 | Production and stock | | Monthly | 3 | 90 |
| Current Industrial Reports | M-28-B | Production and stock - Sulfuric acid | | Monthly | 50 | 1500 |
| Current Industrial Reports | M-28-B-1 | Production and stock - Inorganic chemicals | | Monthly | 12 | 360 |
| Plastic Bottles | M-30-E | End use and r/m consumption | | Monthly | 6 | 180 |
| Survey of Oil and Gas | MA-13-K | Oil and gas field activities within U.S. and adjacent offshore areas | | Annually | 100 | 3000 |
| Annual Yarn Production | MA-22-F | Same as name of report | | Annually | 3 | 90 |
| Current Industrial Reports | MA-28-B-E-1 | Annual report of shipments and production of inorganic chemicals | | Annually | 85 | 2550 |
| Current Industrial Reports | MA-28-E-2 | Shipments and production of industrial gases | | Annually | 6 | 180 |
| Census of Manufacturers | MA-29-A | Supports MA-100 | | Quinquennial | 6 | 180 |
| Current Industrial Reports - Plastics Products | MA-30-D | Same as name of report | | Annually | 12 | 360 |

(continued)

| NAME OF REPORT | REPORT NUMBER | SUBJECT MATTER | AGENCY | REPORTING INTERVAL | EMPLOYEE HOURS/YR | ANNUAL COST |
|---|---|---|---|---|---|---|
| Current Industrial Reports | MA-36-N | Units and dollars of sales | Bureau of Census | Annually | 3 | $ 90 |
| Annual Survey of Manufacturers | MA-100 | Summary of yearly plant operations | | Annually | 885 | 26,550[1] |
| Reports on Shipments to or Receipts for Work Done for Federal Government Agencies | MA-175 | Same as name of report | | Annually | 45 | 1,350 |
| Survey of Pollution Abatement Cost and Expenditures | MA-200 | Same as name of report | | Annually | 45 | 1,350 |
| Plastics Products Survey | MA-300 | Same as name of report | | Annually | 3 | 90 |
| Survey of Manufacturer's Alternative Energy Capabilities | MA-400 | Same as name of report | | Annually | 65 | 1,950 |
| Census of Mineral Industries | MC-13-A | Operating statistics, production, sales and cost information by geographical areas of U.S. | | Quinquennial | 35 | 1,050 |
| Textile Type Equipment in Place | MC-22Z | Same as name of report | | Annually | 3 | 90 |
| Water Use in Manufacturing | MCD-13-A | Same as name of report | | Annually | 10 | 300 |
| Inventory and Sales Survey | MQ-1 | Same as name of report | | Quarterly | 10 | 300 |
| Survey of Plant Capacity | MQ-C-1 | Same as name of report | | Annually | 55 | 1,650 |
| Report of Organization | NC-XIA | Update all establishments | | Annually | 15 | 450 |
| Survey of Industrial Research and Development | RD-1 | Research and development expenditures | | Annually | 85 | 2,550 |
| Commodity Transportation Survey | TC-402 | Same as name of report | | Quinquennial | 3 | 90 |

[1]For years that end in either 2 or 7 (i.e., 1972, 1977) this report is expanded to show detail of items reported. The estimated cost for those years is five times the amount above or $133,000.

(continued)

| NAME OF REPORT | REPORT NUMBER | SUBJECT MATTER | AGENCY | REPORTING INTERVAL | EMPLOYEE HOURS/YR | ANNUAL COST |
|---|---|---|---|---|---|---|
| International Transactions in Royalties, Licensing Fees, Film Rentals, Management Fees, etc., With Unaffiliated Foreign Residents | BE-93 | Same as name of report | Bureau of Economic Analysis | Annually | 10 | $ 300 |
| Annual Report Sources and Application of Funds of U.S. Direct Investments Abroad | BE-133 | Same as name of report | | Annually | 45 | [illegible],350 |
| Schedules of Expenditures for Property, Plant and Equipment of U.S. Direct Investments Abroad | BE-133-B<br>BE-133-C | Same as name of report | | Semi-Annually<br>Annually | 55 | 1,650 |
| Plant and Equipment Expenditures | BE-452 | Same as name of report | | Quarterly | 6 | 180 |
| Plant and Equipment Expenditures - Supplement | BE-452-S | Same as name of report | | Quarterly | 6 | 180 |
| Transactions With Foreign Subsidiaries and Affiliated Companies | BE-577 | Value in U.S. dollars of all items received from or paid to foreign subsidiaries and affiliates | | Quarterly | 105 | 3,150 |
| Operation of Foreign Branches or Other Unincorporated Foreign Business of U.S. Reporters | BE-578 | Net investment and changes in net investment of U.S. corporations in foreign countries | | Quarterly | 105 | 3,1[illegible] |
| Report by Fertilizer Exporter | DIB-661P | Exports of certain products | Office of Export Administration | Monthly | 35 | 1,050 |
| Jeurl Bearings and Related Components | DIB-941 | Same as name of report | | Annually | 3 | 90 |

(continued)

| NAME OF REPORT | REPORT NUMBER | SUBJECT MATTER | AGENCY | REPORTING INTERVAL | EMPLOYEE HOURS/YR | ANNUAL COST |
|---|---|---|---|---|---|---|
| Primary Antimony | 6-1016-QA | Stocks, receipts, production and disposition of primary antimony | Bureau of Mines | Quarterly | 6 | $ 180 |
| Consolidated Consumers Report | 6-1109-MA | Catalyst consumed | | Monthly | 12 | 360 |
| Stone Report | - | Stone report (Soda Springs) | | Annually | 6 | 180 |
| Phosphate Rock | - | Same as name of report | | Semi-Annually | 23 | 690 |
| Phosphate Rock | | Same as name of report | | Monthly | 100 | 3,000 |
| Production Estimate | 6-1209-A | Same as name of report (Soda Springs) | | Annually | 3 | 90 |
| Coal Balances & Consumption | - | Same as name of report | | Monthly | 12 | 360 |
| Statement of Production | - | Same as name of report | Geological Survey | Quarterly | 35 | 1,050 |
| Marketable Phosphate Rock Cost Analysis | - | Royalty calculation | | Annually | 15 | 450 |
| Consumption of Copper | 6-1115-AS | Same as name of report | Dept. of Interior | Monthly | 25 | 750 |
| Ferro Alloys | 6-1056A | Same as name of report | Other | Annually | 3 | 90 |
| Operation Report | - | Operations - Soda Springs | | Annually | 10 | 300 |
| Mine Information | 6-1017-A | Same as name of report (Soda Springs) | | Annually | 6 | 180 |

(continued)

| NAME OF REPORT | REPORT NUMBER | SUBJECT MATTER | AGENCY | REPORTING INTERVAL | EMPLOYEE HOURS/YR | ANNUAL COST |
|---|---|---|---|---|---|---|
| Information for Wholesale Price Index | BLS-473 | Same as name of report | Bureau of Labor Statistics | Monthly | 35 | $ 1,050 |
| Statement of Products | BLS-790 | Principal products sold and used | | Annually | 3 | 90 |
| Monthly Report of Labor Turnover | DL-1219 | Same as name of report | | Monthly | 110 | 3,300 |
| Expenditures for Employee Compensation | BLS-2868 | Expenditures by categories of pay including fringe benefits | | Bi-Yearly | 6 | 180 |
| Monthly Report of Employment, Payroll and Hours | BLS-7790C | Same as name of report | | Monthly | 255 | 7,650 |
| Synthetic Organic Chemicals | CD-A1 | Production and sales of synthetic organic chemicals | International trade Commission | Annually | 350 | 10,500 |
| Synthetic Organic Chemicals | CD-M1 | Production and sales of synthetic organic chemicals | | Monthly | 325 | 9,750 |
| | | | | TOTALS | 3,309 | $99,270 |

## APPENDIX II

### FINANCIAL REPORTS

| NAME OF REPORT | REPORT NUMBER | SUBJECT MATTER | AGENCY | REPORTING INTERVAL | EMPLOYEE HOURS/YR | ANNUAL COST |
|---|---|---|---|---|---|---|
| Monthly Report of Assets and Liabilities and Positions in Specified Foreign Currencies of Firms in the United States | FC-3 | Same as name of report | Federal Reserve Bank | Monthly | 10 | $ 300 |
| Quarterly Report of Assets, Liabilities and Positions in Specified Foreign Currencies of Firms in the United States | FC-3A | Same as name of report | | Quarterly | 12 | 360 |
| Quarterly Consolidated Report of Assets, Liabilities and Positions in Specified Currencies of Foreign Branches and Subsidiaries of Firms in the United States | FC-4 | Same as name of report | | Quarterly | 25 | 750 |
| Summary of Federal Income Tax and Social Security Withheld and State Unemployment Compensation by State | 941/941-M or 943 | Report of wages taxable under FICA | Internal Revenue Service | Quarterly | 55 | 1,650 |
| Statements for Recipients of Miscellaneous Income | 1099 | Miscellaneous amounts paid various recipients | | Annually | 500 | 15,000 |
| Identification of Separated Participants with Deferred Vested Benefits | SSA | Same as title - various employee benefit plans | | Annually | 15 | 450 |
| Employee Savings Bond Report | SB-60-A | Same as name of report | Dept. of Treasury Other | Semi-Annually | 40 | 1,200 |
| Disclosure Statement | - | Same as name of report | Cost Acct. Standards Board | Annually | 25 | 750 |

(continued)

| NAME OF REPORT | REPORT NUMBER | SUBJECT MATTER | AGENCY | REPORTING INTERVAL | EMPLOYEE HOURS/YR | ANNUAL COST |
|---|---|---|---|---|---|---|
| Quarterly Financial Report | MG-1 | Same as name of report | Federal Trade Commission | Quarterly | 95 | $ 2,850 |
| Line of Business Report | - | Same as name of report | | Annually | 1170 | 35,100 |
| Corporate Patterns Report | - | Shipments of establishments, classified by SIC Code | | Annually | 60 | 1,800[1] |
| Annual Report General Form | 10-K | Financial report | Securities and Exchange Commission | Annually | 740 | 22,200 |
| Short Form for Securities to be Sold for Cash | S-7 | Financial report | | Annually | 465 | 13,950 |
| Securities to be Sold to Employees Pursant to Certain Plans | S-8 | Financial report | | Annually | 465 | 13,950 |
| Short Form for Certain Securities of Companies Entitled to use S-7 | S-16 | Financial report | | Annually | 185 | 5,550 |
| Current Report | 8-K | Reports "material" events | | As Required | 25 | 750 |
| Quarterly Report | 10-Q | Financial report | | Quarterly | 435 | 13,050 |
| Annual Lease Report | - | Lease and rent paid | | Annually | 100 | 3,000 |
| | | | | TOTALS | 4,422 | $132,660 |

[1]Not included is a charge of $4,300 from Haskins and Sells for reviewing this report.

## APPENDIX III

### PERSONNEL & BENEFITS

| NAME OF REPORT | REPORT NUMBER | SUBJECT MATTER | AGENCY | REPORTING INTERVAL | EMPLOYEE HOURS/YR | ANNUAL COST[1] |
|---|---|---|---|---|---|---|
| Annual Report | 5500 | Salaried (001), hourly (002), and hourly extended (007) pension plans | Dept. of Labor | Annually | 2,715 | $61,450 |
| " | 5500 | Savings and Investment Plan (004) | | " | 105 | 3,150 |
| " | 5500 | Employee Stock Ownership Plan (011) | | " | 3 | 90 |
| " | 5500 | Salaried supplemental pension plan (101) | | " | 45 | 1,350 |
| " | 5500 | Travel Accident Insurance Plan (501) | | " | 6 | 180 |
| " | 5500 | Salaried Employees Group Life Insurance Plan, Sickness, and Medical Benefits Plan (502) | | " | 6 | 180 |
| " | 5500 | Organized hourly Group Life Insurance, Sickness, and Medical Benefits Plan (503) | | " | 6 | 180 |
| " | 5500 | Unorganized hourly Group Insurance, Sickness, and Medical Benefits Plan (504) | | " | 6 | 180 |
| " | 5500 | Dental Assistance Plan (505) | | " | 6 | 180 |
| " | 5500 | Disability Income Plan (506) | | " | 6 | 180 |

[1] These costs do not include field and subsidiary preparation nor do they include insurance premiums required by statute

(continued)

| NAME OF REPORT | REPORT NUMBER | SUBJECT MATTER | AGENCY | REPORTING INTERVAL | EMPLOYEE HOURS/YR | ANNUAL COST |
|---|---|---|---|---|---|---|
| Premiums and Annual Report Filing | PBG-C-1 | Salaried and hourly pension plans | Dept. of Labor | Annually | 10 | $ 300 |
| Affirmative Action Plans | - | Same as name of report, prepared and filed for each location | | Annually | 1500 | 45,000 |
| Equal Employment Opportunity-Employer Information Report | EEO-1 | Statistics of employment of minorities and women | Equal Employment Opportunity Commission | Annually | 855 | 25,650 |
| | | | | TOTALS | 5,269 | $158,070 |

# APPENDIX IV
## ENVIRONMENTAL REPORTS

| NAME OF REPORT | SUBJECT MATTER | AGENCY | REPORTING INTERVAL |
|---|---|---|---|
| Source Construction Permits | Request authority to construct air emission sources | City, State, or Federal Air Control | 3/yr/plt |
| Source Operating Permits | Request authority to operate emission sources | " | 10/yr/plt |
| Emission Reporting | Self-reporting of actual air emissions | " | 1/mo/plt |
| NPDES Application Forms | Request to discharge water borne wastes to U.S. waters | State or Federal Water Control Agency | 1/plt/5 yr |
| Monthly Discharge Reporting | Report discharge quantities | " | 1/plt/mo |
| 308 Questionnaires | Technical and Economic information regarding water discharges | Federal EPA | 1/plt/yr |
| Dredge and Fill Permits | Authority to remove or add structures or fill material in navigable waters | " | 1/plt/6 yr |
| Notification Hazardous Waste | Notify State or EPA of activity generating hazardous waste | State EPA | 5/plt/yr |
| Manifest for Each Waste Shipment | Bill of Lading | " | 100/plt/yr |
| Disposal Site Permit Application | Request authority to operate solid waste disposal facility | " | 30/Company |
| Deep Well Permits | Request authority to operate deep well | State | 6/Company |
| Injection Rates Reporting | | State | |
| Well Water Supply Permits | Authority to operate water supply wells | State | 1/plt (one time) |
| Withdrawal Rates Reporting | | State | 1/plt/quarter |
| Pesticide Annual Reports | Listing of prod. of pesticides | EPA | 1/plt/yr |

## APPENDIX V

### ENERGY REPORTS

| NAME OF REPORT | REPORT NUMBER | SUBJECT MATTER | AGENCY | REPORTING INTERVAL | EMPLOYEE HOURS/YR | ANNUAL COST |
|---|---|---|---|---|---|---|
| Producers and Wholesale Purchaser Reseller Report for Propane and Butane | FEA-100A | Production and Sales for propane, butane and natural gasoline for all gasoline plants | Dept. of Energy | Monthly | 36 | $ 1,080 |
| Refiners Monthly Report | P-102-M-1 | Domestic crude oil entitlements program | | Monthly | 72 | 2,160 |
| Refiner's Monthly Cost Allocation Report | FEA-P110 M-1 | Natural gas liquid cost and price data applicable to crude oil refiners | | Monthly | 865 | 25,950 |
| Domestic Crude Oil Purchase Report | FEA-P124 M-1 | Domestic crude oil purchases | | Monthly | 24 | 720 |
| Domestic Crude Oil Purchase Report | FEA-P124 M-1 (Schedules D & E) | Domestic crude oil purchases | | Annually | 75 | 2,250 |
| Petroleum Industry Monthly Report for Product Prices | FEA-P302 M-1 | Selling prices and volume of price controlled products | | Monthly | 385 | 11,550 |
| Propane Sales Volumes to Ultimate Consumers | FEA-315 MO | Total volume of propane sales by state which were made to ultimate consumers | | Monthly | 36 | 1,080 |
| Refinery Report | FEA-P320 M-0 | Refinery stocks, receipts, inputs production and shipments | | Monthly | 24 | 720 |
| Crude Oil Stocks | FEA-P323 M-0 | Location and origin of crude stocks | | Monthly | 12 | 360 |
| Energy Conservation Report | - | Same as name of report | | Semi-Annual | 2440 | 73,200 |
| Certification of Prices & Base Production Control Levels to Purchases | - | Same as name of report | | As Required | 24 | 720 |
| Application for Exception of Price Regulations | - | Application for exceptions on properties with loss positions and/or operating problems | | Once Per Property | 400 | 12,000 |

(continued)

| NAME OF REPORT | REPORT NUMBER | SUBJECT MATTER | AGENCY | REPORTING INTERVAL | EMPLOYEE HOURS/YR | ANNUAL COST |
|---|---|---|---|---|---|---|
| Rate Schedule Analysis on a Continuing Basis | 108 | Initial applications, all changes relative to price | Dept. of Energy | Initial, Quarterly, Annually | 920 | $27,600 |
| May, 1977 Crude Report | - | Total crude oil transactions for May, 1977 by tiers | | One Time | 130 | 3,900 |
| Monthly Fuel Consumption Report | 614-M-1 | Same as name of report | | Monthly | 15 | 450 |
| Report of New Non-jurisdictional Sales of Natural Gas by Natural Gas Companies Subject to the Jurisdiction of the FPC | 45 | Same as name of report | | Monthly | 24 | 720 |
| Natural Gas Reserve Report | 40 | Domestic natural gas reserves | | Annually | 200 | 6,000 |
| Natural Gas Company Report | 64 | Reporting of producer expenditures, exploration and development activity, production, reserve additions and revenues | | Annually | 235 | 7,050 |
| Independent Producer Natural Gas Summary | 0501 | Price and volume summary | | Annually | 6 | 180 |
| Independent Producer Rate Schedule Sales of et al Parties | 0505 | Price and volume detail by well, by rate schedule | | Annually | 120 | 3,600 |
| 1099 Forms | 1099 | Gross Royalties from oil and gas | | Annually | 250 | 7,500 |
| Certified Prices/Base Production | - | Same as name of report | | As Required | 25 | 750 |
| Price Exceptions | - | Same as name of report | | As Needed | 400 | 12,000 |

(continued)

| NAME OF REPORT | REPORT NUMBER | SUBJECT MATTER | AGENCY | REPORTING INTERVAL | EMPLOYEE HOURS/YR | ANNUAL COST |
|---|---|---|---|---|---|---|
| Major Fuel Burning Installation | FEAC-607-S-0 | New combustion installation | Dept. of Energy | Each new unit over 100 M̄ BTU | 16 | $ 480 |
| Early Planning Identification Report | Schedules A1 & A2 | Same as above | | Same as above | 32 | 960 |
| Status Coal Stocks | EIA-1 | Same as name of report | | Weekly | 210 | 6,300 |
| Status Coal Stocks | EIA-3 | Same as name of report | | Monthly | 24 | 720 |
| Cost and Feasibility Report | - | Related to converting plant to coal | | One time | 24 | 720 |
| Allocation; Petrochemical Plants | SEC 213.9 | Application for an allocation & license to import crude, fee free, on the basis of having a petrochemical plant | | Annual | 16 | 480 |
| Allocation; Based on Exports | SEC 213.10 | Application for an allocation & license to import crude, fee free, on the basis of production & exportation of eligible petrochemicals | | Semi-Annual | 48 | 1,440 |
| Allocation; Based on Heavy Liquids Feedstock Plant | SEC 213.11 | Application for an allocation & license to import crude, fee free, on the basis of converting heavy feedstocks to petrochemicals | | Annual | 48 | 1,440 |
| Old Oil Entitlement Program Transaction Report | P-103-M-0 | Report on Selling/Buying Entitlements | | Monthly | 24 | 720 |
| Report of Oil Imports | P-113-M-0 | Oil Imports into U.S. | | Monthly | 24 | 720 |

(continued)

| NAME OF REPORT | REPORT NUMBER | SUBJECT MATTER | AGENCY | REPORTING INTERVAL | EMPLOYEE HOURS/YR | ANNUAL COST |
|---|---|---|---|---|---|---|
| United States Geological Survey Royalty Transmittal Forms | 9-614-A | U.S. royalty payments | U.S. Geological Survey | Monthly | 135 | $ 4,050 |
| United States Geological Survey Royalty Transmittal Forms | 9-I431 | Royalty payments by state | | Monthly | 65 | 1,950 |
| Monthly Report of Sales & Royalty | 9-361 | Sales and Value for Royalty to U.S.G.S. | | Monthly | 672 | 20,160 |
| Application for Establishment of Royalty Value | 9-1926 | Assessment of Royalty Value W/Gas Contract | | One report per federal well on stream | 85 | 2,550 |
| Sundry Notices: Reports on Wells | 9-331 | Notice of intention to do any work-over, reparis, abandonment or change in plans | | 3 per well drilled | 9 | 270 |
| Application for Permit to Deepen or Plug Back | 9-331-C | Permit to deepen or plug back | | 1 per well drilled | 16 | 480 |
| Natural Gas Processing Report | G-1343-A | Natural Gas Processed and Disposition of Residue Gas | Bureau of Mines | Annually | 6 | 180 |
| | | | | TOTALS | 8172 | $245,160 |

## APPENDIX VI

### MISCELLANEOUS REPORTS

| NAME OF REPORT | REPORT NUMBER | SUBJECT MATTER | AGENCY | REPORTING INTERVAL | EMPLOYEE HOURS/YR | ANNUAL COST |
|---|---|---|---|---|---|---|
| Report of Tax Free Alcohol Use | ATF-1451 | Same as name of report | Bureau of Alcohol, Tobacco & Firearms | Annually | 3 | $ 90 |
| Shipments and Receipts of Denatured Alcohol and Rum | ATF-1473 | Same as name of report | | Daily (1) | 315 | 9,450 |
| Users Report of Denatured Alcohol and Rum | ATF-1482 | Same as name of report | | Annually | 10 | 300 |
| Users Report of Denatured Alcohol and Rum | ATF 1482 | Same as name of report | | Monthly | 1075 | 32,250 |
| Application and Withdrawal Permit | ATF-1485 | Same as name of report | | Annually | 3 | 90 |
| Contractors Report of Orders | GSA-72 | Same as name of report | General Services Administration | Monthly | 15 | 450 |
| Renegotiation of Government Contracts | RB-1 | Same as name of report | Renegotiation Board | Annually | 390 | 11,700 |
| | | | | TOTALS | 1811 | $54,330 |

(1) Completed and filed an estimated 75% of working days.

## Notes

[1]See, for example, "The Impact of Government Regulation on the Dow Chemical Company," published by Dow Chemical U.S.A. While this study deals with the total costs of government regulation, paperwork is a separate category. See also "Reports Submitted to Federal Agencies, State Agencies, Trade Associations, and Other Organizations," published by Exxon Company, U.S.A., May 1975.

[2]U.S. Commission on Federal Paperwork, *Final Summary Report*, p. 5. The yearly paperwork costs to the major segments of society were estimated as follows:

| | |
|---|---|
| federal government | \$43 billion |
| private industry | \$25-\$32 billion |
| state and local government | \$5-\$ 9 billion |
| individuals | \$8.7 billion |
| farmers | \$350 million |
| labor organizations | \$75 million |

[3]Testimony of Senator Thomas J. McIntyre, Co-Chairman, Commission on Federal Paperwork, before Senate Committee on Government Operations, May 3, 1976.

[4]National Archives and Records Service, General Services Administration, as reported in U.S. Commission on Federal Paperwork, *Study of Federal Paperwork Impact on Small and Large Businesses,* p. 12.

[5]These costs are for the federal government only--they do not reflect private sector costs. It seems safe to assume, however, that as paperwork costs within government increase, the costs to the private sector also increase (ibid., p. 10).

[6]These efforts began in 1887 and continue to the present. A complete listing of these attempts to control paperwork is shown below (ibid., p. 9):

Federal Government Efforts to Control Paperwork
1887-1975

| Year | Effort | Major aim |
|---|---|---|
| 1887 | Cockrell Committee | High cost of copying, paperwork |
| 1893 | Dockerz-Cockrell Commission | Carbon paper letterpresses |
| 1905 | Keep Committee | Filing; establish National Archives |
| 1913 | Taft Commission | Records depositories, filing, mechanization |
| 1942 | Federal Reports Act | Forms control and clearance |
| 1949 | Hoover Commission I | Better organization for record management |
| 1950 | Federal Records Act | Promote records management |
| 1955 | Hoover Commission II | Reduce paperwork and cost |
| 1965 | Paperwork Jungle Hearings | Reduce paperwork burden and red tape |
| 1972 | Paperwork Burden Hearings | Reduce paperwork burden and red tape |
| 1975 | Commission on Federal Paperwork | Reduce paperwork burden and red tape |

[7]Ibid., p. 14.

[8]James T. Bennett and Manuel H. Johnson, "Federal Government Paperwork and Bureaucratic Behavior," p. 4. The agency in OMB used to be called the Statistical Policy Division.

[9]Ibid., pp. 7, 8.

[10]U.S. Commission on Federal Paperwork, *Overview of Impact Studies*, p. 2.

[11]U.S. Environmental Protection Agency, Office of Toxic Substances, *Reporting for the Chemical Substance Inventory*, p. 1.

[12]The need for this activity is illustrated by the definition of a chemical substance contained in the act (ibid., p. 4):

> "Chemical substance" means any organic or inorganic substance of a particular molecular identity, including any combination of such substances occurring in whole or in part as a result of a chemical reaction or occurring in nature, and any chemical element or uncombined radical; except that "chemical substance" does *not* include:
>
> (1) any mixture [710.2(q)]{31-36}.
>
> (2) any pesticide when manufactured, processed, or distributed in commerce for use as a pesticide [710.2(b)]{37-39}.
>
> (3) tobacco or any tobacco product, but not

including any derivative products,

(4) any source material, special nuclear material, or byproduct material [710.2(c)],

(5) any pistol, firearm, revolver, shells and cartridges, and

(6) any food, food additive, drug, cosmetic or device, when manufactured, processed, or distributed in commerce for use as a food, food additive, drug, cosmetic or device [710.2(a)]{37, 40-42}.

[13]These costs were estimated by the TSCA Administrator for the company based on his analysis and record-keeping.

[14]Roland N. McKean, "Avoidance and Enforcement Costs in Government Regulation."

[15]Appendix I to Premanufacture Notification Draft Guidelines, *Chemical Regulation Reporter,* p. 1124.

[16]Ibid., p. 1123.

[17]U.S. Congress, *Toxic Substances Control Act,* p. 2015.

[18]Ibid., pp. 2020-21.

[19]U.S. Environmental Protection Agency, *The Toxic Substances Control Act,* p. 2.

[20]Ibid., p. 3. The interagency committee is composed of representatives from the Departments of Labor, Commerce, Health, Education, and Welfare (including the National Cancer Institute, the National Institute for Occupational Safety and Health, the National Institute of Environmental Health Sciences), the National Science Foundation, the Council on Environmental Quality, and the EPA.

[21]Sam Peltzman, "An Evaluation of Consumer Protection Legislation: The 1962 Drug Amendments," *Journal of Political Economy* (October 1973): 1049-91.

[22]U.S. Commission on Federal Paperwork, *Study of Federal Paperwork Impact on Small and Large Businesses,* pp. 39-40.

[23]U.S. Commission on Federal Paperwork, *Final Summary Report,* p. 2.

[24]Ibid., p. 3.

## References

Appendix I to Premanufacture Notification Draft Guideline. *Chemical Regulation Reporter*, September 1978, pp. 1118-25.

Bennett, James T., and Johnson, Manuel H. "Federal Government Paperwork and Bureaucratic Behavior," Manuscript, George Mason University, 1977.

Benston, George J. "Public (U.S.) Compared to Private (U.K.) Regulation of Corporate Financial Disclosure." *The Accounting Review* (July 1976): 483-98.

Dow Chemical U.S.A. "The Impact of Government Regulation on the Dow Chemical Company."

Exxon Company U.S.A. "Reports Submitted to Federal Agencies, State Agencies, Trade Associations, and Other Organizations." May 1975.

McKean, Roland N. "Avoidance and Enforcement Costs in Government Regulation." Working Paper 16, Center for the Study of American Business, Washington University. October 1976.

U.S. Congress. *Toxic Substances Control Act*. Pub. L. 94-469, 94th Cong., 1976.

U.S. Commission on Federal Paperwork. *Final Summary Report*. Washington: U.S. Government Printing Office, 1977.

U.S. Commission on Federal Paperwork. *Overview of Impact Studies*. Internal draft paper prepared by the staff of the Commission on Federal Paperwork. July 1976.

U.S. Commission on Federal Paperwork. *Study of Federal Paperwork Impact on Small and Large Businesses*. Internal draft paper prepared by the staff of the Commission on Federal Paperwork. July 1977.

U.S. Environmental Protection Agency. Office of Toxic Substances. *Reporting for the Chemical Substance Inventory*. Washington: Office of Toxic Substances, 1977.

U.S. Environmental Protection Agency. *The Toxic Substances Control Act*. Washington: U.S. Government Printing Office, 1977.

# Federal Paperwork Compliance Costs: A Comment On Rogene A. Buchholz's "Corporate Cost For Compliance With Government Regulation Of Information"

Yuji Ijiri

Carnegie-Mellon University

"Corporate Cost for Compliance with Government Regulation of Information," by Rogene A. Buchholz, presents the results of a case study on compliance costs for federal information requirements. The study was carried out at a large chemical company. This type of study is now underway at a number of corporations, sponsored by Business Round Table and by Arthur Andersen & Co. as a part of a nationwide study on the costs of complying with government regulations.

Costs of compliance with government information requirements has been growing at such an alarming rate that the U.S. Commission on Federal Paperwork was established to investigate the situation. Figure 1 of Buchholz's paper presents the trend very well. The $30 billion cost of compliance with federal information requirements estimated by the commission in 1975 is twice as much as a similar estimate made by the General Accounting Office for 1972, nearly four times the estimate of the House Committee on Post Office and Civil Service for 1965, and 7.5 times that of the Second Hoover Commission for 1955.

While these various estimates may define and calculate costs of compliance somewhat differently, the acceleration shown in the growth rate of paperwork compliance costs is consistent: 7 percent a year in 1955-65, 9 percent a year in 1965-72, and 25 percent a year in 1972-75.

Buchholz's study is based on a set of questionnaires sent to various parts of a selected company in order to identify federal information requirements and to obtain estimates of annual employee hours spent on each requirement. Accountants' charges, computed on average salaries, fringe benefits, and overhead, are estimated to be $30 an hour, which is then applied to the employee hour data to arrive at the cost of paperwork. A total of 120,000 employee hours--the equivalent of 64 full-time employees--was spent on such paperwork. Applying the $30 hourly cost, Buchholz estimates total annual compliance costs of federal paperwork to be approximately $3.6 million for the company under study. Excluded from this total are costs of recording and reporting income tax data, since the function of the Internal Revenue Service is more revenue-raising than regulatory, and costs of compliance with information requirements by state and local governments. Appendixes to the paper by Buchholz present a detailed list of specific federal information requirements with estimated employee hours and costs.

## Interpretations

While it is easy to criticize any factual study for lack of this and that, on the whole the Buchholz paper is informative and presents an interesting set of data. An argument may be made for the need for a more sophisticated approach in estimating employee hours or in estimating cost per employee hour, although the roughness of available data may not warrant more sophisticated approaches. Nonetheless, the distinction between total cost of paperwork compliance and incremental cost of compliance is a difficult one and deserves a more detailed discussion, since at least some portion of information presented to the federal government is also needed for managerial uses. In any event, the estimate of 64 full-time employees exclusively for compliance with federal paperwork requirements may be treated as a reasonable figure, even though some may disagree with the approach taken by the author.

What is the significance of this figure? While use of 64 full-time employees at a cost of $3.6 million is not insignificant, some may consider it to be a small fraction of the total cost of running a controller's department. This multinational chemical company under study must have at least several hundred employees all over the world carrying out some portion of the controllership function. If this is ture, 64 employees are less than 10 percent of the total work force of the controller's department.

Complaints about paperwork arise not only for external information requirements but also for internal ones. Disputes between the headquarters and divisions on the proper amount of data the latter should supply to the former are perhaps common to most large companies. A five percent saving in the controller's work force may very well be feasible at many companies by eliminating peripheral data requests for internal purposes and by applying techniques of statistical inferences judiciously.

However, what is truly alarming is the *rate* of increase in federal paperwork. If the rate observed during recent years continues, the controller's department of a corporation soon will have to devote 20 or 30 percent of its work force to federal paperwork requirements.

The $30 billion estimate given by the Federal Paperwork Commission in 1975 is roughly two percent of the 1975 GNP. If paperwork costs double every few years as indicated by past trends, the proportion could reach 10 percent by the mid- to late 1980s, after taking into account an estimated growth rate of the GNP.

Undoubtedly there are benefits associated with information gathered by the federal government in public and private decision-making. There are also indirect benefits from gathering information: compliance with operating regulations is reinforced since disclosure shows compliance or its absence.

However, one may wonder whether it is desirable to have an economy in which 10 cents out of each dollar of goods and services produced are spent for federal paperwork compliance. Certainly this is a public policy issue with no clear-cut answer, but, as Buchholz makes clear, Congress and the Office of Management and Budget must give serious thought before they grant a government agency the power to collect information from the private sector.

## Legal Exposure

While cost of preparing information to meet federal information requirements is increasing exponentially, other costs seem to be increasing as rapidly as paperwork. In particular, what Buchholz calls "avoidance cost" may perhaps be even more significant than paperwork costs.

The author includes in avoidance cost such costs as those for determining possibilities of averting requirements from being established, for additional legal and clerical staff, for advertising and public relations, and for bargaining, lobbying, litigation, and research.

In particular, legal exposure is something with which controllers of corporations are most concerned. Many forms filed with governmental agencies have to be signed by responsible corporate officials. Controllers are often charged to take this responsibility and legal risk.

Even if a controller files information based on the best of his knowledge, an honest mistake may later be judged to be fraudulent if circumstantial evidence happens to build against him or her. Even if litigation is won, the cost to the corporation can be enormous. Class action suits can be filed against a corporation if there is a shred of evidence that a group of people were misled by information provided by the corporation. Many such suits are settled out of court even when the corporation believes it can win in order to minimize the costly time of having top executives tied up in court. Legal exposure is particularly serious in the case of ambiguously stated information requirements or those calling for subjective estimates, unless the supplier of information is specifically protected by a safe harbor rule.

Considering these points, cost of legal exposure and time which top executives must spent to avoid the risk or to respond to inquiries or legal challenges is considerable although it is certainly difficult to quantify. Some of these costs of litigation are justifiable since dishonest controllers are not nonexistent. But for each such dishonest controller, there are an overwhelmingly large number of honest controllers wasting their time just to protect themselves and their corporations from possible casualties of disclosure.

## Effects on Innovation

The single most expensive part of cost associated with federal information requirements is likely to be the stifling effect it could have on innovation. Buchholz provides an example of intervention by the Environmental Protection Agency based on the provisions in the Toxic Substances Control Act and the effects of such intervention on company plans to introduce a new chemical product.

Two factors damage innovation. One is delay in the implementation of innovative ideas due to existing red tape. This type of cost, discussed in detail in the paper, includes cost of regulation itself, since it is not just paperwork but the agency's participation in the decision-making process of introducing a new product that causes delay in the entire process.

The second factor is the fear that proprietary

information filed with a governmental agency may be leaked to the hands of the company's competitors. The Freedom of Information Act requires a governmental agency to disclose information to the public if a request for such information is made. Although the agency can refuse disclosure for some company-specific information, the supplier of information is at the mercy of the agency to decide which information is proprietary and which is not. Thus innovation and new product development become less attractive due to information requirements, because of the threat that the innovator might not be able to enjoy the reward from the innovative activity. The potential deterrent effects on innovation are perhaps the most serious cost of compliance with information requirements and could be many times the $3.6 million cost of paperwork calculated for the company under study.

## Prospects

Needless to say, information requirements by the federal government are established with good intent. Government intervention on new product introduction, for example, is meant to reduce risk of potential hazards from new products. Cost of paperwork or cost from delaying or withholding new product introduction may perhaps be necessary to achieve the overall national objectives these governmental agencies are charged to carry out.

The key issue is the implicit reward structure placed on many governmental agencies. An agency can go wrong in two ways: by imposing unnecessary information requirements or by not imposing necessary ones. Following the terminology of statistical decision theory, we can call the former Type I error (or alpha error) and the latter Type II error (or beta error). An agency may reject introduction of a harmless and beneficial product (Type I error) or may accept introduction of a harmful product

(Type II error).

Good decision-making calls for identification of losses associated with each type of error and balancing of probabilities of the two types of errors. Unfortunately, however, most agencies seem to operate in an environment in which the loss to the agency from committing Type II error is far greater than the loss from committing Type I error.

If an agency rejects a new product which could potentially save a number of human lives, it can account for its action relatively easily by attributing it to some uncertainty associated with the product's benefits or possible hazardous effects even if later the product is found to be perfectly harmless and effective (Type I error). However, if an agency allows introduction of a new product which then kills one person (Type II error), the agency has a hard time defending its decision.

The same imbalance can be observed in information requirements. Requiring information that turns out to be unnecessary (Type I error) is far less embarrasing to the agency than not having needed information on hand (Type II error).

The ratio of the two types of losses that are perceived by the agency seems, therefore, overly unbalanced in favor of more conservative actions (reject a new product, impose more information requirements) than may be called for.

What should be done to reduce this tendency? The matter seems to be entirely in the hands of officials and staff of governmental agencies, who need to exercise good sense to save the economy from being completely subdued under bureaucratic paperwork. However, Congress, the news media, and the public can and should make efforts to provide an environment in which governmental agencies can make an objectives assessment of the two types of errors and associated losses.

# A Comment On Rogene A. Buchholz's "Corporate Cost For Compliance With Government Regulation Of Information"

Raymond E. Perry

Touche Ross & Co.

I found the Buchholz paper interesting to read, and I believe that it is a useful contribution to the attempt to quantify the cost of collecting and using information for government regulation. Its usefulness would be enhanced by similar studies for a representative group of companies, but it is a good start. The paper provides insights that stimulate thoughtful reflection on the costs and benefits of government regulation of business. Reading this paper was my first contact with serious discussion of the mounting costs of complying with government regulation, and I was pleased to find that there are concerned people working in this area. However, I also noted some deficiencies in the paper, some of which can easily be addressed and others probably requiring additional research.

Some of my comments might be different if I had read the sources cited by the author, and both my general observations and comments specific to the paper should be read in the light of my limited knowledge of what has been done and written in this field.

## General Observations

### The Benefits of Government Regulation

The author, while rightly pointing out the burdens placed upon business as a result of government regulations, lacks balance in failing to mention beneficial aspects of regulation. Admittedly these are even harder to quantify than the costs of compliance. It appears to me that, in part, government regulation is one of the "hidden costs" of technological advances that have been made in the past generation. The benefits of technology by way of a higher standard of living have been quite evident for a long time. However, only in recent years are we beginning to realize the costs, such as the damage to the environment and imprudent use of available natural resources. The insistent demand that we should avoid undesirable air pollution, water pollution, and distribution of dangerous and unhealthful products is sound and cannot be denied.

But Buchholz gives no recognition to the fact that in some cases the cost of regulation is well worth it, both to the public and the companies involved. If the paper could analyze and separate regulatory nonsense from usefulness, it would go a long way toward encouraging both regulators and others to think seriously about the burden of unnecessary regulation. Often the gathering of information by regulators is a way of evading the need to consider seriously what is required by way of regulatory action. As the author rightly points out, regulators do not have responsibility for "bottom line" results and therefore can avoid the discipline of the marketplace. Accordingly, the aim of regulation should be to achieve a proper balance between "protecting the public" and maintaining economic productivity.

From the point of view of individual companies, there are undoubtedly benefits to regulation. Adequate attention to researching the potential harmful effects of new products can be a significant saving to a business in the long run, in that it avoids the significant costs of future litigation brought by individuals who have been harmed or alleged that they have been harmed. For example, a number of years ago a drug marketed overseas was not allowed to be marketed in the United States. The drug caused a number of birth defects, resulting in significant adverse publicity for the drug company concerned as well as the incurrence of significant legal liabilities. This same drug had been forbidden in the United States under regulations being analyzed in this paper. Sound research programs can both minimize the possibilities of distributing harmful products and, at the same time, provide valuable evidence in defending invalid law suits against the company.

## Time Value of Money

The author misses the significant cost of the time value of money, which may indeed equal or exceed some of the costs identified. The time value of money cost, in essence, is the difference between the time when a product would be ready to be marketed and the time at which it is marketed multiplied by the applicable interest rate and cost invested to develop the product. For example, if a particular drug required a research and development investment of $2 million and the time lapse between when the drug was ready to be marketed and when approval of marketing was actually given was two years, the $2 million times two years times the incremental borrowing rate would be used to indicate cost incurred by the company because of the delay in marketing its product.

## The Term "Paperwork"

Throughout the discussion the term "paperwork" is used although much more is involved than literally handling paper, especially under current computerized information handling techniques, and perhaps some broader term than "paperwork" would be better.

## Recent Developments

Since the period studied in the Buchholz paper, new legislation has continued to impose new information burdens on the economy. The most pervasive of these new developments may well be the developing requirements for compliance with the Foreign Corrupt Practices Act of 1977.

The disclosures of questionable, unethical, and often illegal acts by American corporations, combined with the Watergate episode and other disclosures of similar practices in government, created a series of legislative actions to eliminate such conduct in the future. The culmination of this legislation, the Foreign Corrupt Practices Act, makes it illegal for all American companies to engage in foreign bribery and for all publicly held companies not to maintain an adequate system of internal accounting controls for safeguarding the company's assets and properly recording transactions. The act provides large fines and imprisonment for violations. This act and similar legislation are of great concern to American businesses and to their auditors because of vastly increased legal exposure--both civil and criminal--for any violations. In the same sense, the creation of more government regulation and "paperwork" is of great concern, not only because of the costs studied in the Buchholz paper but because violations, however inadvertent, may be deemed to be illegal acts. There are already many government agencies which have the power to seek civil and criminal actions against corporate executives, as shown in figure 1.2 on the next page. The chart was originally printed in *Business Week* and reprinted in the 1977 issue of *The Dow Jones--Irvin Business Almanac*. Although this chart was developed prior to the act, it illustrates the pressures that government regulation brings (see figure 1.2).

There are two basic goals which must be achieved by all segments of society--government, industry, and the public: to maintain and increase economic productivity and to protect the public from fraud and from unhealthy and unsafe products. To achieve these goals society must balance them. There is a tendency to create regulation every time there is some type of abuse in order to alleviate the causes of the abuse in the future. What is seldom understood is that regulation itself can be an abuse and sometimes it may be better to risk an occasional abuse rather than to create more and more regulations and more and more "paperwork." If both the government and industry would understand and acknowledge the need for a balance between regulation and productivity, both could work toward more beneficial and meaningful reporting requirements in the future.

## Specific Comments

### Paperwork Costs: Background

The background discussion of information taken from federal government studies is interesting but lacks perspective. It seems to suggest that the biggest "paperwork" costs occur within government since only a relatively small portion of the total cost to society appears to be imposed upon businesses. Also, it is evident that a significant part of the growth in costs from 1950 into the 1970s is due to price inflation. If data are available, it would be helpful if the figures could be related to some meaningful base, such as gross national product, total cost of government, total output of business, and so on. Also it would be interesting to consider how much of the "paperwork" costs to businesses relate to their internal needs compared to the additional costs imposed solely by government regulation.

The author states, "There is no evidence to suggest that this review process [by OMB] has helped decrease federal paperwork" and cites in support the fact that only a negligible percentage of requests for new forms are turned down by OMB. However, it may be that the presence of the review process itself deters the submission of forms that might otherwise be sent out and that the process encourages more careful consideration of the forms that are submitted for review to OMB. These factors should be considered.

Paperwork Costs: Categories of Information Disclosure

The author says that "Much of the information requested is simply *statistical information* that goes, for example, to the Bureau of Census or the Bureau of Labor Statistics." I believe this information is largely basic input, along with income tax return information and certain financial information, to national income and products accounts. While it is difficult to evaluate the benefit to an individual company, this information provides the data upon which virtually all macroeconomic analysis, both by government agencies and by business, is based. The costs involved for this kind of information may not seem so great when looked at in the broader perspective of probable benefits to both business and society.

Paperwork Costs: Types

The author discusses the possibility of allocating start-up costs for new reports over the life of a report. I seriously doubt the validity of this kind of allocation and, since new reports are constantly being developed to replace old ones, it probably makes more sense simply to look at costs incurred annually for a period of time in order to judge their trend.

Paperwork Costs: Methodology of Costing Paperwork

In describing the methodology, the author notes that a 30 percent factor is added to salary costs for salary overhead and then the sum is doubled in order to take into account indirect costs. It is not clear to me whether this is a methodology developed for this specific company or whether it was simply used by the author based on some other studies. In either event, it would be interesting to know the basis for the factors and whether they were valid for the particular company studied.

### Paperwork Costs: Reporting Costs by Category of Information Disclosure

I presume that the objective of the data compiled in this section of the paper is to determine the incremental costs of maintaining records and preparing reports for the government. It is difficult for me to believe that none of this information, or reports similar to those filed with the government, would be maintained and prepared for company use. In other words, it is my impression that copies of many of these government reports are in fact used in day-to-day management of business. For example, one would assume that, aside from government requirements, most companies would want to keep plant accidents at a minimum in order to keep down insurance costs and downtime and would maintain safety logs to assist in this endeavor. Accordingly, it would be useful to know if this aspect was considered in making the study. If so, some commentary on it would be useful.

### Paperwork Costs: Summary

It is not completely clear to me what the relationship is between the data summarized in Table 1.10 and the data in Table 1.11.

### Other Costs: Avoidance Costs

Avoidance costs could be better analyzed. As

described here, they seem to indicate costs incurred by management to avoid doing what they should do, whereas I presume in most cases management feels that the legislation is somewhat misguided and sees avoidance costs as necessary to mitigate what the company believes are the legislation's unreasonable effects. If indeed the paper intends to define one cost of regulation as a company's cost to frustrate that legislation, this is a particularly burdensome way of accumulating costs to be charged toward regulatory agencies. The section really should be reconsidered and segmented to indicate, if appropriate, those costs which companies take to circumvent legislation and the reasons for that circumvention and to change legislation or its enabling regulations or forms because they do not reflect the intent of the regulation; that is, the companies are not attempting to circumvent the legislation as much as to comply with it through interpretation.

## Other Costs: Effects on Innovation

The section of effects on innovation requires more analysis and balance as well as an indication of the time value of money involved in the various time schemes discussed. The balance to be drawn would interrelate the loss of innovation against unchecked and dangerous innovation. Obviously the function of the regulatory agency is not to frustrate innovation but to protect the public from inadequately considered products. Some balance of the purpose of the regulation and its successes and failures would go a long way toward improving this section. In addition, the discussion tends to be excessive as it relates to a particular program; it could be summarized. Further, if we gathered information from companies on the number and significance of times additional consideration by management initiated by regulation has resulted in products being aborted for one reason or another, a more reasoned case might be made as to the cost-benefits of regulation. This is particularly true where the term "defensive research" is used, with no recognition of possible benefits to a company in discovering unexpected side effects of dangers related to a product.

## Author's Conclusions

The recommendation at the end of the paper has two deficiencies. First, the information addressed in the concluding section is not covered in the paper. For example, the paper sets up and argues a proposal being considered by the federal government relating to a "service management concept" and finds the concept deficient. However, the concept is not developed in the body of the paper but only discussed and dismissed in the conclusion section.

Second, the call for a form to be prepared on the economic impact of regulations is weak. The impression one gets from reading the paper is that we have too many forms already, so that recommending yet another form may not reflect positive thinking. What is not missing is a commonality of purpose and objective required in the information requested by governmental agencies; one gets the feeling that many forms call for the same or similar information. A much more positive recommendation would be that government agencies study their own information request or hire "outsiders" to study their information needs and determine how these can be met using existing data as much and as often as possible--in effect, a meeting of the minds as to the base information that is required and could be supplied in a more general way within the normal business stream of information. If this need were met, only exceptions to what business people must accumulate for their own purposes would represent the burden of regulation.

Figure 1.2. The risks executives face under federal law

| Agency | Year Enforcement Began | Complaint May Name Individual | Maximum Individual Penalty | Maximum Corporate Penalty | Private Suit Allowed under Applicable Statute |
|---|---|---|---|---|---|
| Internal Revenue Service | 1862 | Yes | $5,000, three years, or both | $10,000, 50% assessment, prosecution costs | No |
| Antitrust Division (Justice Department) | 1890 | Yes | $100,000, three years, or both | $1 million, injunction, divestiture | Yes |
| Food and Drug Administration | 1907 | Yes | $1,000, one year, or both for first offense; $10,000, three years, or both thereafter | $1,000 for first offense; $10,000 thereafter; seizure of condemned products | No |
| Federal Trade Commission | 1914 | Yes | Restitution, injunction | Restitution, injunction, divestiture, $10,000 per day for violation of rules, orders | No |
| Securities and Exchange Commission | 1934 | Yes | $10,000, two years, or both | $10,000, injunction | Yes |
| Equal Employment Opportunity Commission | 1965 | No | | Injunction, back-pay award, reinstatement | Yes |
| Office of Federal Contract Compliance | 1965 | No | | Suspension, cancellation of contract | Yes |
| Environmental Protection Agency | 1970 | Yes | $25,000 per day, one year, or both for first offense; $50,000 per day, two years, or both thereafter | $25,000 per day, first offense; $50,000 per day thereafter; injunction | Yes |

(continued)

| Agency | Year Enforcement Began | Complaint May Name Individual | Maximum Individual Penalty | Maximum Corporate Penalty | Private Suit Allowed under Applicable Statute |
|---|---|---|---|---|---|
| Occupational Safety and Health Administration | 1970 | No* | $10,000, six months, or both | $10,000 | No |
| Consumer Product Safety Commission | 1972 | Yes | $50,000, one year or both | $500,000 | Yes |
| Office of Employee Benefits Security (Labor Department) | 1975 | Yes | $10,000, one year, or both; barring from future employment with plan; reimbursement | $100,000, reimbursement | Yes |

*Except sole proprietorship

Source Reprinted from the May 10, 1976 issue of *Business Week* by special permission © 1976 by McGraw-Hill, Inc., p. 113.

## 2

# The SEC And Financial Reporting: The Sand In The Oyster

John C. Burton

Columbia University

The pearl is one of nature's most beautiful creations. It is formed by the reaction of certain oysters to an irritant, usually a grain of sand, which becomes imbedded inside the shell. The oyster coats this grain with layers of nacre, and, ultimately, a pearl is formed. The pearl is the joint result of the irritant and oyster, for without both it cannot be created.

The professional standards and practices of the accounting world may not achieve the lustre of the oyster's product, but the process of their development has many similarities. Both currently and historically, the accounting world has tended to exhibit comfotable conservative commitment to the status quo in the absence of external stimulus for change. Unlike the law, the accounting profession has not seemed to attract those with the desire to make over either the world or the professional environment in which they exist. At the same time, there has been a willingness to react to external forces in a fashion such that the power to influence the nature of change has not been lost. Thus the profession has shown the ability to implement change, if not to instigate it.

The process of innovation in accounting, therefore, has required the cooperative effort of a creative irritant providing the stimulus for change and responsive body to build upon it. Since its inception in 1943, the Securities and Exchange Commission has been a principal source of creative irritation in accounting, and the practicing public accounting profession has generally served as the host that builds upon it. It is the hypothesis of this paper that this combination of SEC stimulation and professional reaction is one which emerges logically from the historical and economic forces at work, that it is likely to continue, and that the result is likely to be a satisfactory balancing of diverse interests and objectives. In the financial reporting environment as it exists today, substantial change will not occur in the absence of SEC stimulation. If there is to be innovation, the Securities and Exchange Commission must be a principal source; at the same time, it must operate within the limits of a general consensus which the various parties involved in financial reporting help to define.

It is only fair to report that there are many who do not see this process in particularly pearly terms. On one hand, there are those such as George Benston, who suggest that the SEC has been neither creative nor a force for improvement but rather an organization that has hampered the development of financial reporting by its excessive omnipresence and its disregard of market factors without concomitant benefit to the investors.[1] At the other end of the spectrum are those such as Robert Chatov who suggest that the SEC has been captured by the accounting profession, and hence has not accomplished its mission due to its inaction.[2] In his testimony before the Metcalf Committee, Chatov summed up his views as follows: "SEC participation in the development of corporate financial reporting standards primarily has been ceremonial and caretaker, rather than leading and innovative."[3] There are also wide differences in perception regarding the result of the process. Some view financial reporting in the United States today as a model to be emulated, while others see primarily deficiencies and shortcomings.

It is difficult for many to accept the view that a government agency should be the catalyst for change while the private sector and the marketplace seem to stand as defenders of the status quo. They suggest that leadership and dynamism should come from creative individuals responding to the incentives of the marketplace.

While this is an appealing model, it does not reflect the realities of the present day. If the government were a neutral force, it is conceivable that the marketplace could be the source of risk-taking innovation in the financial reporting world. In fact, this is not the case. The structure of securities regulation in the United States has been legislatively designed to protect against perceived abuse by raising the cost of error in auditing and financial reporting through the imposition of substantial liabilities on both registrants and professionals involved in the process. In addition, the courts and the SEC have liberally interpreted congressional intent in this regard, and the plaintiff's bar has been creative in its litigation thrusts. The commission's increased enforcement activity aimed at professionals who fail to maintain professional standards has also added to the pressure. Even with a number of recent Supreme Court decisions which have limited liability to some degree,[4] the aggregate result of securities legislation and its judicial and regulatory interpretation has been to impose on registrants and experts a substantial burden to avoid any presentation which might be deemed to be misleading.

A logical result of the economic forces brought to bear by this regulatory structure has been substantial pressure to find means of reducing risk of liability. Accountants have been urged to define standards with greater precision, and the SEC has been asked to specify its requirements with ever increasing detail. Auditors have expanded their work and their quality controls to decrease the likelihood of undiscovered error. At the same time, companies have been very hesitant to experiment with new and untried accounting and disclosure techniques, particularly those that require uncertain estimates that may later turn out to be incorrect. The possible benefits of such estimates to investors are far outweighed by the potential costs to the corporation and, more specifically, to the particular decision makers involved. A strong tendency has developed to value objectivity above relevance in financial reporting. For many years, the SEC's policy was also a force in this direction.

In preregulatory days, it was not unusual for an enterprise to perceive market advantage in presenting data in an innovative way. Some presentations might then be emulated by others and ultimately become common practice, while others would prove to be without value or even misleading and would generally gradually disappear. In this environment standards were developed from practice. While abuses existed and there was a lack of commonality among presentations, the system was a dynamic one and resulted in substantial development in accounting and reporting during the early decades of the century (although this development was selective and uneven across companies).

As the environment changed and greater emphasis was placed on uniformity and the avoidance of abuse, economic incentives changed in favor of protection rather than innovation. This was not necessarily a bad social result, as the abuses of the 1920s had high social costs, but it did change the behavior of those reporting financial results. They sought certainty and avoidance of liability.

This tendency had the effect of changing the standard setting process as well. Originally standards were developed from what was seen as the best practice and evolved as practice developed, but increasingly standards were viewed as authoritative pronouncements which were imposed on all enterprises and enforced. This approach provided protection but made evolution more difficult. Standards themselves also tended to emphasize objectivity and conservatism.

Since private sector standard-setting is largely in the hands of those who are exposed to the costs of disclosure, it is not surprising that the role of standards had been largely to enshrine the status quo and to minimize uncertainty and risk. Only under external pressure have standard-setting bodies demonstrated significant innovative spirit.

Thus standards have become the only source of "safe" new methods of accounting. Changes in practice have tended to result from changes in standards rather than the other way around. At the same time market incentives for setters of standards to avoid change and endorse the most conservative practices have increased.

Abuses have not been avoided entirely by this approach, since circumstances still exist where the potential benefits of "creative accounting" outweighs possible costs. Such circumstances tend to exist in new and high risk businesses, and it was here that the application of principles designed for other circumstances provided much material for the accounting critics of the 1960s. Computer leasing and franchise operations are two of the principal examples. It is unfortunate that economic incentives for innovation only become substantial enough to outweigh potential costs in those cases where the potential for abuse is particularly high.

Another reason why the SEC's regulatory mandate has provided countervailing incentives to the development of an efficient information market as an alternative to prescription is the underlying commitment of the securities laws to fairness in the disclosure process. In order to make the capital markets fair, and perceived as fair, the SEC has been required to prohibit the disclosure of significant information to one investor in preference to another. Insider trading rules have been carefully developed and the use of inside information to obtain economic gain in securities transactions has been made illegal. The SEC has been largely successful in making information a public good, and thus the incentive for investors to seek out and pay for new kinds of disclosure has been substantially diluted. Incentives for change have therefore been reduced on both the supply and the demand side of the market for information.

While it may be asserted that, in the absence of regulation, suppliers of information would have an incentive to produce the socially optimum amount of information based on their own economic self-interest, this is neither analytically nor empirically demonstrable. The incentives and the time horizon of those incentives are not always consistent with an informed investor. Under conditions of economic stress, for example, an enterprise seeking capital may have powerful short-run incentives to hide the current state of its affairs from potential investors. In addition the fragmentation of the market of capital suppliers is such that it is not evident that the necessary cost-saving and power-centralizing coalitions would take place to make the bargain for information an effective one in light of the frictions that exist. In addition, even if market forces would work well in a historically unregulated market, they are unlikely to be as effective in a world in which behavior patterns have been shaped by 45 years of regulation.

A major role of the regulator in this setting must be to provide additional incentives for necessary change when market forces fail to do so. In a sense the regulator must replace the very market which its own activities have biased in favor of the status quo, when its regulatory objectives of a fair and efficient capital market requires a dynamic system of information exchange to reflect an ever changing world.

To do this the SEC must take the role of advocate for investors, in order to offset the preparer bias that institutionally exists in the standard-setting process. This requires subjective judgments as to the needs and interests of investors. In reaching such judgments, the SEC has relied on the representation of analysts and investor organizations expressed in letters of comment, appearances at hearings and informal contacts, plus a continuing survey of the literature of security analysis, such as the *Financial Analysts Journal*. In addition, the experiences of members of the SEC and its staff play a significant role.

In making these judgments, the SEC has as its objective achieving a level of public disclosure at least equivalent to the disclosure that would likely be sought by a provider of capital negotiating at arm's length and with power equivalent to that of a capital user. If it errs in this objective, it seeks to do so on the side of providing more information rather than less, since an underlying premise of its regulatory purpose is to assure the existence of adequate information so that the capital-allocating mechanism of the marketplace will work effectively. The potential benefits of such a mechanism are substantial, although they are difficult to demonstrate empirically. Compared to these benefits, the costs of providing additional information are likely to be small. It is clear, however, that the SEC does not disregard cost factors in reaching its judgments. It regularly requests comments on the costs of its proposals from information preparers, including both out-of-pocket costs and possible costs arising from competitive disadvantage. The staff is also asked to do research on these matters.

This representation of the investor viewpoint offsets the fact that the investment community is made up of many investors, where the benefits to any one of devoting substantial resources to the gathering of information would not have economic justification, perhaps even without the constraint of insider information rules. Thus, the SEC acts as a countervailing force to offset the economic weakness of investors in the pursuit of adequate information.

In developing its policies, the SEC does not limit itself to those disclosures that would be demanded by powerful investors in short-run bargaining. One of the purposes of regulation is to conform short-run to long-run behavior. Both investors and managers may have their behavior dominated by short-run influences, while the regulator seeks to smooth the impact. This requires judgment as to the long-run interests of investors and suggests that one of the functions of the SEC is to anticipate investors' needs and to provide the means by which investors can educate themselves on uses of various types of data. Many innovations in accounting and disclosure can only be justified by reference to anticipated use when a user learning curve has been satisfied and comparative data provided for a period of time. The requirement for replacement cost disclosure, for example, was an action of this kind. The SEC did not expect by its adoption to have dramatic short-run effects on the process of capital allocation. Rather, it concluded deductively and subjectively that the disclosures had the potential for providing information that would help users perform their analytical function while at the same time giving preparers of the data the opportunity to develop methodologies for its preparation. After a suitable period of time, use and preparation of the data would become part of the analytical and reporting processes. There seems to be some evidence that this process is occurring, but only after a period of years will it be possible to attempt a reasonable cost/benefit judgment; even at that time it is doubtful whether empiricism will provide conclusive answers.

The SEC inserts itself into the negotiation for investor information in a number of ways. In part, it offers suggestions through the speeches of its chairman, its commissioners, and its senior staff. While each speech carries the traditional disclaimer that the speaker is presenting individual views and not those of the commission, major policy addresses serve as a significant means of communication. It was Chairman Cohen's speech to the AICPA annual meeting in 1966[5] which expressed strong discontent with the profession's standard-setting efforts and served as a significant stimulant to the creation of the FASB and an increasing activism in standard setting. Similarly, Chief Accountant Blough's 1937 speech to a meeting of the New York State Society of CPAs[6] brought pressure on the profession to begin the narrowing of accounting differences and led to the activation of the Committee on Accounting Procedures. Chairman Casey's 1971 speech[7] signaled the end of the SEC's opposition to forecasting, while his 1972 speech at the AICPA annual meeting[8] outlined his expectations of a more active profession in partnership with the SEC.

In addition to speeches, the SEC exercises the rule-making powers granted by Congress under the Securities Act of 1933 and 1934. In the accounting area, it has chosen to use these powers with considerable discretion, because it has consistently recognized the difficulty of taking over the standard-setting mechanism and the importance of its resources by the utilization of the private sector. Governmental rule-making has inflexibilities that do not exist in the private sector, and in addition, the human and financial resources of the SEC have historically been less than those the private sector could bring to bear. The Securities Acts give the SEC permissive rather than mandatory standard-setting authority and left the audit role explicitly to independent public accountants. The importance of the permissive nature of the SEC's power provided by securities legislation is great. If the SEC had been directed to establish standards it would have done so, and it is likely the results would have been quite different. In the one example that presently exists, the SEC was mandated to deal with the oil and gas accounting issue, with results that are demonstrably different, both in process and outcome, from the SEC's normal dealings with accounting standard-setting bodies.[9]

In a number of cases where no mandate existed, the SEC has exercised its discretion and concluded that it was necessary to enter the rule-making forum. There are a number of reasons why it has done this, and they exist in varying degrees in the case of different rules. Most important, the SEC acts when it concludes that important data are not generally being made available to investors on a voluntary basis. Without such a conclusion, rules are not adopted. The adoption of a rule may also be designed primarily to provide protection to registrants who would otherwise fear liability from such disclosures. By creating a disclosure requirement, the SEC provides assurance that particular classes of disclosure may not be deemed by a court to be misleading per se. When a new kind of disclosure is required, this may be important. Replacement costs, the capital value of leased assets, and forecasts are examples.

Recently the SEC has moved more explicitly to reduce risk by adopting "safe harbor" rules, which attempt to offer additional legal protection by recognizing the uncertain nature of some disclosures and providing that good faith errors in estimation will not be viewed as violations of certain sections of the securities laws.

In addition to reducing legal risk, rule-making provides protection against comparative competitive disadvantage. Companies are often hesitant to make disclosures because they believe that making certain disclosures where their competitors do not will put them at a disadvantage. If everyone must make the disclosures there is less concern, although the impact of disclosure requirements may still fall with unequal weight on competitors. Line-of-business profit disclosure is an example of an area in which voluntary efforts were not making much progress until the SEC's rule-making authority was brought to bear.

Legal risk and competitive disadvantage are two of the most common risks that deter disclosure initiatives in the absence of rule-making or clear economic incentives.

Other fears of a less specific nature are also significant. The law of anticipatory multiplication, which provides that both the probability and the potential cost of unpleasant possible outcomes are multiplied whenever change is being considered, suggests that the estimation of the expected value of change is likely to be biased in favor of the status quo. Thus the SEC, by rule-making, has often played the role of the person who pushes a reluctant swimmer into the water to demonstrate that the experience will really not be as bad as it may appear from the dock. In this way, corporations will be able to observe the lack of disastrous impact that is sometimes predicted from disclosure initiatives.

While disclosure requirements serve an end in themselves, they may also create an environment which is more sympathetic to the development of basic reporting standards by private sector entities. In addition to breaking the ice, such rules may also provide standard setters with a data base to support subsequent actions. This was the case, for example, in lease accounting, where the SEC mandated the use of present-value techniques to compute a lease liability figure[10] and in the area of replacement cost accounting where a rule[11] was adopted to require certain companies to provide replacement cost information. In both of these the FASB has been provided with information and has been able to adopt or propose more extensive rules which bring these disclosures into a more systematic framework.

Rule-making powers have also been used as a means of preventing the erosion of current accounting standards and practices. There seems to be at least anecdotal evidence that, in the application of accounting principles, techniques develop and become commonly used which accelerate the recognition of income or create other effects desired by management which may not be consistent either with economic reality or with the conventional application of the accounting models. These developments are widely perceived as abuses and raise questions about the validity accounting measurement in general. Some of these cases arise when the interpretation of an established standard makes possible results not anticipated by the standard setters. Accounting series releases have been issued to provide interpretations of standards when the SEC was dissatisfied with the development of practice. Examples are the releases on lease capitalization,[12] business combinations,[13] the preferability of accounting methods when a change in method is made,[14] and segment reporting.[15]

There are also cases where accounting principles are applied to new or changing circumstances with creative but not necessarily realistic results. In AST 95, for example, the SEC dealt with problems arising from real estate transactions and cautioned against the premature recognition of revenue. In ASR 142, a prohibition was imposed on the disclosure of cash flow per share. Staff accounting bulletins have also been used for this purpose, as for example in the case of exchanges of assets between debtors and creditors[16] and REIT accounting.[17]

On two occasions, rule-making powers were used to put a moratorium on new applications of an accounting principle (catastrophe reserves[18] and interest capitalization[19]), which the SEC believed was being selectively adopted in cases where the validity of the application was in doubt. In these cases, the issue was specifically referred to the Financial Accounting Standards Board for consideration and resolution.

Beyond its rule-making powers, the SEC extensively uses its review and comment process, together with the power not to accelerate the effectiveness of a registration statement, to discourage accounting applications in specific cases which its staff believe to be inappropriate in the circumstances.

In addition to the adoption of formal rules, the SEC sometimes uses accounting series releases as a vehicle for identifying general problems which it urges registrants and public accountants to address in financial reporting. These releases may deal with limited topical problems (e.g., ASR 133, Disclosure of Contingent Liabilities Arising under the Economic Stabilization Act of 1970), or they may identify problems of great breadth and very general application, such as disclosure of inventory profits[20] and disclosure of unusual risks and uncertainties in financial reporting.[21] Such exhortation is frequently a means of calling attention to a problem which it believes ultimately should be dealt with by a private standard-setting body.

Beginning in 1978, after the Metcalf and Moss hearings, a new means of formal communication with standard-setting bodies came into existence through the SEC's undertaking to make an annual report to the Congress on the accounting profession and the SEC's oversight role. While there had always been a brief section on accounting in the SEC's regular report, this new report requires a focus on attention matters. While the first report, a monumental 1,200-page document, emphasized reforms occurring in the structure of the profession, it is likely that subsequent reports will be used as a means to influence accounting standards.

While speeches, rule-making, and public releases and annual reports are all effective techniques in the SEC's stimulation of standard setting, direct formal and informal contact with standard-setting bodies in the private sector is also an essential part of the exercise of its oversight role. The SEC and its staff spend a great deal of time monitoring professional standard-setting activities. They attend meetings of task forces, advisory committees, and standard-setting bodies, and they frequently receive visitations from representatives of such bodies seeking communication, counsel, and sometimes approval of proposed actions. In addition, the SEC's Chief Accountant frequently discusses current problems from his vantage point and urges actions of various sorts. In a few cases, the standard-setting body has been asked to take a specific action to deal with specific problems, with the clear alternative of formal SEC action if no professional standard was promulgated. These cases are the exception, and in most circumstances the informal communications between the bodies are simply part of a cooperative effort to achieve the best solutions to difficult problems.

In the case of accounting standards, the SEC does not make formal responses to FASB proposals. This decision was reached because it was felt that the SEC's statutory authority was such that it could not express an official view on a standard and then accept a significantly different result. In the case of auditing and other kinds of standards, however, the Chief Accountant, with the authorization of the SEC, does sometimes offer specific comments, and from time to time these comments may forcefully express concern. Such expressions are normally given considerable weight by the bodies involved.

Beyond its impact on standard-setting, the SEC has exercised significant influence on financial reporting by its oversight over the audit function and the activities of the public accounting profession. It has devoted substantial resources to the assurance of audit quality and independence, and it has encouraged the expansion of the auditor's role. This has been done in part through enforcement activities, where the staff has investigated and sought to correct shortcomings by developing remedial sanctions and extensive reports of the SEC's view of audit deficiencies. In addition the SEC has sought to reduce cases of "auditor shopping" to obtain less rigorous application of accounting standards by requiring disclosure of disagreements between auditor and client prior to auditor changes, and to strengthen the hand of the auditor in such circumstances. It has also steadily supported the formation of corporate audit committees from the time of its opinion on the McKesson-Robbins case in 1940 to the present day, by a series of exhortative releases and proxy disclosure rules. It has encouraged the profession to develop improved concepts of auditor independence, and it has led the profession in a number of respects in imposing its own guidelines in this respect. In addition the SEC has moved to develop the concept of continuous auditing and the more regular involvement of auditors with corporate reports, both through its requirements for timely auditor evaluation of the accounting treatment of material unusual charges and credits to income[22] and subsequently in its requirements for auditor involvement with interim financial reporting.[23] It has recently proposed that for 1980 and subsequent years auditors be required to report on a statement of management on the subject of internal accounting controls.[24]

In summary, then, the SEC's role has been an extremely active one and one in which its encouragement of innovation and change has contributed to the development of financial reporting. In looking to the future, it seems likely that the importance of the SEC's role will continue. The basic economic forces that impinge upon standard setters seem to point in this direction.

To suggest this, however, is not to suggest a dominant position for the SEC. The SEC's role is to contribute to an environment in which standard-setting bodies can work with greater imagination, and creativity than would be the case in its absence. Traditionally, the more active the SEC the more active has been the private sector in developing accounting methodology and disclosure approaches. The dynamism of accounting in the 1980s, therefore, is likely to be dependent upon the joint action of the private sector accounting institutions and their creative irritant, the Securities and Exchange Commission.

## Notes

[1]See, for example, George J. Benston, "The Effectiveness and Effects of the SEC's Accounting Disclosure Requirements," in *Economic Policy and the Regulation of Corporate Securities,* edited by H. Manne (Washington: American Enterprise Institute, 1969), pp. 23-79.

[2]Robert Chatov, *Corporate Financial Reporting--Public or Private Control?* (New York: The Free Press, 1975).

[3]Hearings before the Subcommittee on Reports, Accounting, and Management of the Committee on Governmental Affairs, U. S. Senate, 95th Cong., p. 81.

[4]Ernst & Ernst v. Hochfelder, 425 U.S. 185, is the conspicuous case.

[5]Manuel Cohen, "The SEC and Accounts: Cooperative Efforts to Improve Financial Reporting," printed in the *Journal of Accountancy,* December 1966.

[6]Carman G. Blough, "Some Accounting Problems of the Securities and Exchange Commission," printed in *The New York Certified Public Accountant,* April 1937.

[7]William J. Casey, "Responsibilities and Liabilities in Corporate Life," November 18, 1971.

[8]William J. Casey, "The Partnership between the Accounting Profession and the SEC," October 2, 1972.

[9]*Accounting Series Release No. 253,* August 31, 1978.

[10]*Accounting Series Release No. 147,* October 5, 1973.

[11]*Accounting Series Release No. 190,* March 23, 1976.

[12]*Accounting Series Release No. 132,* November 17, 1972.

[13]*Accounting Series Release No. 130,* September 29, 1979; *No. 135,* January 5, 1973; *No. 146,* August 24, 1973.

[14]*Accounting Series Release No. 177,* September 10, 1975.

[15]*Accounting Series Release No. 244,* March 3, 1978.

[16]*Staff Accounting Bulletin No. 5,* February 13, 1976.

[17]*Staff Accounting Bulleting No. 4,* January 29, 1976.

[18]*Accounting Release No. 145,* August 2, 1973.

[19]*Accounting Series Release No. 163,* November 14, 1974.

[20]*Accounting Series Release No. 151,* January 3, 1974.

[21] *Accounting Series Release No. 166,* December 23, 1974.

[22] *Accounting Series Release No. 138,* January 12, 1973.

[23] *Accounting Series Release No. 177,* September 10, 1975.

[24] *Securities Exchange Act Release No. 15772,* April 30, 1979.

A Comment on John C. Burton's "The SEC and Financial Reporting: The Sand in the Oyster"

George R. Catlett

Arthur Andersen & Company

Sandy Burton seems to think the accounting profession is under water--either as an oyster looking for a grain of sand or as a reluctant swimmer who has been pushed in. Such characteristics are colorful but hardly pertinent. He also refers to the SEC as a "creative irritant," but some persons might contend that this term is only 50 percent accurate.

Let me say at the outset that I have respect for the SEC as a regulatory agency that is making a conscientious effort to carry out its mission. It is one of the better agencies in Washington, and it has played a role in the standard-setting process. However, the SEC is not infallible, and the profession is not going to be "saved" or made into a vibrant force in our society by government regulation.

Burton's case in support of the imperative need for the SEC to push the profession toward desirable goals is overstated when the says, "In the financial accounting environment as it exists today, change will not happen in the absence of SEC action to stimulate the profession. If innovation is to occur, the SEC must be the principal source." While it is true that SEC action has stimulated professional developments at various times, the record does not show that such action is necessary for change to occur. Quite the contrary: the SEC, with its emphasis on uniformity and "general acceptance," has stifled innovation and experimentation in accounting standards and financial reporting more often than not. For example Arthur Andersen & Co. was prepared to accept the capitalization of financing leases by a client before such capitalization was customary and in a manner similar to that now required. The SEC refused to permit the capitalization because it was not in accordance with generally accepted accounting principles. Another example is the prohibition by the SEC for many years of any value information or price-level data in or with the financial statements or any place else in a registration statement.

I question whether the SEC always knows what is best for investors. Burton indicates that "one of the purposes of regulation is to conform short-run to long-run behavior" and that the SEC should decide what new information investors need and then persuade them to learn to use it whether they want to or not. But the SEC rarely analyzes its regulation in terms of cost-benefit. The information explosion as reflected in lengthy and complex registration statements is not necessarily productive and useful. More and more information, regardless of cost, is not necessarily better. Selectivity and quality of information are important, and no one has a corner on wisdom in this regard. One real danger of too numerous government regulations and rules is that efforts to cure the sick may result in infecting the healthy.

While I agree with some of Burton's observations about the relationship of the profession and the SEC, my greatest disagreement is with his conclusion that the 1980s will be the same as the 1970s. Many changes are going to occur in the profession and probably in the SEC, and this relationship is certain to be affected in various ways that cannot now be anticipated.

Several developments could have significant effects in

the 1980s. I will mention three possibilities.

*Further government regulation of the accounting profession.* The question of further government regulation of the accounting profession will be resolved one way or the other during the next few years. The profession needs to be independent of government as well as of clients if it is to carry out its proper functions. The FASB cannot be isolated from the threat of government regulation. If it carries out its function well enough, it could survive and be reasonably independent of the SEC. If the FASB does not perform well enough, the "creative irritant" of the SEC is not going to overcome the deficiency, and we could end up with a new government agency apart from the SEC. At the present time, the FASB is doing an increasingly better job as an organization in the private sector, and we can hope that this improvement continues.

I have been involved with the American Institute's self-regulatory efforts since the inception of the SEC Practice Section and am quite encouraged about the progress that has been made, particularly by members of the Executive Committee of the SEC Practice Section and other related committees. The Public Oversight Board of that section has five outstanding members who are doing an excellent job.

*Large arena for accounting profession.* The arena with which the accounting profession is involved is much larger than that of the SEC. The SEC is concerned with financial information for investors in publicly owned companies, whereas the profession is also concerned with nonpublic companies, nonprofit organizations, and governmental entities. All three of these latter areas are huge and involve many different problems relating to accounting standards and financial information. There is considerable debate at the present time about whether the FASB or some other agency should establish standards for the accounting of state and local governmental entities. I believe that the FASB should take the lead, with the cooperation of such organizations as the Municipal Finance Officers Association.

*The public interest.* Last, and perhaps most important, is what might be called "the ascendancy of the public interest." Current public attitudes are influenced by consumerism, demands for more social responsibility, inflation, the energy crisis, and many other matters. This also involves the economic consequences and political ramifications of accounting standards, which is a subject that has been much discussed during the last year. (David Solomons had an interesting article on this subject in the November 1978 issue of the *Journal of Accountancy.*) The profession is going to have to consider the public interest as well as investor interest in the future.

Accounting and financial reporting should not be used as a tool to distort the facts in order to achieve social or political objectives or national goals, and this is one of the reasons for keeping the standard-setting functions out of government agencies. And it does not follow that standards which cause undesirable economic consequences necessarily result in improper accounting. There may also be a question about what consequences in fact occur and whether those that do occur are desirable, because those making the judgments have different and conflicting interests. On the other hand, if the public interest is ignored in a democracy, the public will eventually assert its influence through the political process, which is the only course of action available.

Examples of accounting standards that have significant economic effects are those involving mergers, research, pension plans, lease financing, translation of foreign currency financial statements, and oil and gas exploration and development. In the case of oil and gas, it was the potential economic effects that caused political intervention that resulted in the SEC overruling the FASB conclusion. One lesson we should have learned is that the greater the potential economic consequences, the more necessary it is for the alternative standard selected to be clearly superior to other alternatives. Deploring political intervention will not eliminate such intervention. It must be dealt with--in a positive and constructive manner--as a fact of life in a democracy.

There is an important difference between the public interest and politics. They get mixed up because politicians cloak themselves with the public interest and because the public interest tends to be asserted through politicians. The accounting profession should keep the distinction clearly in mind.

The accounting profession has had the sextant but no fixed star, the techniques but no destiny, the material but no blueprints, the means but no clear ends. These goals are on the horizon and could be realized in the 1980s--and without any grains of sand.

# Beauty is in the Eye of the Beholder: A Comment on John C. Burton's "The SEC and Financial Reporting: The Sand in the Oyster"

Ross L. Watts

The University of Rochester

Beauty is in the eye of the beholder. Those who wear pearls, those who consume them, undoubtedly consider pearls to be beautiful. However, I doubt if oysters think pearls are beautiful. The oyster bears the cost of creating the pearl and receives none of the benefits.

I think Sandy Burton's comparison of the development of accounting standards to an oyster's creation of a pearl is apt. A chief accountant of the Securities and Exchange Commission consumes regulations just as the person wearing pearls consumes pearls. Consequently it is not surprising that Sandy considers the standard-setting process beautiful. Since I both observe and feel some empathy for the oysters who pay the costs of creating the pearl, I do not regard the standard-setting process as beautiful. Beauty is in the eye of the beholder.

In his thought-provoking paper, Sandy argues that disclosure regulation has restricted private innovation in disclosure. The increased liability of corporate managers and accountants has made them reluctant to depart from the status quo. Sandy suggests that as a consequence the preparers do not sufficiently consider investor interests. Consequently, the SEC has had to step in to protect investor interests and be the driving force for innovation in disclosure.

I agree with some of the empirical propositions put forward by Sandy in his paper. For example, I agree that disclosure regulation and the concomitant increase in liability for corporate managers and accountants has reduced innovation in disclosure. However, I disagree with his explanations of the acts of the SEC and of Congress. Undoubtedly, Sandy's and my differing interpretations are colored by our backgrounds as a consumer of pearls and an observer of oysters, respectively. Some of these differences follow.

## Examples of Differences in Interpretation

### The Motivation for the Securities Acts

Sandy argues in his paper that the structure of securities regulation established in the Securities Acts was designed to protect investors against perceived abuses in financial disclosure. You will note that he uses the term "perceived abuses" instead of just "abuses." Undoubtedly, he is aware that there was no evidence of frequent abuses in the disclosure system prior to the Securities Acts.[1] Further, he is aware that there was no attempt to determine the frequency of abuse and the costs and benefits of reducing that frequency in the hearings which preceded the Securities Acts. Hence, it is difficult to argue that the legislation was concerned with actual abuses. Instead his argument is that Congress was concerned with abuses perceived by the electorate.

There does seem to be a flaw in this argument. The argument suggests the cost of information in the political process is substantial enough to cause politicians to be concerned with perceived rather than actual abuses. If so, then surely those same costs would now cause politicians to be concerned only with being *perceived* to be doing something about perceived abuses rather than actually doing something.

I hypothesize that in fact what caused the enactment of the Security Acts was the incentive for politicians to appear to be acting to prevent another great crash. Those individual politicians were not concerned with the realities of the situation or the public interest (whatever that is); they were merely acting in their own self-interest by actions which would increase their probability of being reelected.

Incidentally, the argument that there are substantial information costs in the political process was first advanced by Downs in 1959. He argued that the probability of an individual voter's vote affecting the outcome of an election is almost zero. Hence, the value of the voter's vote is almost zero and the voter has little incentive to gather information about political issues.

Burton appears to make a similar argument about investors by stating that no single investor would want to bear the costs of gathering information when he is only one of the many investors who will benefit. However, he ignores one important difference between the marketplace and the political process. The marketplace has lower costs in the sense of higher gains to individuals expressing their intensity of beliefs and preferences than does the political process. For example, if the manager of corporation A has information that leads him to B is not acting in the shareholders' interest and has consequently reduced the value of B's shares, the manager of A can express this belief by making a bid to take over B. If the manager of A is successful and then manages B in the shareholders' interest, he (and his shareholders) can capture a capital gain from the changed actions.[2] This concentration of benefits via the market for securities gives a larger incentive to gather information. In the political process, however, it is more costly to concentrate such gains from changes in actions. There isn't an effective market for votes, and this reduces the desire for information in the political process.

In general I would characterize the political process as competition among individuals pursuing their own self-interest. There is evidence to support this position in the economic literature.[3] However, my interpretation is at odds with Burton's view that the disclosure legislation was designed to meet perceived abuses.

## Motivation of the SEC

Burton suggests, "the SEC has as its objective achieving a level of public disclosure at least equivalent to the disclosure that would likely be sought by a provider of capital negotiating at arms length and with equivalent power to that of a capital user." He also suggests in closing that the SEC does consider costs and benefits, including out-of-pocket costs and costs of competitive disadvantage.

I don't think the evidence supports the impression given that the SEC objectively assesses the costs and benefits of alternative disclosure rules. Certainly, the replacement cost requirement appears (from the outside) to have been a hasty decision with little thought given to the costs and benefits.[4] Further, the groups charged with calculating costs and benefits do not appear to be important within the SEC. The proportion of the budget spent on cost/benefit analysis is probably trivial relative to the total SEC budget.

To me the behavior of the regulators in the SEC seems to be more consistent with the view of the political process expressed above. If the SEC's budget is determined by politicians more concerned with appearances than substance, I would expect the SEC's actions to be more concerned with appearance than fact. The SEC's function is to issue regulations and to prosecute--to appear to be acting to remedy "perceived" abuses. Allowing serious calculation of costs to affect those regulations would be dysfunctional. That is why the SEC spends a small fraction of its budget on estimating costs and benefits and a large fraction on the lawyers who produce and enforce regulations.

## The Effect of the SEC on Disclosure

Burton suggests that the SEC's "encouragement of innovation and change has contributed to the development of financial reporting." In effect he suggests the SEC has been an active rather than passive stimulator of change.

I question that interpretation. I do not see the SEC as the initiator of actions. I see the SEC's actions as the response to competing pressures in the political process. There are many examples that support this view. At first glance, it may appear that the threat delivered by Chairman Budge in 1969 that the SEC would dictate rule-making if the Accounting Principles Board did not present a satisfactory opinion on business comibnations and goodwill was instrumental in the appearance of APB Opinions 16 and 17.[5] However, even before Budge's threat, there had been considerable political pressures generated by attacks on the methods of accounting for business combinations in the financial press. Consequently, a better interpretation is that the SEC was merely an agent in the process.

Other examples abound. The SEC's effective over-ruling of APB Opinion 2 was associated with considerable congressional lobbying by business. There was also political pressure for inflation accounting at the time of the replacement cost requirement.

Since the SEC's actions are determined by the political process, and the objective of those actions is to appear to be improving financial disclosure rather than to improve disclosure, it would only be by chance that the SEC has improved disclosure from the investors' point of view.

I suspect there has been very little benefit to the investor from the accounting standard-setting process.

Formal empirical evidence has indicated that the imposition of an accounting standard reduces the value of the shares in corporations using alternative accounting procedures.[6]

There is even more direct evidence that the disclosure system imposes costs. We actually observe arms-length borrowers and lenders contracting out of imposed accounting standards. For example, we observe lending agreements requiring that net income be calculated using the cost basis of accounting for subsidiaries instead of the equity method.[7]

## Disputes over Evidence

There are some statements in Burton's paper which appear to be at variance with available evidence. For example, his suggestion that one of the purposes of the disclosure regulation is to conform short-run investor behavior to long-run behavior implies that investors would not act in their own long-run interest without the SEC's help. But all of the evidence on capital markets suggests maximizing behavior by investors (i.e., maximizing wealth), and this implies that investors correctly trade off current and future benefits. I know of no formal evidence which suggests the opposite.

In general it seems ludicrous to suggest that a few lawyers in the SEC know the demands of investors better than the investors themselves. After all, the investors lay their own bucks on the line.

## Summary and Conclusions

Clearly Sandy Burton and I view the pearl in the oyster differently. Naturally, I consider my view of the world to be more consistent with the evidence, i.e., that investors are oysters irritated by the disclosure arrangements.

## Notes

[1]See Benston (1969).

[2]The extent of the capital gain captured by firm A's manager and shareholders depends on the number of other firms which could also takeover B and capture the gain and whether or not those other firms know of the opportunity.

[3]See Posner (1974).

[4]Other examples of hasty decisions abound. Given the evidence on the efficient markets hypothesis, the recent moratorium on writing options would appear hasty. Further, the recent proposals to require firms planning to take over other firms to reveal their plans would seem likely to inhibit the market for corporate control and reduce the efficiency of the capital market.

[5]See Zeff (1972), p. 213.

[6]Collins and Dent (forthcoming); Holthausen (1979); Leftwich (1979).

[7]Watts (1977), p. 62.

## References

Benston, G. J. "The Effectiveness and Effects of the SEC's Accounting Disclosure Requirements." In *Economic Policy and the Regulation of Corporate Securities,* edited by H. G. Manne, pp. 23-79. Washington: (American Enterprise Institute, 1969).

Collins, D. W., and W. T. Dent. "The Proposed Elimination of Full Cost Accounting in the Extractive Petroleum Industry: An Empirical Assessment of the Market Consequences." *Journal of Accounting and Economics,* forthcoming.

Downs, A. "An Economic Theory of Political Action in a Democracy." *Journal of Political Economy* (1957).

Holthausen, R. W. "Bond Covenants and the Choice of Accounting Techniques: The Case of Alternative Depreciation Methods." Manuscript, Graduate School of Management, University of Rochester, 1979.

Leftwich, R. W. "The Impact of Mandatory Changes in Accounting Principles on Corporate Loan Agreements." Manuscript, Graduate School of Management, University of Rochester, 1979.

Posner, R. A. "Theories of Economic Regulation." *The Bell Journal of Economics and Management Science* (Autumn 1974): 335-58.

Watts, R. L. "Corporate Financial Statements, A Product of the Market and Political Processes." *Australian Journal of Management* (April 1977): 53-95.

Zeff, S. *Forging Accounting Principles in Five Countries: A History and Analysis of Trends 1971.* Arthur Andersen Lecture Series. Champaign, Ill.: Stipes Publishing Company, 1972.

3

# Regulation of Accounting: Practitioner's Viewpoint

Robert K. Elliott and Walter Schuetze

Peat, Marwick, Mitchell & Co.

Governmental regulation of economic activity, by definition, is partial control of that activity. Complete control is the Marxist concept of state-run economic activity. Thus, when considering economic regulation, one is necessarily drawn to an evaluation of the appropriate balance between governmental and private-sector control of economic decisions affecting the activity in question. Whatever the merits of complete governmental control of an economic activity, they are not germane to a realistic assessment of the question of regulating accounting. Thus the basic issue in regulating accounting is twofold: how much regulation is necessary and what proportion of such authority and responsibility should be in public-sector hands and what proportion in private-sector hands.

In this paper we place the issue of regulation of accounting in the broad context of regulation in general. We define some basic principles by which regulation can be evaluated. Today accounting is largely, but not wholly, regulated by the private sector. For instance SEC disciplinary actions that deny accountants the privilege of practicing before it constitute a form of governmental regulation of accounting; so does state licensing of CPAs. Other examples could be cited. We need a framework of regulatory principles to judge the efficacy of the regulatory responsibilities now applicable to accounting, to consider whether additional regulatory responsibilities are necessary, and to determine the appropriate parties to administer regulatory responsibilities.

Setting the issue of regulation of accounting in the context of regulation in general also may help to divorce the issue from the problem of improper payments. It does not diminish the social importance of the improper payments question to say that it is virtually irrelevant, or at best tangential, to a sound assessment of regulating accounting. Accountants are not now and never have been professionally or legally responsible for the detection or prevention of improper payments immaterial to the financial statements. Yet concern over improper corporate payments probably has been the major cause of the reconsideration in recent years of regulating accounting. The issue has stimulated criticisms and reform proposals by congressional committees, the SEC, and spokesmen for the public interest. It is time to set out criteria for regulating accounting that are more relevant and enduring than concern over improper payments or other specific situations that arise from time to time.

The issue of regulation of accounting also is sometimes distorted by the narrow view that governmental regulation is innately superior to private-sector regulation; under this assumption, the mere criticism of private-sector regulatory institutions can lead to a call for public-sector intervention. But this assumption is illogical and unrealistic. Government can do a worse job than an imperfect private-sector institution, and reforming the private-sector institution may be a more cost-effective, socially desirable alternative, if indeed reform is needed.

The assumption that all governmental encroachment on or regulation of the private sector is, ipso facto, an evil as narrow as the assumption that it is superior. Governmental regulation of economic activity in non-Marxist states is neither new nor necessarily evil. Paradoxically the assumption that governmental regulation is to be avoided at all costs can lead private-sector groups to an approach to regulation based on political concessions. Armed with no support for their opposition other than their narrow assumption, individuals may be tempted to cut their losses by compromises. They may concede governmental regulation in some areas in order to render less likely a larger measure of governmental regulation or adopt private-sector regulation solely to demonstrate that governmental regulation is unnecessary. These are unworthy approaches to the question of regulation. We shall not discuss them, although we hope that putting the issue of regulation in the context of broad principles demonstrates the irresponsibility of what might be called the "horse-trader" approach.

Complete private control of economic activity, in which the marketplace is absolutely undisturbed by the active presence of the state, is incompatible with modern organized society. It is a species of anarchy. Adam Smith, who championed the free market, recognized this: "Commerce and manufactures can seldom flourish long in any state which does not enjoy a regular administration of justice, in which the people do not feel themselves secure in the possession of their property, in which the faith of contracts is not supported by law, and in which the authority of the state is not supposed to be regularly employed in enforcing the payment of debts from all those who are able to pay."[1] In short, in Adam Smith's "free" market, the economic decisions to steal, to evade contractual obligations, and to renege on debts are prohibited, and the prohibitions are enforced by the state. Now it is unreasonable to say Adam Smith's free market is greatly compromised by these admissions. They simply indicate the fallacy of postulating a marketplace uninfluenced by government. Smith argued even more fervently and eloquently against too much government influence, as in the regulatory system that existed and was called mercantilism.[2] What role would Smith consider proper for the state after two centuries of rapid economic and social change? Would he, for instance, extend the concept of justice to include equal employment opportunity or the concept of security to include security from toxic pollutants visited without consent?

Economic regulation by government preceded the mercantilist system that Adam Smith attacked. For example, in fourteenth-century England, Parliament passed the Statute of Labourers, which mandated that wages and the cost of food should be set at the rates prior to the increases caused by the impact of the Black Death. The measure was a response to the economic dislocation caused by the plague, which had so reduced the supply of labor that its market value was often double, sometimes more, what it had been before the calamity.[3] In 1497 Parliament set the fee for membership in the Fellowship of the Merchant Adventurers of London, which had attempted to exclude provincial competitors from its preeminent position in the Antwerp cloth trade by a far higher membership fee.[4] The Statute of Artificers in 1563 authorized Justices of the Peace to set wage rates yearly, graded for different occupations and based upon the cost of living.[5] The justices were to consider "the plenty or scarcity of the time and other circumstances necessary to be considered."[6]

The history of regulation in our country is properly traced back to the Constitution. Ours has always been a concept of limited government, limited, for instance, by separation of powers and inviolable individual rights and liberties. The Constitution contains language authorizing future regulation of economic activities and language that sets limits on the way government may pursue its purposes, including regulation. The preamble states that the purpose of government is to promote the general welfare, and article 1, section 8, empowers Congress to regulate interstate and foreign commerce. However, the preamble also states that the purpose of government is to ensure citizens the blessings of liberty, and the fifth amendment holds that no person should be deprived of property without due process of law and that property cannot be taken for public use without just compensation. Moreover, no attempt to regulate in the interest of the general welfare can infringe on other rights enumerated in the Constitution, such as free speech.

In our history, regulation of economic activity most often has been intended to serve two basic purposes, protecting consumers and protecting persons who, while not parties to an economic transaction, are nevertheless affected by it (especially by external *dis*economies). Rate regulation and antimonopoly measures, for instance, are intended to protect consumers. The FTC is authorized to protect consumers by administering laws that prohibit monopoly, restraints on trade, false advertising, and other deceptive practices. The Consumer Product Safety Commission develops uniform safety standards for consumer products in order to protect consumers from unreasonable risks of injury. The Federal Energy Regulatory Commission has power to regulate rates and charges for transportation and sale of natural gas and electricity.

The consumer-protection regulatory functions just cited may be contrasted with those intended to regulate economic decisions because of their effects on external parties. Those who suffer from pollution, for example, are primarily external to the economic decision makers who pollute. The Environmental Protection Agency develops standards to reduce and prevent pollution of air and water resources. The agency's regulations affect public health, in the case of toxic emissions into the atmosphere; public enjoyment of natural resources, in the case of polluted streams and waterways; and public comfort, in the case of noise emissions.

The SEC was formed to serve both direct consumers and the public welfare in general--the former by protecting purchasers of securities from fraud and insufficient information and the latter by rekindling confidence in the capital markets, which, by contributing to economic growth and stability, benefits parties external to securities transactions.

There is little doubt about the legitimacy of public-sector regulation, long since a part of our traditions and our constitutional framework. Few can doubt the importance of the goals regulatory agencies are designed to achieve. Even critics of governmental regulation recognize its successes, as George Stigler did when he wrote: "The delay in introducing thalidomide in the United States presumably was a splendid success, and should receive full credit. But . . . if the policies which delayed thalidomide would delay a new penicillin at least as long--as seems highly probable--we must recognize this in the costs of the programs."[7] Thus, the critical point is not the concept of regulation by the government but whether and in what circumstances governmental regulation is necessary and whether and to what degree those circumstances apply to accounting.

There are certain general principles by which governmental regulation may be judged. First, regulation must not violate constitutional rights or statute. Second, it should be designed to prevent real or probably social damage. Third, regulation must be in the public interest. A corollary to this principle is that costs not exceed benefits and the regulation itself not be superfluous. If the forces of the marketplace can resolve a question adequately, regulation is superfluous. Fourth, regulation should not be adopted by the public sector if its purpose can be achieved by private-sector institutions. Fifth, the potential regulatee should not bear the burden of proving regulation is unwarranted; rather, advocates of regulation must demonstrate that regulation is warranted. Sixth, regulatory action should not be used to correct occasional lawbreaking, which is the task of law enforcement; nor should regulatory responsibilities be established to combat occasional antisocial behavior that can be proscribed by statute.

The principles we have cited are consistent with our country's legal history and traditions. The first principle simply states that regulation should be consistent with the law, and the fifth--no burden on the potential regulatee--is in harmony with the legal tradition that presumes innocence. The fact that regulation affects property rights makes this concept of due process still more relevant. The priority given to private-sector solutions to problems that might be addressed by governmental regulation (principle four) is in our tradition of limited government. That regulation must be in the public interest is virtually a restatement of the constitutional concept that government should "promote the general welfare." The cost-benefit corollary is the operative element in the principle. The notion of the public interest is also consistent with the purposes of most previous regulation, as is the second principle concerning social damage. As we have noted, previous regulation has been designed chiefly to protect consumers or to protect third parties from injury caused by transactions executed by others.

Table 3.1 contains a statement of these principles translated into prerequisites for the adoption of federal regulation. As conditions change, however, any specific regulation adopted to satisfy these prerequisites may become unnecessary and unjustifiable because it ceases to satisfy them.

Before we illustrate these principles, we must point out that regulating accounting is not directly analogous to regulating the purchase and sale of products and privately consumed services or regulating the external effects of private economic decision-making, such as toxic emissions from factories. Regulating accounting includes setting accounting and auditing standards, disciplining professionals for errant performance, and prescribing quality controls and ethical standards for a private profession. It involves novel and complicated sets of interests. The auditor's service is purchased by the client, but the auditor has well-known responsibilities to third parties. Those responsibilities are not externalities but rather an essential element of the audit function. Auditors are legally liable for their performance, in varying degrees, both to clients and the third-party users of their reports. Setting accounting standards, the task now performed in the private sector by the FASB, affects preparers of financial statements who apply the standards, auditors who examine the preparer's application of the standards, and third parties who use the financial statements and auditors' reports. Setting auditing standards also affects all three groups. Although in these and other ways, regulating accounting is not directly analogous to any other field of regulation, the general principles described above are still applicable. Moreover, they assume greater importance precisely because arguments from analogy to other economic activities have so little relevance.

Table 3.2 illustrates the application of the prerequisites in Table 3.1 to selected regulatory issues. The table is deliberately set up so that decisions about applying earlier prerequisites (reading left to right) affect decisions about the application of subsequent prerequisites. Thus, the item "Some CPA firms are large," is given a "no" in column 1 because no empirical data indicating damage have been brought out in the public dialogue on this subject. Accordingly, the entries for the next four prerequisites are "no" and "not applicable."

Item 7 is worth singling out because it helps clarify the principle that regulatory action should not be used to correct occasional lawbreaking, which is the task of law enforcement, and that regulatory responsibilities should not be established to combat occasional antisocial behavior that can be proscribed by statute. The Foreign Corrupt Practices Act of 1977, which prohibits bribes to foreign officials, was a response to identified cases of what many considered to be antisocial behavior. A statutory proscription of such behavior is an appropriate response. However, the same statute that prohibits certain foreign bribes establishes general regulation of all companies registered with the SEC through the "accounting provisions" (which require accurate records and adequate internal controls). This is a case where an entire class of businesses is regulated because of the transgressions of a few, a regulation manifestly inappropriate under the principles described above.

The principle that regulation must not violate statute may be illustrated by the Supreme Court decision in the Hochfelder case. The court addressed the question of whether a cause of action against accountants in a securities fraud could be maintained under Section 10(b) of the Securities Exchange Act of 1934 and SEC Rule 10b-5 in the absence of an allegation of intent to deceive or defraud. As is well known, the Court found that such an allegation was necessary. The justices held that the language and history of Section 10(b) indicated that it was intended to encompass only intentional behavior. Our interest is in the Court's findings with respect to the SEC's argument in an amicus brief that Rule 10b-5 does not require intent to deceive.

The Court agreed with the SEC that the language of Rule 10b-5 could be read as proscribing conduct that has the effect of defrauding investors, whether or not the conduct is intentional. Nevertheless, the Court held that the SEC had no authority to exceed by rulemaking the power granted to it by Congress in the enabling statute, the 1934 Act:

> The rulemaking power granted to an administrative agency charged with the administration of a federal statute is not the power to make the law. Rather

> it is "'the power to adopt regulations to carry into effect the will of Congress as expressed by the statute.'" [sic] . . . Thus, despite the broad view of the Rule advanced by the Commission in this case, its scope cannot exceed the power granted the Commission by Congress under Section 10(b).[8]

The constituional right to legal due process and the prohibition against unreasonable search and seizure have been asserted in the courts in opposition to certain governmental regulatory activities. Some believe that the Barlow case (May 1978), in which it was held that a plumber had the right to eject inspectors from OSHA from his shop because they did not have a search warrant, may become a landmark, and related actions have been brought. Regardless of the merits of such cases, they illustrate that in our society regulatory agencies may not violate constitutional rights.[9]

The principle of nonviolation of constitutional rights and liberties also applies to the question of whether a governmental body or the private sector, through the FASB, should set accounting standards. Since setting accounting standards affects the way financial reports present corporate results (reports used in turn for analysis of the health of our economy), the power to set accounting standards is also power to control information about the success or failure of national economic policies. It would therefore violate the spirit of the right of free speech if government set accounting standards. The right of free speech functions not only as a liberty enjoyed by individuals but also as a check on government. It ensures that information and opinions unfavorable to government can be produced and disseminated.

The investment tax credit fiasco of 1971 demonstrates government's vested interest in accounting standards that can reflect on national economic policies. On October 6, 1971, the House passed a tax bill reinstituting the investment tax credit, which was proposed by the administration to bolster a sagging economy. While the bill was being considered, the Accounting Principles Board developed a draft Opinion, which was issued for public comment on October 22. It would have required deferral of the credit and amortization over the life of the related asset. On November 9, the Senate Finance Committee report on its version of the bill expressed the view that companies should have free choice in selecting the accounting treatment for the new credit. This would ensure that the "flow-through" method, which results in higher reported earnings in the year the credit is available, could be used. Although AICPA leaders met with administration and congressional officials and explained the benefits to investors and creditors of the profession's approach, emphasizing the desirability of uniform accounting requirements, the law that emerged expressly forbids taxpayers from being required to use any particular method of accounting for the investment tax credit. This effectively killed the proposed APB Opinion and established a statutory barrier to eliminating a set of accounting alternatives.[10]

The administration had argued that businessmen would have greater motivation to purchase new equipment--the government's goal--if they were not obligated to use deferral--in other words, that they would be motivated by the prospect of reporting higher earnings (although, of course, the underlying economics are not affected at all by the accounting treatment selected).[11] It may be argued that it is odd to attempt to influence individual decisions by regulating what is reported about them instead of trusting the effect of economic incentives, but that is not the critical point here. The point is that the legislative decision was made in virtual disregard of the notion that financial accounting should report the substance of economic events and the concept that reducing alternative accounting principles facilitates analysis of reported data by enhancing their comparability. The one incident alone demonstrates why government should no more control accounting standards than it should specify the editorial standards or content of newspapers.

The principle that regulation should be in the public interest is not always easy to apply to regulating accounting. Despite the work of men like George Benston and George Stigler, too little research has been done on the consequences of regulatory policy. Interest in the subject has recently become more widespread, but much work remains. It is hard to measure the costs and benefits of regulation, and this of course bequeaths difficulties to those who wish to compare the respective cost-benefit advantages of public- and private-sector regulation. However, it is best to face this problem squarely rather than to allow arguments to degenerate into assumptions and assertions. This difficulty was addressed by the Advisory Committee on Corporate Disclosure, charged "to assess the costs of the present system of corporate disclosure and to weigh those costs against the benefits it produces." But its report to the SEC in 1977 acknowledges that, despite the efforts of its staff, it was "generally unable" to perform the task.[12] Until we have improved means to measure the costs and benefits of regulation, there will be limits on the precision of comparisons between public- and private-sector regulation. For the same reason, there will be limits on comparisons between the effectiveness of pursuing desirable objectives by regulation (public or private) and the effectiveness of achieving such objectives through the natural forces of the marketplace. For instance, if the marketplace, by rewarding full disclosure and penalizing inadequate disclosure, provides an effective incentive for adequate disclosure, there is less necessity for mandatory disclosure. The Advisory Committee on Corporate Disclosure wrestled openly with this question, and a majority concluded that there was at this time an insufficient basis for dismantling the existing system.[13]

The limitations on assessments of the costs and benefits of regulation highlight the importance of requiring regulation not be superfluous, that is, not duplicative of other regulation, serving no useful purpose, or serving a purpose already fulfilled by the marketplace. In addition, regulation is less likely to be superfluous if it is designed to eradicate an identified abuse rather than to prevent a potential abuse.

Consider the case of management advisory services performed by auditing firms. There has been much talk of adding to the restrictions already imposed on the provision of such services. The November 1977 report of the Senate Subcommittee on Reports, Accounting and Management expressed concern over the impact on audit independence of performing certain management advisory services.[14] Both the SEC and a private-sector regulatory body, the SEC Practice Section of the AICPA, have taken up the question, and the SEC has prescribed disclosures as a result of its deliberations.[15] Such regulatory activity concerns potential abuse rather than identified ones. The issue did not rise out of any instances of abuse but with the encouragement of critics who would benefit by increased business if accounting firms curtailed their provision of management advisory services. There is no body of data showing that audit engagements have been compromised by performing management consulting. The Cohen Commission wrote, "If empirical evidence were the only consideration, the Commission's conclusion would be clear: The evidence does not support the theory. No prohibition of management services is warranted."[16]

Now it is true that the appearance of independence is important to auditors, and this is the primary ground on which many have supported reexamining auditing firms' management consulting practices. Again, however, no empirical evidence has been adduced; that is, no data indicate that auditors' public appearance of independence has been damaged materially by performing management advisory services. All these factors suggest that superfluous regulatory activity has been pursued. Nor was the effect of the marketplace openly considered by those who advocated reevaluating the propriety of providing management advisory services. The marketplace rewards auditors for being independent. Without a reputation for independence, an auditing firm would not last long in public practice.

To summarize this episode in regulatory activity, the recent ongoing reconsideration of auditors' provision of management advisory services has shown inadequate regard for defining the public interest through research. Responsiveness to publicly expressed criticism does not translate directly into responsiveness to the public interest. Certainly one of the major responsibilities of a regulatory body should be to examine the empirical validity of criticisms calling for regulatory action. There has been too little examination of the empirical validity of the recent criticism by congressional committees that accounting and auditing standard-setting is deficient and would be remedied by public-sector standard-setting. Our firm performed an analysis of the quality of U.S. accounting and auditing standards as compared to the quality of the standards in other major countries. Figures 3.1 and 3.2 summarize the findings.[17] Three facts are immediately apparent from the figures.

* The U.S. has the highest quality accounting and auditing standards in the world.
* The falloff in quality is rather abrupt, and aside from a few countries the rest of the world does not even approach the level of quality in the U.S.
* There is a strong correlation between high quality and private-sector standard-setting.

These findings do not, of course, indicate that private-sector standard setting is perfect, but they suggest that it is more effective than public-sector standard setting would be. Although this is vitally important, it is not what we wish to emphasize here. The point is that when considering governmental regulation, the search for empirical evidence should take priority over acceptance of critical, unsupported assertions.

The principle that governmental regulation should not be adopted if there is a private-sector remedy to a problem calling for regulation has been supported as consistent with our tradition of limited government. Let us for the moment abandon this justification and answer the following hypothetical question: if an activity or action is needed in regulating accounting, and both private- and public-sector bodies can perform it equally well, which course is preferable?

One might cite the impropriety of spending tax dollars when private-sector funds could be used instead. However, if the number of dollars were the same in each case, this would not be a decisive point. Private-sector costs eventually are borne by consumers and thus become diffused to a rather broad constituency. The decisive issue, we believe, is whether the public- or private-sector body is more flexible, can adapt the new regulatory action or activity to changing circumstances more readily, even, if need be, rescinding rules. This is largely a question of accountability. The more accountability is built into the system, the more likely it is to respond to changing circumstances.

We believe regulation of accounting by independent federal government agency would be, and is, less accountable than that by private-sector institutions. This position is based on two arguments. First, such agencies *are* "independent," occupying and exercising in this respect a role unique in our constitutional framework, and their independence carries with it an important measure of insulation from public accountability. Second, with the current mix of regulatory responsibilities, private-sector bodies regulating accounting are more responsible to the public than public-sector bodies. In short, the general assumption that in a democratic society governmental institutions are the most accountable of institutions does not necessarily apply to independent agencies, such as the SEC, which would bear the brunt of additional federal regulation of accounting.

The independence of regulatory agencies continues to be the subject of much debate. Except for the president's power of appointment and informal relationships between the executive branch and the agencies, the agencies are independent of the executive. This has the advantage of removing regulatory agencies in some measure from the "politics"--in the negative sense of the term--of the executive branch. It has the disadvantage that the agencies do not share with the executive its quadrennial accountability to the electorate. It also has the disadvantage that the activities of regulatory agencies are not readily coordinated with national economic policy as directed by the executive.[18] These issues have been intensified as President Carter seeks to coordinate his attack on inflation,[19] but they are not new. President Roosevelt's Committee on Administrative Management (the Brownlow Committee), famous for calling the agencies a "headless fourth branch" of government, put the problem this way: "No administrative reorganization worthy of the name can leave hanging in the air more than a dozen powerful, irresponsible agencies free to determine policy and administer law. Any program to restore our constitutional ideal of a fully coordinated Executive Branch responsible to the President must bring within the reach of that responsible control all work done by these independent commissions which is not judicial in nature."[20]

Some would quarrel with the notion that the agencies are "irresponsible," holding that they are responsible to Congress. As William L. Cary has shown, Congress can have a significant impact on regulatory agencies through oversight, appropriations, and regulators' beliefs that agencies are responsible to Congress.[21] But constitutional theory on this question is somewhat confusing. If independent agencies, which exercise administrative, judicial, and legislative functions (whether prefixed by "quasi" or not), are tucked into any of the three branches of government, including the legislature, the principle of separation of powers is breached. In reality, independent agencies are chiefly limited by their legislative mandate, and the ebb and flow of congressional oversight, interest, and influence, along with the power to revise enabling legislation, does not constitute a regular check on agency independence. If it did, there probably would not have been a recommendation by the House Subcommittee on Oversight and Investigations in 1976 that congressional oversight be strengthened "to increase the accountability of the agencies to elected representatives of the public."[22] Thus, without delving deeply into the constitutional argument about degrees of independence that obtain or should obtain in the federal regulatory framework, it is clear, partly from the very fact of the long-standing debate on the subject, that federal regulatory agencies are not directly and absolutely accountable for their behavior. It follows that when comparing the accountability of private-sector regulatory bodies to public-sector regulatory bodies, one cannot assume that governmental institutions represent optimal accountability. Indeed, one scholar who analyzed the agencies concluded, "Unfortunately, the commissions operate under conditions which appear to maximize the obstacles to the achievement of democratic political responsibility."[23]

In contrast to independent agencies, private-sector institutions that regulate accounting, in particular the FASB, the Auditing Standards Board, and the Firms Division of the AICPA, are notable for their accountability. It is demonstrated by the nature of the institutions and by the reforms adopted in recent years, which we shall review selectively and briefly.

The FASB was set up as a result of the report of the Study Group on Establishment of Accounting Principles, issued in March 1972, which recommended that the new standard-setting body, "to the fullest extent possible, carry out its functions in public."[24] In addition, the report stated that the new board should be "free of any private interests which might conflict with the public interest."[25] To assure that a broad spectrum of views are available to the board, the study group recommended the establishment of an Advisory Council composed of members from various occupations.[26]

The FASB's structure, its bylaws, and its rules of procedure gave institutional form to the study group's recommendations. The board's personnel policies to ensure that members do not have conflicts of interest compare favorably to those in government,[27] and its history demonstrates the openness of its operating procedures. The board actively solicits comments and views from all interested parties, through hearings and letters of comment. For all practical purposes, the FASB's due-process requirements always have been at least as demanding as those set forth in the Administrative Procedures Act.[28]

In December 1976 the Financial Accounting Foundation exercised its responsibilities under its bylaws to review the basic structure of the FASB. It charged the standing committee on structure to review the organization, operation, and mission of the board.[29] The resulting report led to several improvements, including the following:

* Meetings of the trustees, Advisory Council, task forces, and the FASB are open to public observation.
* The Advisory Council now has its own salaried chairman, independent but supportive of the board.
* The requirement that four of the seven members of the board must be practicing CPAs has been changed. The only requirement is: "Knowledge of accounting, finance, and business and a concern for the public interest in matters of financial accounting and reporting."
* FASB statements that have been in effect at least two years are now subject to formal postenactment review.

* The AICPA no longer has veto power over the selection of trustees. Selection of trustees is now the responsibility of the six sponsoring organizations.[30]

These measures demonstrate an ongoing concern that the FASB be open to the scrutiny and views of the board's constituencies and that the standard-setting apparatus appear independent.

The Auditing Standards Board (formerly the Auditing Standards Executive Committee) was reorganized as a result of a report by a special committee established in June 1977.[31] One of the changes was to set up an Advisory Council to assist the board. The sole qualification for service on the council is capacity to contribute to the work of the board. The chairman is an attorney, and only five of the remaining 13 members are CPAs in public practice. The other members are from academia, industry, internal auditing, and government. The council has the responsibility to bring to the board's attention problems calling for new standards, to provide guidance on agenda priorities, to review proposed pronouncements in an advisory capacity, and to report at least annually on the board's work and the extent to which it has fulfilled its charge. The report is to be made public.

The SEC Practice Section of the AICPA is the key institution in the private sector governing firms in SEC practice. The section was created in 1977 as an addition to the AICPA's governing structures, which had applied to individual CPAs rather than firms. The section's objectives are to improve the quality of members' practices and to regulate members by peer review, quality control requirements, and sanctions for failure to meet membership requirements. The structure, functioning, and progress of the section is worth a paper in itself, but we need only focus on the Public Oversight Board, which is composed of five members, chosen for their prominence, integrity, and reputation. Their charge is to monitor and evaluate the activities of the section, and there is virtually no limit on their oversight activities. They are to publish periodic reports on the results of their oversight work and to recommend operating improvements to the section's Executive Committee. Obviously, the board could destroy the section by public criticism or public opposition to a course of action.

This power derives from the integrity of the board members, of course, but also from the accountability of the profession and its institutions. Public outcry by the board would immediately arouse the SEC and congressional oversight committees. These groups play an important role in the accountability of the private-sector regulatory bodies. The SEC, congressional oversight groups, and spokesmen for the public interest who are critics of the profession would be moved to action immediately if they found the profession had violated its public trust. The last decade provides evidence of that likelihood, just as surely as the openness of the private-sector regulatory bodies makes certain that violations become part of the public record.

These examples demonstrate, first, that the profession recently has adopted new measures to assure its public accountability, and, second, that the profession is sufficiently accountable when under heavy criticism, sufficiently flexible to adapt to a new level of public demand for assurances of accountability. It is often assumed that there is some sort of unbridgeable gulf between public-sector and private-sector regulatory authorities. But in fact, despite institutional separation, occasional jealousies, conflicts, and sniping, there is also cooperation between the two, and the public benefits from a constructive relationship between the public and private sector.

We have just pointed out the role of SEC and congressional oversight in the accountability of private-sector institutions that regulate accounting. The constructive relationship goes further than that, however, and it is not hidden from public view. The SEC provides input to the processes by which accounting and auditing standards are set. Many believe it does this to excess, but far fewer, we trust, would argue that an informal dialogue is not constructive. The report of the Structure Committee on accounting standard-setting said, "We encourage the board (FASB) to continue to maintain a close, but open working relationship with the SEC. The present informal board-to-commission relationship is just about the best relationship we could expect to have between the SEC with its congressional mandate, and the FASB with its mandate from its constituency."[32]

The purpose of this paper has been to articulate a framework of principles in which regulation of accounting can be considered. The principles can be applied to specific issues to determine whether regulation is warranted and, if so, whether it should be undertaken by the public or the private sector. If a proposal for federal regulation of accounting is determined to be in accordance with the principles, the profession should accept it. If it is not, the profession should oppose the recommendation strenuously. We believe that no radical alternative to the present mix of private- and public-sector regulatory responsibilities is now warranted. The soundness of this conclusion rests not only on our perception of the facts that obtain in the world of accounting but also on the validity of the principles we have outlined. We hope they will be discussed and reexamined by others so that the subject of regulating accounting can be brought into sharper focus.

Table 3.1

Prerequisites for Adopting Federal Regulation

1. There must be a real or probable social damage.

2. The damage must not be the result of occasional lawbreaking, which is appropriately remedied by law enforcement, nor occasional antisocial behavior, which is appropriately proscribed by statute.

3. There must be <u>no</u> cost-effective private-sector or market-based remedy.

4. There must be a cost-effective regulatory remedy.

5. The regulatory remedy must not violate any laws or constitutional rights or liberties.

6. The burden of proving the need for regulation should be on the complainant or on government; the prospective regulatee should not have the burden of disproving the need.

Table 3.2. Applying the prerequisites for adopting federal regulation: selected examples[a]

| Preregulatory Situation | Social Damage? | Occasional Lawbreaking or Antisocial Behavior? | Market-Based or Private-Sector Remedy? | Cost-Effective Governmental Regulatory Solution? | Regulatory Remedy in Violation of Laws or Constitutional Rights? | Comment |
|---|---|---|---|---|---|---|
| 1. Workers injured in factories | Yes | No | Yes | N/A | No | Make employers responsible for job-related injuries (including substantial penalties) and eliminate OSHA (note: state law already provides some restitution for job-related injuries) |
| 2. Automobiles pollute | Yes | No | No | Yes | No | Require pollution control equipment |
| 3. Pension funds inadequate to meet payments | Yes | No | No | Yes | No | ERISA |
| 4. Minorities can't get jobs | Yes | No | No | Yes | No | EEOC, affirmative action |
| 5. Unqualified accountants in practice | Yes | No | No | Yes | No | State boards license CPAs |
| 6. Companies use nonuniform financial reporting standards | Yes | No | Yes | N/A | Yes | FASB sets standards |

(continued)

TABLE 3.2 - Continued

| Preregulatory Situation | Social Damage? | Occasional Law-breaking or Antisocial Behavior? | Market-Based or Private-Sector Remedy? | Cost-Effective Governmental Regulatory Solution? | Regulatory Remedy in Violation of Laws or Constitutional Rights? | Comment |
|---|---|---|---|---|---|---|
| 7. Some companies make foreign bribes | Yes | Yes or Maybe | No | N/A | N/A | Proscribe foreign bribery by statute, enforce law, do not add so-called accounting provisions |
| 8. CPA firms offer consulting services | No | No | N/A | N/A | N/A | No action required |
| 9. Some CPA firms are large | No | No | N/A | N/A | N/A | No action required |
| 10. Some CPA firms have poor quality controls | Yes | No | Yes | N/A | N/A | AICPA Practice Section Peer Reviews |
| 11. CPAs use nonuniform standards in performing audits | Yes | No | Yes | N/A | N/A | Auditing Standards Board sets standards |
| 12. Some CPAs report fraudulently | Yes | Yes | No[b] | N/A | N/A | Criminal prosecution and civil damages adequate |

[a]Most of the entries are for illustration only, and some readers may disagree about them. Prerequisite No. 6 from Table 1 is deliberately excluded because it is so difficult to apply without considerable information and because although it would result in injustice if violated, the violation would not change the application of the other five prerequisites.

[b]Although ultimately the truth outs, and they are no longer engaged to do audits.

Figure 3.1

Comparative Accounting Quality[a]

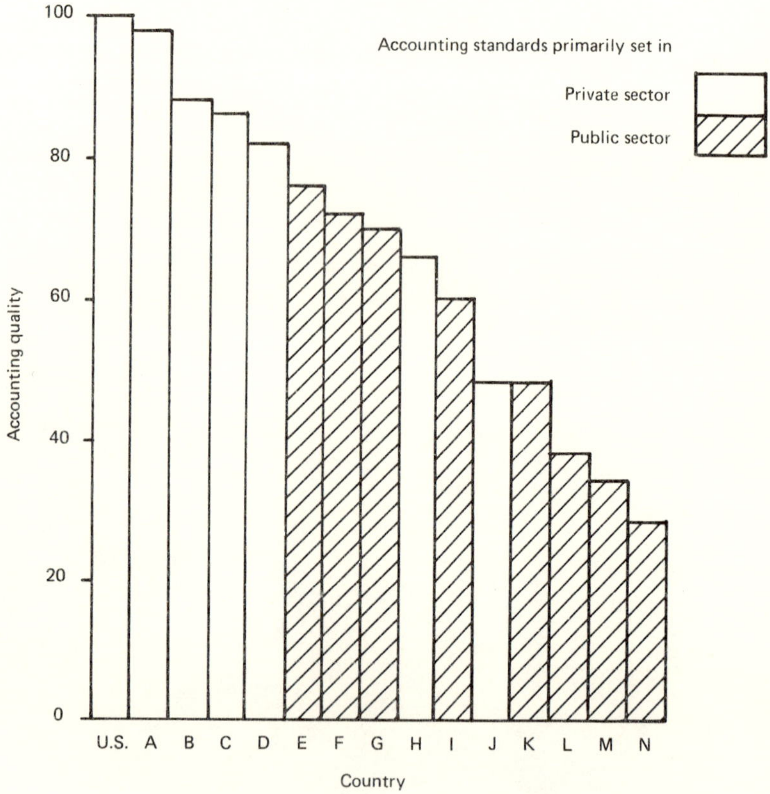


The countries ranked in this figure are all non-Communist countries with 1974 Gross National Products greater than $50 billion.

[a]The fact that we show the U.S. with an accounting quality of 100 does not mean that U.S. accounting is perfect. Nor does it mean that the U.S. was used as the standard. The countries are ranked on the basis of their adherence to standards recognized as important by international accounting groups. Countries other than the U.S. are identified by letter because the purpose is only to make comparisons, not to criticize the accounting of any other countries.

Figure 3.2

Comparative Auditing Quality*

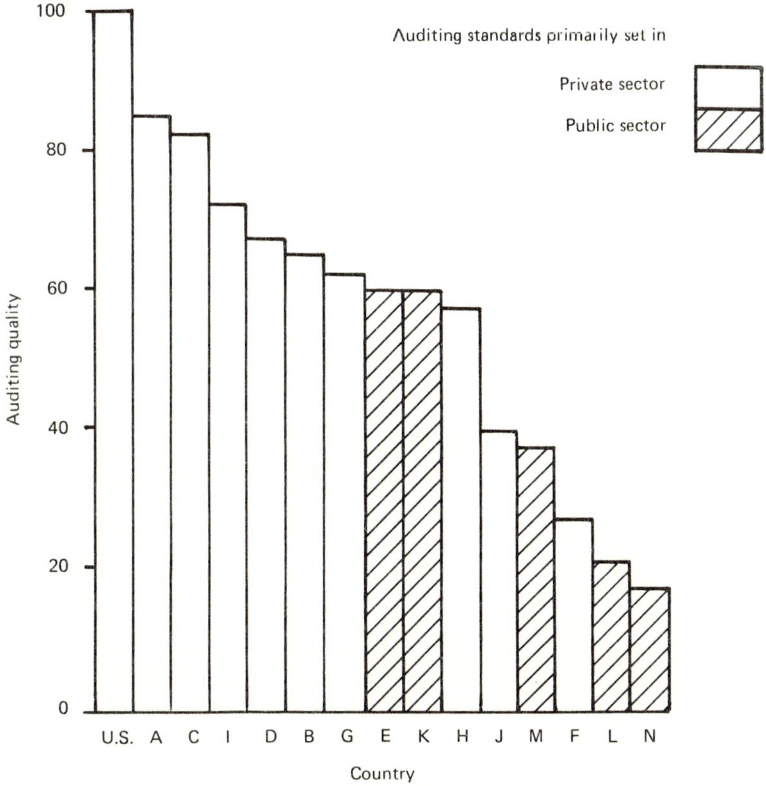


The countries ranked in this figure are all non-Communist countries with 1974 Gross National Products greater than $50 billion.

*The explanation regarding Figure 3.1 also applies here, except that, in the absence of international consensus on auditing standards, auditing performance was ranked on criteria that were judged most important. However, use of other comparable criteria would not be expected to change the results significantly.

## Notes

[1]Adam Smith, *Wealth of Nations*, Everyman edition, vol. 2 (London, 1962), pp. 392-93.

[2]The *New Dictionary of American Politics*, eds. Edward Conrad Smith and Arnold John Zurcher (New York, 1952), p. 241, defines mercantilism as "A term designating various policies and practices of European states between the 16th and 18th centuries, the chief aim of which was to unify and strengthen the state in competition with other states through public control over economic activities, thus securing a 'favorable' balance of trade, exporting commodities and importing specie and gems, building a merchant fleet, extending colonies, and planning the domestic economy to conserve and increase wealth."

[3]G.M. Trevelyan, *England in the Age of Wycliff, 1368-1520* (New York, 1963; 1st pub., 1899), pp. 186-87; *Sources of English Constitutional History*, ed. and trans. Carl Stephenson and Frederick George Marcham (New York, 1937), pp. 225-26.

[4]S.T. Bindoff, *Tudor England* (Harmondsworth, Eng., 1950), pp. 18-20.

[5]Ibid., pp. 200-202.

[6]Stephenson and Marcham, p. 349.

[7]George J. Stigler, *The Citizen and the State: Essays on Regulation* (Chicago, 1975), pp. 185-86.

[8]*Ernst & Ernst v. Hochfelder*, March 30, 1976, No. 74-1042. The Court also argued that the administrative history of Rule 10b-5 made clear that it was originally intended to apply to situations involving intentional misconduct.

[9]See Leonard M. Apcar, "More Companies Bar Regulatory Agencies from Factories, Files," *Wall Street Journal*, January 22, 1979.

[10]For details see Gilbert Simonetti, Jr., "Accounting for the Investment Credit," *Journal of Accountancy* (February 1972): 75-77.

[11]Ibid., p. 76.

[12]*Report of the Advisory Committee on Corporate Disclosure to the Securities and Exchange Commission* (Washington, 1977), D-3, D-6, D-7.

[13]Ibid., Introduction, pp. I-XLIX.

[14]*Improving the Accountability of Publicly Owned Corporations and Their Auditors* (Washington, 1977), pp. 16-17.

[15]SEC *Accounting Series Release No. 250*, June 29, 1978.

[16]The Commission on Auditors' Responsibilities, *Report, Conclusions, and Recommendations* (New York, 1978), p. 102.

[17]To conserve space, we are not reprinting here the rationale and methods used to assemble Figures 3.1 and 3.2, which run 17 pages. They are part of the public record. See *Accounting and Auditing Practices and Procedures*, Hearings Before the Subcommittee on Reports, Accounting and Management of the Committee on Governmental Affairs, United States Senate (Washington, 1977), pp. 927-43.

[18]On the relationship of the agencies to the executive, see Marver H. Bernstein, *Regulating Business by Independent Commission* (Princeton, 1955), chap. 5; William L. Cary, *Politics and the Regulatory Agencies* (New York, 1967), chap. 1.

[19]See, for example, Martin Tolchin, "Battle Intensifies over Authority of President to Control Agencies," *New York Times*, January 17, 1979; "Should Presidents Bend the Rules?," *New York Times*, February 14, 1979.

[20]Quoted in *Federal Regulation and Regulatory Reform*, Report by the Subcommittee on Oversight and Investigations of the Committee on Interstate and Foreign Commerce, October 1976 (Washington, 1976), p. 8.

[21]William L. Cary, *Politics and the Regulatory Agencies* (New York, 1967), chap. 2.

[22]*Federal Regulation and Regulatory Reform*, pp. 3, 544-47.

[23]Bernstein, p. 154.

[24]*Establishing Financial Accounting Standards: Report of the Study on Establishment of Accounting Principles*, AICPA (New York, 1972), pp. 9, 74.

[25]Ibid., pp. 10, 72.

[26]Ibid., pp. 75-77.

[27]The FASB's testimony (April 1977) to the Senate Subcommittee on Reports, Accounting and Management makes a convincing comparison. See *Accounting and Auditing Practices and Procedures*, pp. 202-4, 280-83.

[28]See FASB, *Rules of Procedure* (Stamford, Conn., 1973).

[29]*The Structure of Establishing Financial Accounting Standards*, Report of the Structure Committee, Financial Accounting Foundation, April 1977, p. 11.

[30]The changes are summarized in a speech by FASB Chairman Donald Kirk (*FASB Viewpoints*, August 4, 1978, p. 2).

[31]See AICPA, *Report of the Special Committee of the AICPA to Study the Structure of the Auditing Standards Executive Committee* (New York, 1978).

[32]*Structure of Establishing Financial Accounting Standards*, p. 52.

# A Comment on Robert K. Elliott and Walter Schuetze's "Regulation of Accounting: Practitioner's Viewpoint"

Raymond C. Lauver

Price Waterhouse & Company

Elliott and Schuetze's paper is useful because it invites examination of the very difficult and very important question "When and in what circumstances should government resort to regulation?" Answers range from frequently to not at all. But before selecting an answer, perhaps we ought to decide on a working definition of the term "government regulation." Without being too precise, we can think of it as administrative agency control or promotion of a part of private industry for stated public purposes, such as the public good. Because these activities encompass executive, legislative, and judicial functions, it is often said that the regulatory agencies constitute a fourth branch of government. Although the title of this conference suggests that we are considering only governmental regulation, this working definition is equally descriptive of private sector regulation.

As an abstract analysis of the basic question of regulation, this paper may be useful in determining whether new areas of society should be regulated. In the accounting area it may be useful for consideration of regulation in the event of a sunset legislation program. The heart of the paper lies in the authors' list of prerequisites for governmental regulation of activities--a thought-provoking list, although it may not be the only such list that could have been drawn up.

Given the degree of regulation that now exists, the most fruitful approach may be to discuss, challenge, and criticize the effect of existing regulation rather than to debate whether society has followed a rational course of action in setting that structure into place. Accordingly, I propose to add a number of other facets to the question, both to broaden this consideration and to better evaluate the conclusions reached by the authors.

## The Subject of Regulation

One particular aspect of the paper which leaves this reviewer unconvinced and struggling is the almost entirely negative definition of what is or ought to be the subject of regulation, a definition based on what must <u>not</u> be present if an activity is to be regulated.

The second prerequisite established by the authors, again in the form of a negative condition, is that, even when a cause exists (prerequisite number one) consisting of real or probable social damage, there should not be resort to regulation if the damage is the result of lawbreaking subject to law enforcement. But regulation is frequently just the imposition of another set of rules or laws. This prerequisite leaves the reader with a feeling of being lost in a type of circularity: regulation shouldn't be permitted if laws and enforcement will remedy the damage, but when regulation is permitted it will provide its own laws, which in turn will be enforced in order to remedy the damage. Little help there!

This leaves us with the question of just what it is that distinguishes activities with a potential for regulation from those without such potential. Isn't it that the nature of the activity does not lend itself easily to a statute articulating with assurance either the social damage or harm or the conduct which must be proscribed but rather that the nature of the activity can only be dealt with by the ongoing exercise of qualitative judgments encompassing executive, legislative, and judicial judgments? Think of some of the Solomon-like decisions entailed in regulating activities and described by words such as *over-charge, improve, fair, equal, not misleading, safe, honest*--all common enough words but each of them, like beauty, existing only in the eye of the beholder. Even with the utmost intent and integrity, who can be sure whether an action by the regulated party, for example, a corporation issuing a registration statement, is in conformity with the law, or whether an action by the regulator, for example, the setting of tariffs, is in conformity with the law? Each frequently results in litigation. All this seems to say is that the most likely subject matter of regulation involves matters of equity, about which judgments may change from time to time.

## Auditing vs. Accounting

The paper, while entitled "Regulation of Accounting," is concerned also with the role of the public accountant--the auditor, the attestor. In fact, the paper is heavily weighted toward auditing. Would it not have been useful to consider both topics but to consider them separately? The accounting subject would involve the "if," "what," "when," and "how" of reporting financial information. The auditing subject would involve many of the same kinds of questions, such as what should be audited, when and how--but would also consider the qualifications of the auditor.

One of the interesting aspects of the separation of the two subjects would be the greater ability to probe the reason for the implicit conclusion that financial information being regulated needs to be attested but that other kinds of information regulated by different agencies need not be attested. Several references are made in the paper to the Food and Drug Administration and the regulation of new medicines and drugs. I am unaware of any attesting by an independent party of the reports filed with FDA relative to requests for licenses to manufacture and sell, even though those reports are voluminous, important to society and the conclusions in them must to some degree involve estimates and judgments. What is it that requires an attest of financial information but not of the new drug license request? Is the economic well-being of society more critical than its physical well-being? Is there a presumption that management behaves less honorably in preparing reports describing the need for and the effectiveness of a new medicine? If that presumption were true in 1933, is it equally true forty-six years later? Or have we somehow deceived the public, and perhaps ourselves, that accounting information has qualities of precision that the report on the effectiveness of a new medicine cannot have? If so, have we therefore paved the way for the notion that bad judgments in one are more likely to be evidence of misconduct than bad judgments in the other, thus laying the groundwork for greater regulation of one activity than the other? Whatever the answers to these questions, one stark fact stands out: of all the myriad regulatory reports, financial accounting information is subjected to far more attesting than other reports I have been able to discover, and any study of accounting regulation needs to consider why this should be so.

## Some Pragmatic Questions

My pragmatic mind wants to leap over the abstract and theoretical considerations and grapple with the question of whether the regulation of accounting and auditing in existence at present seems to work for better or for worse. Many subjects could be used as a basis for this kind of consideration. Let us take innovation.

If we start with the observation that accounting is conventional, we are more likely to accept the fact that accounting standards and practices will change over time as attitudes and the environment change. The question then is whether regulation stimulates or inhibits innovation and whether the effect is good or bad.

Clearly, regulation precludes innovation in those areas in which regulatory rules have been prescribed--a very negative sounding statement. But not all innovation is progressive, forward-looking, and aimed at enhancing the public good. Accordingly, it is not easy to generalize about the desirability of precluding or inhibiting innovation; it depends on a judgment about the desirability of the subject of the innovation.

In addition to precluding or inhibiting innovation, regulation also stimulates or forces innovation. This is obvious when it imposes a requirement for a new disclosure against someone's wishes, but it is probably equally true for those in the regulated group who concur in the new disclosure requirement. Accounting today is an area in which companies compete. Therefore, if a particular disclosure or a particular accounting practice is seen as something that might have a detrimental effect on the company as a result of a comparison with a competitor, the company may well not innovate even after it concludes that something should be changed but will rather wait for the change to be prescribed by the regulator. When the innovation is prescribed by a regulatory authority, all companies are affected concurrently and no competitive disadvantage occurs.

## The Effects of Rule-making

One of the frequent observations about the regulatory scene is that, given an activity to be controlled or prompted, an enormous structure of rules will be forthcoming. There are two common reactions to a complex network of rules and regulations. On one hand it is argued that the numerous rules are necessary to deal with the numerous circumstances in an equitable fashion. It is easy to state a general rule, but general rules usually are inadequate to deal with all of the circumstances encountered in any part of the business world--hence the cry for exceptions and clarifications. On the other hand, a complex rules structure is regarded as undesirable because it gives rise to complexities which are not cost-efficient and which produce somewhat absurd results. In OSHA, for instance, anecdotes demonstrating the absurd are legion. The most recent concerns the one-man mine in Wyoming, miles from the nearest town, which is required to keep a stretcher on the premises for use in the event of an accident. We might be able to match that in the accounting area if we examined carefully the layers of existing rules and interpretations, especially unstated administrative interpretations. Recent experiences suggest that rulemaking becomes an endless effort with less and less additional value created for each additional rule as requests are made for narrower and narrower exceptions and clarifications.

## Public vs. Private Regulation

The authors conclude their paper confident that private sector regulation is more desirable than public sector regulation. This is not a conclusion likely to be widely questioned, certainly not by this reviewer. Intuition and a widespread suspicion of big government and bureaucracy suggest that conclusion. However, the paper itself is not that convincing.

Interest in the public good is both an objective of regulation and one of the characteristics of our profession. Because of this commonality, there ought to be less need for regulation of activities within the accounting profession. Any desirable changes within the profession need to be accomplished within the private sector by the profession itself, out of this concern for the public good and as a mark of its own professionalism.

Another basis is that public regulation is less accountable, less answerable for its actions. This need not be so. Accountability is related to independence; an excessive amount of one becomes an insufficiency of the other. Acknowledging the need for accountability cannot be the end of the debate. We need to balance the two qualities of accountability and independence that are always in tension.

While we are discussing accountability, I must express my disagreement with one comment in the paper which is in fact inconsistent. The paper deplores the role of the federal government in the investment tax credit debate of the early 1970s. On the other hand, it characterizes as a disadvantage the fact that "activities of regulatory agencies are not readily coordinated with national economic policy as directed by the executive." Disadvantage indeed! If, with respect to accounting, that condition were ever to become a serious risk, it alone would be evidence enough to support the conclusion that regulation of accounting should be a private sector matter; a healthy fear of that possibility is always appropriate.

Finally on this subject, the lengthy discussion of FASB, the Auditing Standards Board, and the SEC Practice Section of AICPA strongly argues that the private sector contains good mechanisms. I share the authors' conclusions, but the arguments presented are unlikely to convince a healthy skeptic that private is better than public regulation of accounting. The best argument continues to be the constant demonstration, via the practice of all concerned, that the private sector is acting responsibly and in the public interest.

A Comment on Robert K. Elliott and Walter Schuetze's "Regulation of Accounting: Practitioner's Viewpoint"

Douglas H. Thompson, Jr.

Florida State Board of Accountancy

As indicated in the program, I am executive director of the Florida State Board of Accountancy. I have served in this job for over 11 years, thus, at least in some people's eyes, becoming the worst of all creatures: a career government regulator at 35! My father is a farmer in the Glades who believes the best government is no government. For years when his friends asked what I did for a living, he said I was a CPA instead of a state employee. He still feels the only thing worse than working for a government is collecting unemployment compensation--which he thinks most government employees really do anyway.

The following remarks do not represent the opinions or positions of my employers, the Florida board, collectively or individually.

Lee Loevinger, partner of Hogan & Harston, recently said, and I concur, that "The spectrum of opinion about government regulation is probably as broad as toward any current social issue."[1] Mr. Loevinger quoted Bill Rasberry, a Washington columnist, as saying the way to tell the difference between a conservative and a liberal with respect to government regulation is to observe the reactions when caught in an inexplicable traffic jam. The conservative will say, "There must be a damn fool traffic cop ahead screwing things up." The liberal will tell you, "Somebody ought to call a traffic cop to straighten these damn fools out." While simplistic, those two responses probably represent the extremes of the views on the extent of government intervention in the accounting profession. All of us probably agree that some government intervention is necessary. However, most likely none of us will agree as to the degree of government involvement in the regulation of accounting and information. Perhaps this conference will further enlighten our thinking and move us closer together on this subject.

Basically, Elliott and Schuetze have discussed broadly the regulation of accounting, identified prerequisites that must be satisfied if the profession agrees to federal regulation, and concluded that no radical alternatives to the present mix of the private-public sector regulation is warranted. I concur with their conclusions, with certain conditions, but I get there a different way. Most important, the authors have failed to distinguish between the regulation of accounting (the *practice* of accounting) and the regulation of "accounting" information (the promulgation of accounting principles and auditing and standards), which, in my opinion, are two entirely different matters. In my view, such distinction is essential to discussion on the extent of government regulation of the accounting profession.

First, I do not feel that concern over improper corporate payments has been the major cause for the reconsideration in recent years of regulating accounting. Quite frankly, I believe the various state legislatures, Congress, and particularly the public don't really care that much about who promulgates professional standards. They have confidence that the various professions will adopt (and have adopted) high practice standards. They also are primarily concerned with the failure to enforce the standards of practice and with high costs of professional services caused by monopolies made legal by state licensure to practice. These monopolies are justified by professionals as being "essential to the public safety." Furthermore, prices are felt to be higher due to anticompetitive provisions in practice acts, regulations, and professional ethics codes. Adam Smith, quoted in the paper as championing the free market system, also stated, "People of the same trade seldom meet together even for merriment and diversion, but the conversation ends in a conspiracy against the public, or in some contrivance to raise prices." Perhaps I err in my reasoning for the current "public scrutiny." However, I can't help but feel if the public believed CPAs were making $15,000 instead of over $50,000 a year ($400,000, if you read some firms' annual reports) and if they read of $1,000 law suit settlements instead of $1 million and more, we wouldn't be having this conference today. The profession's success and accomplishments have placed it in the limelight, and the public, especially the news media, are just like auditors in that they don't dwell on accomplishment but on shortcomings. I'm afraid the public has agreed, rightly or wrongly, with the observation long ago of Bernard Shaw that "a self-governed profession is a conspiracy against the laity."

I concur that the history of regulation in the United States can be traced to the Constitution. In fact, professions, including public accounting, are regulated by the various states under the police power granted them by the tenth amendment: "The powers not delegated to the United States by the Constitution, nor prohibited by it to the States, are reserved to the States respectively, or to the people." Here is the authority for state laws concerning certification of certified public accountants, medical doctors, dentists, and other professionals. Is there anyone here today who holds a CPA certificate issued by a body, public or private, *other* than a state board of accountancy or its equivalent under a state law? However, we sometimes forget that the impetus for state regulation came *from* (not outside) the profession.

In the beginning, at least in the U.S., there was the

American Association of Public Accountants (1887), a direct predecessor to the present American Institute of Certified Public Accountants. This association had as its initial objectives "establishing a high standard of professional attainments in accounting through general education and knowledge and otherwise" and "legislative recognition." The early profession was concerned about and wanted to prevent unauthorized use of a professional accountant designation. The best way to accomplish this goal was by state statute. Early initiative for regulation by state laws did not come from the public, but from the organized groups of accountants who wanted to promote professional esteem and enhancement. The first Accountancy Law became effective in New York in 1896. The rest is history. When our forefathers chose to seek licensure by state government, they gave up the privilege of total self-regulation.

The early profession recognized "self or voluntary" discipline had its limitations as evidenced by the following: "In the 1930s it was becoming clear that in areas involving the public interest the only alternative to self-discipline in the long run is discipline imposed by the public through government. The task of leadership in a professional organization, whose members are highly individualistic and cannot be coerced, is to explain, and to persuade; explain the relationship between self-imposed rules and maintenance of public confidence, persuade members to adopt such rules before they are compelled to do so by external authority."[2]

I was disappointed (perhaps for reasons of self-pride) at the authors' failure to give state boards of accountancy deserved status in the regulatory scheme. While I recognize the thrust of the paper is "federal regulation" as related to promulgation of standards, many fail to recognize when considering the question of "accounting" regulation that only 5 to 10 percent of accounting profession practitioner units have any association with the SEC. *The Report of the Commission on Auditors' Responsibilities* (1978) contains the statement "State boards may provide the only means of removing demonstrably incompetent CPAs from public practice." The AICPA, in *The Institute Responds* (1978), stated, "Of course the institute, which can, at most, expel a member from a voluntary organization, is not the only instrument for discipline in the profession. Disciplinary matters are handled by state boards of accountancy since they are the only governmental authorities which license accountants and which can effectively suspend or terminate an accountant's right to practice." This was in response to an earlier staff report issued by the U.S. Senate Subcommittee on Reports, Accounting, and Management.

The word "regulation" is defined in the *Random House Dictionary of the English Language* as "A rule or order prescribed by authority to regulate conduct; a governing direction or law; the act of regulating; the state of being regulated." The definition implies an outside authority. Can in fact the regulated be the regulator? Is the popular term "self-regulation" really contradictory? Do we really mean "self-discipline" or "self-determination" or some other term? Can I regulate myself? Can the profession of accounting or any profession regulate itself? No. Simply put, the CPA profession or any of the other professions where standards of admission, continued practice, and technical requirements are prescribed by state law and regulations are not self-regulated. They are government-regulated.

No doubt there is misunderstanding on the part of the public, the profession, state legislators, and Congress over the use of the term "self-regulation." The AICPA and various members of the profession in responding to recent congressional inquiries have advocated the maintenance of "self-regulated" status. Interestingly, I note that several newspaper articles on the AICPA Council's action establishing the division of firms were titled "Self-Regulation by CPAs is Approved." I thought the CPA profession had been "self-regulated" since its founding!

Basically, this disagrees with one of the authors' prerequisites adopting government regulation that "The burden of proving the need for regulation should be on the complainant or on government; the prospective regulatee should not have the burden of disproving the need." Just the opposite is occurring in sunset hearings before various state legislatures. The professions are fighting to keep regulation, not to become "de-regulated."

While the Constitution is the basis for professional state regulation, it also may be the best deterrent to increased federal regulation of professional practice. I read with interest an article that appeared in the *Florida Bar News* (March 15, 1979) titled "Florida Bar Files Objection to FTC's Investigation of State Bars." The article reported that the Florida Bar and several other state bars will oppose responding to an FTC questionnaire based upon their inherent and constitutional authority to regulate the practice of law within their respective states. The cited comments of Chief Justice H. E. Nichols of the Supreme Court of Georgia may set the tone for increasing opposition by state professional regulatory bodies to federal encroachment: "To fail to object to this investigation by the FTC may be to acquiesce in a fundamental modification of your court's power to regulate lawyers and the practice of law in your jurisdiction..."

The authors describe the regulation of accounting to include "setting accounting and auditing standards, disciplining professionals for errant performance, and prescribing quality controls and ethical standards for a private profession." I have a problem with the term "private profession." I don't believe any profession is private. Two of the seven criteria used by John L. Carey to distinguish professions from other pursuits are a public interest in the work that practitioners perform and recognition by the professionals of a social obligation. AICPA Ethics, ET Section 51, begins, "A distinguishing mark of a professional is his acceptance of responsibility to the public. All true professions have therefore deemed it essential to promulgate codes of ethics and to establish means for ensuring their observance." A profession by its very nature is public. Personally, I prefer the following four elements of a system of accounting regulation as identified by the Commission on Auditors' Responsibilities: high educational standards for entering and continuing in the profession; high technical standards; quality control policies and procedures to monitor practice; an effective disciplinary system to impose penalties for infractions of standards established by law, SEC or the profession. I submit that to the extent that either CPAs, the AICPA, or state societies are doing these things, self-discipline exists in the accounting profession. To the extent that these elements are imposed by state and federal agencies or the courts, the accounting profession is government-regulated, not self-regulated.

To what extent are these four elements of the system of accounting regulation set by the accounting profession or government? Educational standards for entering the profession, i.e., qualifying for the Uniform CPA Examination and receiving a CPA certificate, are prescribed by state law and rules in every state (and in four territorial jurisdictions) and administered by state boards of accountancy. Standards for continuing the profession, or continuing professional education, likewise are required by state law and regulations in 27 states. In those states where it is not required, few practitioners are complying with the voluntary standards of the AICPA or state CPA society.

Technical standards in accounting and auditing are, for the most part, promulgated by the private sector, i.e. the Financial Accounting Standards Board (FASB) and the Auditing Standards Board of the AICPA (ASB). However, few may recognize that standards promulgated by FASB and ASB are made effective by state laws and regulations (see Exhibit 1). Examples of typical language are reflected in Exhibit 2. It should be observed that in all but three states and the District of Columbia every certified public accountant (whether or not a member of the AICPA or a state society) is required by state law and regulations to follow generally accepted auditing standards and conform to generally accepted accounting principles when associated with financial statements. Failure to do so could (and has) result in suspension or revocation of the CPA certificate. Such adherence is likewise required by the federal government, the SEC, for those CPAs and firms associated with financial statements to be filed with that body.

As indicated earlier, I believe one of the main causes placing the public accounting profession under such scrutiny is the public's perception of no effective disciplinary system. I believe this is a major weakness of the paper under review in that the authors failed to discuss the "quality" of the existing system and its performance. Is this perception by the public justified? I invite you to make your own conclusions from the following:

Certainly, the organized profession has attempted to establish quality control procedures and policies for the purpose of monitoring practice. However, the "Voluntary Quality Control Program" initiated in 1975 by the AICPA has been met with what could best be described as lukewarm acceptance and certainly cannot, at this time, be termed a success. I expect that the "public practice section" of the AICPA Division of Firms will be effective. The SEC will see to that. However, there are some infirmities that could prove terminal: lack of a public oversight board to have disciplinary authority, determination of scope of review, lack of SEC to have access to review working papers, and so on. Serious questions exist as to whether a substantial number of local practitioner firms will join the "private practice" section. At the AICPA annual meeting in October 1979, it was reported that approximately 10 percent of the eligible AICPA member practice units had joined the private practice section. Practice review committees of the various state societies also have proven to be ineffective in monitoring the quality of accounting services. This is not to say that individuals involved with these efforts have not been dedicated and worked diligently to promote their acceptance. Experience has shown that a majority of those individuals who most need to participate simply will not respond to a voluntary quality control program. And, while I may be wrong, my discussions with many local practitioners lead me to believe they view the AICPA as being similar to the federal government, i.e. distant, bureaucratic, unresponsive to their needs, representative of the big firms, and so forth. If given the choice, with proper constraints, they might opt for effective state regulation instead of discipline by the AICPA.

As far as an effective disciplinary system requiring adherence to technical standards is concerned, the record shows little, if any, effort by either the voluntary professional organizations or state boards of accountancy. First, professional organizations can only impose sanctions or penalties affecting membership status in that organization. These organizations have no authority or control over an individual member's right to practice. To the best of my knowledge, there have been little if any technical cases pursued by the voluntary professional accounting organizations. I have been advised by a member who served two years on the AICPA Trial Board (1974-76) that only one technical standards case was brought before it during that time. I would like to know how many members of the American Institute of Certified Public Accountants and state societies have been disciplined in the last five years for violations of generally accepted accounting principles and/or generally accepted auditing standards.

Have the private professional organizations, specifically the AICPA and state societies, made an effective disciplinary effort and imposed penalties for infractions of self-established standards? Table 3.3 illustrates an interesting response to this question. Consideration of the table should be coupled with the fact that during the period shown, the Florida Board of Accountancy was responsible for regulating approximately 7,000 CPAs while the AICPA and forty state societies probably had at least 150,000 members. Nevertheless the Florida Board entered 173 individual disciplinary sanctions compared to 77 by the AICPA and state societies. Also, the board disposed of almost 94 percent of matters pending or received during the period while the private organizations completed only 50 percent. Based upon these comparisons, one must question the effectiveness of "self-regulation" by the organized, voluntary accounting professional groups. Simply stated, such regulation hardly exists. However, these organizations are not (and in my opinion should not be) in the regulation/enforcement business. They have no jurisdiction over the right to practice and do not have the necessary authority. Blame for the lack of regulation in the accounting profession must fall directly on state boards of accountancy and indirectly on the voluntary professional organizations. This is a "shared" blame because the accounting profession has not really wanted effective regulation. It has desired, and gotten, the appearance of regulation of the quality of practice instead of regulation in fact.

What about initiative on the part of the private sector for the regulators to do their job? The Operations Manual of the Professional Ethics Division of the AICPA, dated January 1, 1976, contains Appendix I, "Proposed Form of Agreement between the AICPA and State Societies with Respect to the Joint Enforcement Procedures." This exhibit gives objectives of the joint enforcement plan: to eliminate the duplication of jurisdictions and enforcement procedures of state societies and the AICPA, and to provide a means for the profession to initiate appropriate actions before State Boards of Accountancy. In my 11 years as the executive director of the Florida State Board of Accountancy, the board has not received a single initiation from the AICPA or Florida Institute of CPAs relating to a technical matter on which action had not already been taken by the board.

On November 29, 1978, I sent a questionnaire to all state boards of accountancy asking, among other things, "During the period of January 1, 1976, to present, has your board received any referrals from the AICPA regarding AICPA disciplinary actions taken against your licensees <u>on matters your board had not previously taken</u> action?" Of 31 boards responding, 30 answered no.

The Florida State Board of Accountancy in 1977-78 conducted quality reviews of accountants' reports and related financial statements of municipalities and land development/sales companies. These entities are required by law to file reports accompanied by an opinion of an independent audit with the auditor general and the comptroller, respectively. With respect to these reviews our findings were as follows:

For land development and sales companies, 80 out of 585 reports were selected for review. Of those, 29 warranted specific comments on technical matters and 27 resulted in initiation of investigations. Of the sample reviewed, 34 percent contained deficiencies material enough to result in investigation. To date, 15 have been heard with 10 (67 percent) resulting in probable cause findings and disciplinary action.

For municipalities, 80 out of 343 reports were selected for review. Of these, 30 warranted specific comments on technical matters and 20 (25 percent) resulted in investigation. To date, all 20 have been heard with eight resulting in probable cause findings and disciplinary actions. Also, in fiscal years 1976-77 and 1977-78, <u>only 16</u> of the 80 complaints filed against CPAs and firms pertaining to technical standards (20 percent) were received from CPAs. The other 80 percent came from board-initiated quality reviews. CPAs don't turn in their peers for substandard work.

Attached as Exhibit 3 is an article written by Harold L. Monk, Jr., CPA, an investigating officer for the

Florida Board, summarizing the technical deficiencies he discovered during a one-year period. These deficiencies are not minor and must cause concern as to the quality of practice by many who are expected to be "competent" practitioners.

In the beginning of my response I indicated that I concurred with the authors' conclusions that the present discipline/regulation systems of private promulgation of standards and public regulation of standards is adequate with conditions. Although the system is basically sound, it needs both improvements and the support of the profession and government entities so it will work as intended. I suggest the following recommendations to improve the quality of existing systems of accounting discipline and regulation:

AICPA Division of Firms

Membership should be required of all practice units in the section applicable to their practices. The rules of the public practice section should be amended to give the Public Oversight Board more authority to determine scope of reviews and review working papers should be available to SEC. Quality reviews in the private practice section should be made on a sample basis and not required of each member during a specified period. Otherwise, the cost of self-discipline will be prohibitive. For example, the average cost of a technical investigation made by the Florida Board in 1977-78 was $1,300. I understand the first quality review by the private companies practice section cost approximately $3,500.

Securities and Exchange Commission and State Boards of Accountancy

State boards should be encouraged by the private sector to assume their intended role as the regulators of the practice of accounting excepting those engagements filed with the SEC. Here, to avoid duplication, state boards should automatically accept decisions by the SEC and issue appropriate sanctions regarding their respective certificate holders. Also, the model accountancy bill of the AICPA should be amended to provide for random quality inspection by state boards of accountancy. Such amendment should provide for due notice to practitioners selected for review, specify the limits of disciplinary sanctions, and give the option of accepting, in lieu of state inspection, quality reviews conducted by the AICPA under the Division of Firms. This would promote private sector discipline. It would enhance the "threat" of government without making it mandatory and would encourage participation in the private sector quality review system.

### Standards-Setting

The "standards-setting bodies" should remain in the private sector. Their independence should be improved.

### Referral of Disciplinary Matters to SEC and State Boards of Accountancy by Private Sector

The AICPA and state societies should, pursuant to one of the two objectives of the "Joint Enforcement Program," promptly refer disciplinary sanctions to the SEC and state boards of accountancy.

In conclusion, when discussing the subject of regulating accounting we must distinguish "regulating the practice of accounting" and "self-discipline." Also, we must remember that the promulgation of accounting and auditing standards (information) is entirely different from requiring adherence to those standards. The process of standards promulgation should remain with the private sector. The recent changes in this area giving more participation to groups outside of the accounting profession are steps in the right direction. This will lead to greater acceptance and understanding of accounting standards by all concerned parties. State boards of accountancy, the SEC, and (as a last resort) the courts should remain as the "regulators" of public accounting by requiring adherence to the standards promulgated by the private sector as a condition to practice. The *self*-discipline bodies, AICPA, state societies, should continue to encourage adherence to technical standards through peer quality reviews.

The existing system should be improved, strengthened, and made to work as intended. The most important participants in improving the existing system are the practitioners themselves, for they are the true "self" in self-discipline. Practitioners must accept the responsibility stated in the AICPA Code of Ethics, ET 55.03: "A CPA has the obligation to assist his fellows in complying with the Code of Professional Ethics and should also assist appropriate disciplinary authorities in enforcing the code. To condone serious fault can be as bad as to commit it. It may be even worse, in fact, since some errors may result from ignorance rather than intent and, if let pass without action, will probably be repeated. In situations of this kind, the welfare of the public should be the guide to a member's action." Otherwise, there will be increased government involvement in all facets of the regulation of the public accounting profession. This will not be in the best interest of the public.

Two of my favorite quotations support this last statement. Goethe said, "What is the best government? That which teaches us to govern ourselves." And Senator Sam Ervin said, "Some people think government ought to regulate all the affairs of all our people. They overlook the fact that a willingness on the part of the people to assume responsibility for their own life is inseparable from liberty, and whenever you destroy that willingness in people and rob them of incentive, liberty is going to perish."

---

The author would like to acknowledge that "Departures from Generally Accepted Auditing Standards" listed in Exhibit 3 were adapted from an article by Harold L. Monk, Jr., CPA, in Florida Accountancy News entitled "Technical Deficiencies Summarized."

Exhibit 1

Generally Accepted Accounting Principles and Generally Accepted Auditing Standards Required by State Laws and/or Regulations

| By Rule Adopting Identical AICPA Code of Ethics | By Rule Adopting NASBA Code of Ethics | By Rule Adopting Basic AICPA Code of Ethics | Not Specifically Required by State Law or Rule |
|---|---|---|---|
| Delaware | Arkansas | Alabama | District of Columbia |
| Hawaii | Colorado | Alaska | Michigan |
| Massachusetts | Connecticut | Arizona | Minnesota |
| Montana | Indiana | California | New Jersey |
| Nebraska | Iowa | Florida | |
| New Hampshire | Kansas | Georgia | |
| North Dakota | Maine | Idaho | |
| Ohio | Maryland | Illinois | |
| Oklahoma | Missouri | Kentucky | |
| Rhode Island | New Mexico | Louisiana | |
| South Carolina | Oregon | Mississippi | |
| Tennessee | Vermont | Nevada | |
| Virginia | | New York | |
| | | North Carolina | |
| | | Pennsylvania | |
| | | South Dakota | |
| | | Texas | |
| | | Utah | |
| | | Washington | |
| | | West Virginia | |
| | | Wisconsin | |
| | | Wyoming | |

Exhibit 2

Examples of Specific Wording of State Laws and Regulations Requiring and Defining GAAP and GAAS

Florida: F. S. 473.04: "It (the board) shall prescribe a standard of professional conduct and formulate reasonable rules defining unethical practices for persons holding certificates under this chapter. Every person practicing as a certified public accountant. . .in this state under a certificate issued by the board. . .shall be governed and controlled by the rules and standards adopted by the board."

(473.251) Suspension or Revocation of Certificate; Forfeiture of Privilege of Special Permits and Agency Relationships; Grounds.

(1) The certificate of any person to practice as a certified public accountant or as a public accountant may be revoked or suspended for a definite period not to exceed five years when it shall appear to the board:

(g) That such person was guilty of a violation of the provisions of this chapter or any of the rules of the board."

Rules of the Board

21A2.08 - Generally Accepted Accounting Principles

"Generally accepted accounting principles" shall be deemed and construed to mean accounting principles or standards generally accepted in the United States, including, but not limited to, Accounting Principles Board Opinions Nos. 1 to 31 as published by the American Institute of Certified Public Accountants and Statements of Financial Accounting Standards and interpretations thereof as published by the Financial Accounting Standards Board prior to October 1, 1977.

General Authority 473.04, F.S.; Law implemented, interpreted or made specific 473.011(5), 473.04, F.S.

21A-2.09 - Generally Accepted Auditing Standards

"Generally accepted auditing standards" shall be deemed and construed to mean the ten generally accepted auditing standards adopted by the American Institute of Certified Public Accountants, together with interpretations thereof, as set forth in Statements on Auditing Standards as published by the American Institute of Certified Public Accountants prior to October 1, 1977.

General Authority 473.04, F.S.; Law implemented, interpreted or made specific 473.011(5); 473.04, F.S.

21A-4.02 - Auditing Standards

A practitioner shall not permit his name to be associated with financial statements in such a manner as to imply that he is acting as an independent certified public accountant or public accountant unless he has complied with the applicable generally accepted auditing standards. *Statements on Auditing Standards* are, for purposes of this rule, deemed and construed to be interpretations of generally accepted auditing standards, and departures from such statements must be justified by those who do not follow them.

21A4-03 - Accounting Principles

A practitioner shall not express an opinion that financial statements are presented in conformity with generally accepted accounting principles if such statements contain any departure from any such principle which has a material effect on the statements taken as a whole, unless he can demonstrate that due to unusual circumstances the financial statements would otherwise have been misleading. In such cases his report must describe the departure, the approximate effects thereof, if practicable, and the reasons why compliance with the principle would result in a misleading statement.

Ohio: OS 4701.03: ". . .The board may promulgate, and amend from time to time, rules of professional conduct appropriate to establish and maintain a high standard of integrity and dignity in the profession of public accounting. . ."

(OS Sec. 4701.16) Revocation or Suspension of Certificates and Registrations

After a notice and hearing as provided in sections 119.01 to 119.13 of the Revised Code, the accountancy board may revoke, or suspend, any certificate issued under section 4701.06 of the Revised Code, or any registration granted under section 4701.07 of the Revised Code, or may revoke, suspend or refuse to renew any permit issued under section 4701.10 of the Revised Code, or may censure the holder of any such permit, for any one or any combination of the following causes:

(B) Dishonesty, fraud or gross negligence in the practice of public accounting;

(C) Violation of any of the provision of section 4701.14 of the Revised Code;

(D) Violation of a rule of professional conduct promulgated by the board under the authority granted by sections 4701.02 to 4701.22 of the Revised Code.

Ohio Code of Ethics

Published by Accountancy Board of Ohio, effective July 1978, as amended.

(34,301) Ethical Rules

The Accountancy Board of Ohio has adopted the Rules of Conduct, Restatement of the Code of Professional Ethics of the American Institute of Certified Public Accountants, with some changes. The AICPA Code is reproduced beginning at 65.501. The following variations are reflected in both State and AICPA Codes:

Ohio Rules 4701-9-01, et seq.

4701-9-01. Integrity and Objectivity--Variation: Substitute "certified public accountant or public accountant" for "member" (Note: variation appears in all following Rules).

4701-9-02. Competence--Variation: Substitute the following for the amended Rule 201--General Standards--of the AICPA Code: "A certified public accountant or public accountant shall not undertake any engagement which he or his firm cannot reasonably expect to complete with professional competence."

4701-9-03. Auditing Standards--Variations: Omit "promulgated by the Institute"; and substitute "American Institute of Certified Public Accountants, and other pronouncements having similar generally recognized authority, are" for "Institute's Auditing Standards Executive Committee are for purposes of this rule" and "pronouncements" for "statements."

(Rule 4701-9-03, as amended, effective Sept. 1, 1978.)

4701-9-04. Accounting Principles--Insert "financial" between "such" and "statements"; substitute "such accounting principles" for "an accounting principle"; and omit "promulgated by the body designated by Council to establish such principles." Add the following: "For purposes of this rule, generally accepted accounting principles are considered to be defined by pronouncements issued by the 'Financial Accounting Standards Board' and its predecessor entities and similar pronouncements issued by other entities having similar generally recognized authority."

AICPA Form of Regulatory Public Accountancy Bill
(Approved by AICPA Council on May 5, 1970)

Section 2(e) (1) (2) - "The Board shall prescribe rules and regulations not inconsistent with the provisions of this Act which it deems consistent with or required by the public welfare and policy set forth in Section 1. Such rules and regulations may include:

(1) Rules of procedure for governing the conduct of matters before the Board;

(2) Rules of professional conduct for establishing and maintaining high standards of competence and integrity in the profession of public accountancy.

Section 12(a), (b) and (d) - Revocation or Suspension of Certificate or Registration or Permit. "After notice and hearing as provided in Section 14 of this Act, the Board may revoke, or may suspend for a period not to exceed. . .years, any certificate issued under Section 3 of this Act, or any registration granted under Section 5 of this Act, or may censure the holder of any such permit for any one or any combination of the following causes:

(a) Fraud or deceit in obtaining a certificate as certified public accountant, or in obtaining registration under this Act or in obtaining a permit to practice public accounting under this Act.

(b) Dishonesty, fraud or gross negligence in the practice of public accounting.

(d) Violation of a rule of professional conduct promulgated by the Board under the authority granted by this Act.

AICPA Code of Ethics

ET Section 201 - General Standards

01. Rule 201--General Standards. A member shall comply with the following general standards as interpreted

by bodies designated by Council, and must justify any departures therefrom.

A. Professional competence. A member shall undertake only those engagements which he or his firm can reasonably expect to complete with professional competence.

B. Due professional care. A member shall exercise due professional care in the performance of an engagement.

C. Planning and supervision. A member shall adequately plan and supervise an engagement.

D. Sufficient relevant data. A member shall obtain sufficient relevant data to afford a reasonable basis for conclusions or recommendations in relation to an engagement.

E. Forecasts. A member shall not permit his name to be used in conjunction with any forecast of future transactions in a manner which may lead to the belief that the member vouches for the achievability of the forecast. (As amended March 31, 1978)

ET Section 202 - Auditing Standards

01. Rule 202--Auditing Standards. A member shall not permit his name to be associated with financial statements in such a manner as to imply that he is acting as an independent public accountant unless he has complied with the applicable generally accepted auditing standards promulgated by the Institute. Statements on Auditing Standards issued by the Institute's Auditing Standards Executive Committee are, for purposes of this rule, considered to be interpretations of the generally accepted auditing standards, and departures from such statements must be justified by those who do not follow them. (As amended March 31, 1978.)

ET Section 203 - Accounting Principles

01. Rule 203--Accounting principles. A member shall not express an opinion that financial statements are presented in conformity with generally accepted accounting

principles if such statements contain any departure from an accounting principle promulgated by the body designated by Council to establish such principles which has a material effect on the statements taken as a whole, unless the member can demonstrate that due to unusual circumstances the financial statements would otherwise have been misleading. In such cases his report must describe the departure, the approximate effects thereof, if practicable, and the reasons why compliance with the principle would result in a misleading statement.

Exhibit 3

Departures from Generally Accepted Auditing Standards

- The second standard of field work specified that internal control will be studied and evaluated to determine the extent of audit procedures necessary. In 11 of the 14 firms and 22 of the 50 reports, there was insufficient evidence or documentation of internal control. Similarly, there was a lack of documentation as to the effect the internal control review had on the audit procedures performed.

- An apparently incorrect opinion was expressed on 12 of 50 reports issued by nine of the 14 firms. Specifically, unqualified opinions were expressed where qualified opinions were called for, or qualified opinions expressed where an adverse opinion should have been rendered. In one instance, a qualified opinion was properly given but was worded incorrectly.

- No audit programs were found in the workpapers supporting 19 of the 50 statements in seven of the 14 firms reviewed.

- In 11 of the 50 financial statements reviewed, issued by seven of the firms, the auditors' report failed to cover specifically all of the financial statements being reported on. It is imperative that the auditors' report be specific and all-inclusive regarding exactly what the opinion covers.

## Departures from Generally Accepted Accounting Principles

The departures from generally accepted accounting principles were somewhat more varied and accordingly the rate of occurrence for any one departure was somewhat lower. The most frequently occurring items are summarized below.

- Prior period adjustments were improperly reported in eight of 50 statements by six of 14 firms. Either a PPA was included when it should not have been (or vice versa) or the presentation within the statements was not correct.

- In six of the 50 statements issued by five of the 14 firms, there were either no disclosures pertaining to leases or the disclosures were inadequate.

- In 10 reports issued by four firms, there was no summary of significant accounting policies included in the notes to financial statements.

- The components of fixed assets and/or required disclosures pertaining to depreciation were not included in four of 35 reports (municipal reports excluded), issued by three of the 14 firms.

In the same instances, inadequate disclosures were made pertaining to long-term debt.

## Notes

[1] "The Impacts of Government Regulation--The History and the Effect," ITT Lecture Series, New York University, October 25, 1978.

[2] John L. Carey, *The Rise of the Accounting Profession: From Technician to Professional 1896-1936* (New York: American Institute of CPAs, 1969).

Table 3.3

Comparison of Ethics Disposition of AICPA and 40 State Societies of CPAs with Actions of Florida State Board of Accountancy

| | AICPA & State Societies Yr. Ended 12/31/77[a] | SBA (Florida) Yr. Ended 6/30/77 |
|---|---|---|
| Investigations (and complaints): | | |
| Open at start of period | 494 | 18 |
| Opened during period | 714 | 223 |
| Total | 1208 | 241 |
| Dispositions in period: | | |
| Expelled or suspended under automatic provision | 28 | N/A[b] |
| Expelled or suspended | -- | 135[c] |
| Prima facie cases approved for sending to trial board | 16 | N/A |
| Reprimand or censure with and without terms | -- | 17[d] |
| Administrative censures | 33 | -- |
| No violations | 539 | 74 |
| Subtotal number of dispositions | 616 | 226 |
| Open at end of period | 592 | 15 |

(continued)

TABLE 3.3 - Continued



[a]As published in <u>CPA Letter</u>, AICPA (April 10, 1978).

[b]No suspension or other disciplinary action of the board is automatic.

[c]Includes 99 CPAs suspended in May 1977 for failure to satisfy continuing education requirements and 33 CPAs revoked pursuant to F. S. 473.201(2) requiring reciprocal CPA certificate holders to engage in the substantially full-time practice of public accounting in Florida for three consecutive years after licensure.

[d]While the board had 17 actions involving censure and probation, some involved firms and included as many as four individual orders against partners. Actually, 38 individual complaints and orders were entered.

# A Comment on Robert K. Elliott and Walter Schuetze's "Regulation of Accounting: Practitioner's Viewpoint"

Stephen A. Zeff

Rice University

In their paper, Elliott and Schuetze call for empirical evidence to support the assertion that private-sector standard-setting has been unsuccessful and should be conveyed to the public sector. They draw our attention to an analysis which their firm performed and submitted as an appendix to Walter E. Hanson's statement before the Metcalf Committee on May 12, 1977 (PMM Study, 1977; pages to which references are made in this discussion are in the appendix). They allege that their firm's study demonstrates that "The U.S. has the highest quality accounting and auditing standards in the world; the falloff in quality is rather abrupt, and aside from a few countries the rest of the world does not even approach the level of quality in the U.S.; and there is a strong correlation between high quality and private-sector standard-setting." This evidence suggests to them "that private-sector standard-setting is more effective than public-sector standard-setting would be."

An empirical demonstration of the relative degrees of quality of accounting and auditing standards among countries would be a remarkable achievement and success in correlating "quality" with the degree of government involvement in standard-setting even more of one. I am saddened to report, however, that their firm has succeeded in neither endeavor, and I sincerely hope that their data are not cited by readers who think they did so succeed.

In the last couple of years, we have been treated to chauvinistic assertions by several professional leaders, all who strongly believe the first of the three facts which the Peat, Marwick, Mitchell & Co. (PMM) analysis attempted to establish. I have noticed the following statements: "The financial reporting standards in the United States are generally recognized as being the best in the world."--Donald J. Hayes (1977, p. 125; see my reply: Zeff 1977-78), Arthur Young & Company. "This cooperative partnership [between governmental agencies and the accounting profession] has served this Nation well in the development of a disclosure system which is second to none in the world...."--Michael N. Chetkovich (1977, p. 98), Deloitte Haskins & Sells, then Chairman of the Board, American Institute of Certified Public Accountants. "Accounting and auditing in the United States today are the best in the world, not only in the comprehensiveness and soundness of standards, but more importantly in the integrity of their application in practice."--Walter E. Hanson (1977, p. 862), Peat, Marwick, Mitchell & Co. "We in the United States have the best and most credible corporate financial reporting system in the world."--William S. Kanaga (1977, p. 1365), Arthur Young & Company.

Is it true? Do we have the best accounting and auditing in the world? I suggest that it is almost impossible to establish the validity of such a proposition for the very reason that our standard-setting leaders are still struggling to produce a conceptual framework while at the same time trying to determine how to deal with the alleged economic and social consequences of the standard-setting process.

How does one assay "goodness" in such standards? Theorists are in disarray over paradigms, and standard-setters themselves have thus far failed to produce a definitive conceptual framework anywhere in the world. An agreement on the "goodness" in accounting standards therefore presupposes agreement on a paradigm, to say nothing of agreement on how the entailed propositions should be implemented in the myriad practical settings. Auditing standards might present less of a challenge, but no one will deny that the decade of the 1970s has brought profound changes in the norms of accepted auditing practice in the United States. Even if it could be determined which countries have the "best" accounting and auditing standards, it would be much more difficult than is suggested by the model used in the PMM Study to associate quality--in a defensible, rigorous way--with the degrees of government involvement in standard-setting.

To illustrate the problems with the PMM Study to which Elliott and Schuetze refer, let me suggest some of its most serious weaknesses.

How does PMM set about the execution of its study? In the portion devoted to accounting, 25 "accounting standards and reporting disclosures among the accounting practices considered most basic for fair financial statement presentation" are selected. PMM adds, parenthetically, that "Most of these items are drawn from the list of topics being studied by international accounting groups seeking to harmonize worldwide financial statement reporting" (PMM, 1977, p. 175). PMM's selections are as follows (pp. 183-87):

going concern
consistency
accrual
disclosure of accounting policies
inventory
consolidation
equity method
impairment of investments
depreciation
rational allocation of depreciation
pledged assets
receivables and payables to related parties
contingent assets and liabilities
statement of changes in financial position
unusual income statement items
changes in accounting policies
research costs
research and developement cost disclosure
subsequent events disclosure
long-term contracts
deferred taxes
business segments
leases
pensions
goodwill

In 1977, when the PMM Study was presented, about half of these topics were either covered by statements issued by the International Accounting Standards Committee or were under study by it. It is curious, however, that two very topical and controversial matters of that period were omitted from the PMM list: inflation accounting and foreign exchange accounting. Their inclusion, as will be suggested below, might have placed the United States in a less favorable light than was suggested by the PMM Study. The topics which should be included in any such study could, of course, be debated at length, and the validity of PMM's findings will necessarily depend on the soundness of the choices. But it is difficult to defend the omission of these two important areas. (Also, why were business combinations omitted?)

A variable which is not even mentioned in the PMM Study, but which profoundly affects the results, is the characterization of *standard* practice in each of these 25 areas. Naturally, if the practice denoted as standard happens to agree with that prevailing in the United States, other countries may look the poorer by comparison. In describing the equity method of accounting, the PMM Study uses phraseology ("significant influence over the operating and financial policies" of the investee) which, as far as I know, is used only in the American and Canadian pronouncements on the subject. But that is a minor point. Of even more interest is the omission from the standard practice on inventory of any reference to the method of finding cost: LIFO, FIFO, or average. These alternatives are mentioned in the IASC's statement on the subject, but, as is well known, American practice varies widely on the method of cost-finding. The standard for inventory in the PMM Study is confined to the lower of cost or market and the costing of self-manufactured assets.

There is a question of much larger significance, however: Where is it shown that these standard practices are compatible with "the highest quality accounting standards in the world"? What evidence do we have that ingredients in the highest quality accounting include (1) lower of cost or market for inventories, (2) writing off research costs as incurred, (3) recognition of permanent losses but not gains, on investments, (4) recognition and amortization of goodwill against earnings, (5) tax-allocation accounting, and, indeed, even (6) accrual accounting? The PMM Study does not even suggest that these standard practices might constitute less than the quintessence of sound accounting.

Further, the PMM Study weights each of the 25 standard practices equally. Einhorn (1976) is cited as support for this decision, since "In obtaining rank orderings, . . . equal weighting has been shown to be at least as good as unequal weighting" (PMM, p. 176). Einhorn's conclusions are cautiously phrased (1976, p. 11), and I frankly doubt that they would hold for the PMM Study. It would appear that a priori weightings could well be assigned to the 25 standard practices, and it would have been interesting to see whether the results obtained by replicating the PMM Study with the use of unequal weights would have been importantly different than PMM's findings. Unfortunately, since the PMM Study does not identify by name which countries are being compared with the United States, replication is not possible. I find it difficult to accept a study that ranks going concern and accrual accounting on the same plane as the disclosure of pledged assets. Furthermore, it is curious that a general principle such as accrual accounting and an application of that principle such as the systematic assignment of pension cost to earnings are both assigned to categories--and to equally weighted categories, at that.

Finally, each country's "quality accounting" is measured by the degree to which the standard practice is followed in financial statements. I presume the authors refer to published financial statements or to statements published by companies whose shares are traded in organized securities markets. Nothing is said on these points.

A linear point scheme is developed: four points to the country in which the standard practice is "required by professional standards and/or [is] found to a high degree in financial statements"; two points to the country where the standard practice is found "with a frequency of 50 percent or less" (how much less?); and no points to a country where the standard practice is "not required by professional standards and/or [is] not generally found in financial statements" (PMM, p. 176). How does one score a standard practice which is "required by professional standards" but is "not generally found in financial statements"? Is it four or zero? I can think of a number of Third World countries in which this circumstance exists. (The authors of the PMM Study do not disclose whether they confine themselves to industrially developed countries.) In the United Kingdom, moreover, several of the old Recommendations on Accounting Principles (which have never been formally withdrawn) call for practices that are generally not followed. At this juncture, the effect of omitting inflation accounting and foreign exchange accounting can be seen: U.S. practice, as reflected in the secondary sources used in the PMM Study,[1] was in disarray on the latter and oblivious to the former. Furthermore, the specification of FIFO (or LIFO) inventory costing might have resulted in a score of only two for the United States, whereas most other countries (if FIFO had been specified) would have scored four.

Why use a four-two-zero scale? Is acceptance in about half of a country's financial statements a logical median position between uniform compliance and uniform non-compliance? To what extent should the adoption of certain standard practices depend on "circumstances"? Do the authors of the PMM Study suggest that uniform compliance with *any* accounting and disclosure standards is compatible with "highest quality accounting"? Nowhere do they defend the standard practices themselves or the desideratum of compliance. Is it all that obvious?

And, indeed, to what degree do the environments of countries other than the United States even call for practices which the United States has adopted (in some instances, only in recent years)? In how many countries is leasing a widespread financing device? In how many countries do pension plans present the same accounting problems as in the United States? In how many countries do mergers and acquisitions occur with such frequency that an accounting question meriting attention by professional accounting bodies (or the legislature or securities commission) has even been debated? In how many countries are diversified operations a phenomenon of concern? In how many countries does financial accounting diverge from tax accounting, producing a tax allocation "problem"? Indeed, in some (mainly civil law) countries, as suggested in the PMM Study (pp. 177-78), the two might be very close indeed. A question may well be raised: with what factors is PMM correlating U.S. phenomena--with accounting practices in other countries or with the ways in which business is conducted in the other countries? A confounding variable has not been controlled.

Once the ratings were determined, it was found that the United States is "best" (but not "perfect," counsel Elliott and Schuetze) with 100 points. Country A has 98 points, and I wonder whether a slight change in the standard practices might have tipped the scales in favor of that country. Without identifying the countries (other than the United States), PMM reports that in the countries occupying the first five places in the standings, the "predominant group setting the accounting practices" is in the private sector (p. 177). Places 6, 7, and 8 are taken by countries whose practices are predominantly set in the public sector. These rankings evidently form the basis of Elliott and Schuetze's allegation that the PMM findings "suggest that private-sector standard-setting is more effective than public-sector standard-setting would be." Apart from the proviso that it is impossible to show empirically that public-sector standard-setting *would be* more or less effective in a country in which private-sector standard-setting has been practiced--that is, after all, a hypothetical question--how does one determine whether a country falls in one category or the other? And even if two countries were properly classified as "private sector," suppose that one were entirely free of overt (or even covert) government involvement while the other were mixed? How crude can the categories justifiably be?

Is the United States a private-sector country? Chetkovich (1977, p. 98) refers to the "cooperative partnership" between governmental agencies and the profession. Although the initial pronouncements emerge from a private-sector body (the Financial Accounting Standards Board), a public-sector agency (the Securities and Exchange Commission) participates at all stages in their preparation and has been known to reject the private-sector body's recommendations. Furthermore, the public-sector agency has announced its own policies on accounting standards and disclosure practices. What about the influence of Congress, the Federal Trade Commission, the bank regulatory agencies, the Federal Energy Regulatory Commission, the Department of Treasury, the Cost Accounting Standards Board, the Department of Justice, the Department of Energy, and other public-sector agencies which have, from time to time, intervened in the standard-setting process in the United States? Compared with standard-setting practices in Canada, the United Kingdom, and Australia, those in the United States could almost be classified as half-private and half-public.

It may be suggested that the private-sector countries are more like the United States (in terms of traditions, institutions, and even business practices) than are the public-sector countries. If so (and this assertion cannot be verified owing to the nondisclosure of the countries' identities), the interpretation placed on "correlations" between private-sector countries and "best" accounting standards would amount to a tautology.

Additionally, the PMM Study does not allow for the possibility that the securities markets in several of the countries may be less efficient (in the semi-strong form) than the American market, suggesting a different role for accounting information. It also does not allow for the possible existence or nonexistence of other information sources in Countries A-N, and it says nothing, of course, about cost-benefit calculations attendant to providing certain measurements and disclosures. In these respects, an inquiry such as PMM has made raises all of the issues which vex our domestic accounting policy makers.

I do not wish to pursue a similar analysis of the PMM Study's treatment of auditing standards and procedures. The same problems exist. One curiosity, however, might be mentioned. I believe it is true that in only a few countries (including the United States, Canada, and the United Kingdom) is the issuance of interim reports at all common. Yet one of the auditing standards in the PMM list is "interim financial statement reviews." Perhaps it is not surprising that only the U.S. scores above zero on this standard. With regard to most of Countries A-N, if a country does not have interim reports, why should the auditor be asked to review them? And the greatest irony is that a public-sector agency in the United States (the SEC) was the first to prescribe a "limited review" by auditors!

I have not exhausted the problems that emerge in research such as that conducted by PMM. I applaud the firm's courage in essaying such a study. It would be pleasant if the profession is understanding of the role of accounting in society that enabled us to conduct such research in a defensible, rigorous terms. But all we can do today is chip away at small questions. Research with the global implications of the PMM Study is not yet within our grasp, and I think it is unfortunate that this study may be cited by those who believe it establishes the heady conclusions suggested by its authors.

## Note

[1]The secondary sources relied upon by the PMM Study were: AICPA International Practice Executive Committee, *Professional Accounting in 30 Countries* (New York: AICPA, 1975); Institute of Chartered Accountants in England and Wales, *A Survey in 46 Countries* (London: ICAEW, 1976); ICAEW, *Accounting Principles and Practices in European Countries* (London: ICAEW, 1972); and Michael Lafferty, *Accounting in Europe* (Cambridge: Woodhead-Faulkner Ltd., 1975). It is also stated that the authors of the study held "discussions with accounting practitioners in certain of the countries" (PMM 1977, p. 928).

## Appendix A*

## A Comparison of International Accounting and Auditing Standards

It is undeniably difficult to measure the quality of international accounting and auditing standards, for there exists no ideal or optimum system with which to compare such standards. This appendix describes the method we used and its rationale.

For purposes of this comparison, we included all non-Communist countries with total 1974 gross national products greater than $50 billion. These countries are the United States, Japan, West Germany, France, the United Kingdom, Italy, Canada, Brazil, India, Spain, the Netherlands, Australia, Mexico, Sweden, and Belgium.

### Accounting Standards and Reporting Disclosures

To compare the accounting standards and reporting disclosures among these countries, we chose twenty-five items (see Exhibit 1) as significant criteria. The twenty-five accounting standards and reporting disclosures chosen are among the accounting practices considered most basic for fair financial statement presentation. (Most of these items are drawn from the list of topics being studied by international accounting groups seeking to harmonize worldwide financial statement reporting.) Although other standards or disclosures could have been included in the set of basic criteria in place of some actually used, we believe that any other representative criteria list would produce equivalent results and conclusions.

After selecting the criteria, we determined how each country's accounting practices require the criteria items to be treated in financial statement preparation and rated the treatment as follows:

*Source: *Accounting and Auditing Practices and Procedures*, Hearings before the Subcommittee on Reports, Accounting, and Management, U.S. Senate, 95th Cong., 1st sess., May 12, 1977, pp. 927-43.

| Status | Rating[1] |
|---|---|
| If required by professional standards and/or found to a high degree in financial statements | 4 |
| If applied with a frequency of fifty percent or less in financial statements | 2 |
| If not required by professional standards and/or not generally found in financial statements | 0 |

The rating of each item was determined from recent financial statements, recent analyses of generally applied financial practices,[2] and discussions with accounting practitioners in certain of the countries. Although these practices are in a state of change, we have attempted to determine the most currently applied practices. After each criterion was rated, a composite rating was developed by adding the rating points for each country. (It may be argued, of course, that not all criteria selected for evaluation are equally important and should therefore be weighted as to their relative importance. In obtaining rank orderings, however, equal weighting has been shown to be at least as good as unequal weighting.[3])

A schedule of the individual criteria items and each country's practices is shown in Exhibit 2. We have omitted the names of countries other than the U.S. and used letters instead. This was done to avoid any implied criticism of the practices of any specific country. The results, by country, of compliance with the criteria are as follows:

| Country | Composite Total Based Upon Compliance with Criteria | Predominant Group Setting the Accounting Practices |
|---|---|---|
| U.S. | 100 | Private |
| A | 98 | Private |
| B | 88 | Private |
| C | 86 | Private |
| D | 82 | Private |
| E | 76 | Public |
| F | 72 | Public |
| G | 70 | Public |
| H | 66 | Private |
| I | 60 | Public |
| J | 48 | Private |
| K | 48 | Public |
| L | 38 | Public |
| M | 34 | Public |
| N | 28 | Public |

One note of caution should be interjected concerning the results. The financial reporting systems within countries generally evolve to serve the financial needs and practices of the financial markets of those individual countries. For example, Europe's companies may rely less upon the stock markets for financing and more upon the banking system, thus causing some accounting practice variations. However, as investors, creditors, and companies begin to examine financial opportunities on an international rather than local basis, the need for the application of the basic criteria accounting standards and reporting disclosures grows greater.

With this note of caution in mind, it is interesting to note that the U.S. and those other countries with predominantly private standard-setting groups have generally achieved a higher degree of compliance with respect to basic accounting standards and reporting practices than countries with public standard-setting groups. The private standard-setting groups make available a greater amount of financial information.

For those countries with public standard-setting bodies, the lower level of standards may arise because those countries view financial reporting in a legal, rather than economic, sense. For instance, reporting items in accordance with the allowable tax treatment, rather than with a method that reflects the economic use, lessens the quality and usefulness of the financial statements for economic decision-making. In general, the public standard-setting groups appear to respond less quickly to changes needed to reflect changed economic conditions. Also, although the actual financial statements in these countries may be presented in conformity with a required uniform chart of accounts, such prescribed uniformity may mask numerous differences.

We also found that the current movements to harmonize differences in accounting standards in different countries (and generally to <u>increase</u> compliance with basic accounting standards) are usually coming from <u>private</u> accounting groups and from the demands of companies and investors, not from the public regulators. For example, the trend in French financial statements to reflect consolidation and equity accounting from an economic point of view (thus presenting more fairly the financial statements of the company and its subsidiaries as if the group were a single company, with less "smoothing" of income, etc.) is the result not of the public sector, but of France's private accounting bodies' urging companies to comply with the International Accounting Standards Committee's (IASC) recommendations. Also, during the 1970s a number of non-U.S. companies have begun engaging international auditing firms (often on a joint basis with local auditors) to report on financial statements prepared in conformity with Anglo-American accounting principles; thus, these companies have generally moved into closer compliance with the basic set of accounting principles and reporting disclosures. Both of these instances reflect the private sector's flexibility and willingness to reflect the economic results.

## Auditing Standards and Procedures

Accounting principles and reporting disclosures are only one part of a nation's accounting practices; an equally important part is the auditing standards and procedures used by the auditors who report on financial statement presentations. The usual objective of the auditor's examination of financial statements is the expression of an opinion on the fairness with which the financial statements present the financial position and results of operations in conformity with the accounting standards used within a particular country. The auditing standards used in the examination of financial statements are the measures of the quality of auditing procedures performed and of the objectives to be attained by the use of such procedures. Auditing standards also deal with auditors' professional qualities and the judgments exercised by them in the performance of their examinations and in their reports.

The type of auditing standards used in financial statement examinations is not merely of academic interest. Users of financial statements often recognize the differences in auditing standards and demand reporting by auditors with high auditing standards.

There is no international consensus on preferable auditing standards. Therefore, to compare international auditing standards and procedures we had to use our judgment in selecting a set of basic criteria. Although other criteria could have been selected, we believe that the use of any other set of representative criteria would produce equivalent results and conclusions.

Exhibits 3 and 4 are analogous to previous Exhibits 1 and 2 in that we have listed a basic group of auditing standards and procedures and determined how each country's auditing practices address these items. Our rating of the treatment within each country was as follows:

| Status | Rating[4] |
|---|---|
| If required by professional standards and/or found to a high degree in practice | 5.0 |
| If professional standards provide little guidance and/or are applied only fifty percent or less in practice | 2.5 |
| If not required by professional standards and/or not generally found in practice | 0 |

The rating for each item was determined from analyses of current auditing literature and from discussions with auditors familiar with that country's auditing practices. (It is interesting to note that some countries which are dominated by the public sector in the setting of accounting standards allow the auditing standards to be determined predominantly by the private sector.) The results by country are as follows:

| Country | Composite Total Based Upon Compliance with Criteria | Predominant Group Setting the Accounting Practices |
|---|---|---|
| U.S. | 100.0 | Private |
| A | 85.0 | Private |
| C | 82.5 | Private |
| I | 72.5 | Private |
| D | 67.5 | Private |
| B | 65.0 | Private |
| G | 62.5 | Private |
| E | 60.0 | Public |
| K | 60.0 | Public |
| H | 57.5 | Private |
| J | 40.0 | Private |
| M | 37.5 | Public |
| F | 27.5 | Private |
| L | 22.5 | Public |
| N | 17.5 | Public |

Again, before we begin reviewing the results, remember

that auditing standards evolve based on many factors, including the financial markets to be served, auditors' perceived responsibilities, the legal environment, and so forth. For example, our U.S. use of public equity financing may lead to an earlier demand for auditor reviews of quarterly financial statements than in countries where central institutions dominate the financing. As a second example, our U.S. legal environment may lead to greater codification of standards and procedures and efforts to assure audit quality.

The comparison of auditing standards and procedures is also made more difficult by the fact that we had to evaluate the professional requirements within the literature but could not systematically measure actual compliance by auditors. In addition, compliance is not always mandatory in some non-U.S. countries. Thus, the comparison within auditing is less precise than within accounting, where we were able to examine published financial statements.

With these caveats in mind, the results show that for auditing standards and procedures, the U.S. and other countries with predominantly _private_ standard-setting groups generally achieve a higher degree of compliance with the set of criteria than do countries with predominantly _public_ standard-setting groups. Areas of difference among countries include the concept of independence (e.g., absence of any financial interests), confirmation of receivables, and observation of inventories.

The private standard-setting groups appear more in touch with "real world" problems and generally adapt more quickly to changing business circumstances.

## Notes

[1]Rating points were scaled to add to 100 in the case all criteria were required or found to a high degree in a country's accounting practice.

[2]References for accounting standards and reporting disclosures included the following:

- AICPA International Practice Executive Committee. Professional Accounting in 30 Countries. New York: AICPA, 1975.
- Institute of Chartered Accountants in England and Wales. A Survey in 46 Countries. London: ICAEW, 1976.
- Institute of Chartered Accountants in England and Wales. Accounting Principles and Practices in European Countries. London: ICAEW, 1972.
- Michael Laferty. Accounting in Europe. Cambridge: Woodhead-Faulkner (Publishers) Ltd., 1975.

[3]See Hillel J. Einhorn, "Equal Weighting in Multi-Attribute Models: A Rationale, an Example, and Some Extensions," Proceedings of the Conference on Topical Research in Accounting, 1976, Ross Institute of Accounting Research, New York University.

[4]Again, rating points were scaled to add to a total score of 100 in case all criteria are required or found to a high degree in practice.

## Exhibit 1

### Basic Accounting Standards and Reporting Disclosures Chosen as Criteria for Evaluating International Accounting Practices

#### Going Concern

An accounting entity is viewed as continuing in operation in the absence of evidence to the contrary. (If liquidation appears imminent, financial information may be prepared on the assumption that liquidation will occur.)

#### Consistency

Accounting practices and procedures are consistently applied from one period to another.

#### Accrual

The effects of transactions and other events on the assets and liabilities of a business enterprise are recognized (i.e., accrued) and reported in the time periods to which they relate rather than only when cash is received or paid.

#### Disclosure of Accounting Policies

All significant accounting policies of the reporting entity are included as an integral part of the financial statements.

#### Inventory

Inventory is valued at the lower of historical cost or net realizable value. The historical cost of self-manufactured goods includes an allocation of production overhead costs as well as direct costs.

## Consolidation

As a general rule, a parent company includes in consolidation any company in which it owns (directly or indirectly) over fifty percent of the outstanding voting shares. In consolidation, intercompany transactions and balances are eliminated. (Thus consolidation more fairly presents the financial statements of the parent company and its subsidiaries as if the group were a single company. Such financial statements reflect an economic, rather than legal, view of the group.)

## Equity Method of Accounting

The equity method of accounting is followed for unconsolidated subsidiaries and for investments in common stock where the investor has the ability to exercise significant influence over the operating and financial policies of the investee even though the investor owns fifty percent or less of the voting stock. Intercompany profits and losses are eliminated, until realized. (In applying the equity method as opposed to the cost method, an investor generally records his proportionate share of the investor's earnings or loss during the current period. Under the cost basis, recognition of earnings or loss may be postponed with a potential for manipulating the investor's earnings pattern.)

## Impairment of Investments

A loss (which is other than temporary) in the value of an investment is reported when it becomes evident.

## Depreciation

The cost of depreciable assets (e.g., buildings and machinery) is charged to income during the life of the asset.

## Rational Allocation of Depreciation Expense

Depreciation expense is allocated in a rational and systematic manner to the accounting periods during the useful life of an asset. (There are no excessive charges for depreciation in certain periods because of "conservatism" or to comply with tax return reporting.)

## Pledged Assets

Any restrictions on the title to assets or any pledged assets are disclosed.

## Receivables and Payables to Related Parties

Receivables and payables from related companies, officers, and directors are disclosed.

## Contingent Assets and Liabilities

Contingent assets and liabilities are disclosed.

## Statement of Changes in Financial Position

A statement of changes in financial position is included as a part of the financial statements.

## Unusual Income Statement Items

Items unusual to the ordinary activity of the business are disclosed separately and explained.

## Changes in Accounting Policies

Changes in accounting policies that materially affect current or future periods are disclosed. The justification for and effect of the change are stated.

## Research Costs

Research costs are expensed as incurred.

## Research and Development Cost Disclosure

The amount of research and development costs expensed in each period presented is disclosed.

## Subsequent Events Disclosure

Material events occurring between the balance sheet date and the date the financial statements are issued are reflected or disclosed in the financial statements if knowledge of the events might affect interpretation of the statements.

## Long-Term Contracts

Revenue on long-term contracts is recognized on the percentage-of-completion method (i.e., as work on a contract progresses). If a loss on completion is anticipated, the estimated loss is recognized in the current period (i.e., rather than waiting until the completion of the work).

## Deferred Taxes

Deferred tax accounting is used to give effect to those items which affect the determination of financial statement income and taxable income in different reporting periods (i.e., if depreciation allowable for tax purposes is greater than that which would reflect a systematic allocation of the asset's cost for financial statement purposes, a deferred tax expense and liability are recorded to report the tax payments deferred into future periods).

Business Segments

Financial statements include certain types of information concerning the material segments of a company's business if those segments are in different types of businesses.

Leases

Lease commitments are disclosed.

Pensions

Pensions costs are systematically accrued by charges to current periods' earnings over the expected periods of active service of the employees (i.e., pension costs charged to current earnings are not based on cash payments only).

Goodwill

In a business combination, the excess of the cost of the acquired company over the fair values assigned to acquired assets and liabilities is recorded as goodwill. Goodwill is then amortized against earnings over the periods estimated to be benefited.

Exhibit 2

INDIVIDUAL COUNTRIES' TREATMENT OF BASIC ACCOUNTING PRINCIPLES AND REPORTING DISCLOSURES

| Criteria | Country | | | | | | | | | | | | | | |
|---|---|---|---|---|---|---|---|---|---|---|---|---|---|---|---|
| | U.S. | A | B | C | D | E | F | G | H | I | J | K | L | M | N |
| Going concern | 4 | 4 | 4 | 4 | 4 | 4 | 4 | 4 | 4 | 4 | 2 | 4 | 2 | 2 | 4 |
| Consistency | 4 | 4 | 4 | 4 | 4 | 4 | 2 | 4 | 4 | 4 | 4 | 4 | 4 | 2 | 2 |
| Accrual | 4 | 4 | 4 | 4 | 4 | 4 | 4 | 4 | 4 | 4 | 4 | 2 | 4 | 4 | 4 |
| Disclosure of accounting policies | 4 | 4 | 4 | 4 | 4 | 4 | 4 | 2 | 2 | 2 | 2 | 2 | 0 | 0 | 0 |
| Inventory | 4 | 4 | 4 | 4 | 4 | 4 | 4 | 4 | 4 | 4 | 2 | 4 | 2 | 4 | 2 |
| Consolidation | 4 | 4 | 2 | 4 | 4 | 2 | 2 | 4 | 0 | 2 | 2 | 4 | 0 | 0 | 0 |
| Equity method of accounting | 4 | 4 | 4 | 4 | 2 | 2 | 0 | 0 | 0 | 2 | 0 | 4 | 0 | 0 | 0 |
| Impairment of investments | 4 | 4 | 4 | 4 | 4 | 4 | 4 | 2 | 2 | 2 | 2 | 2 | 4 | 4 | 2 |
| Depreciation | 4 | 4 | 4 | 4 | 4 | 4 | 4 | 4 | 4 | 4 | 4 | 2 | 2 | 4 | 4 |
| Rational allocation of depreciation expense | 4 | 4 | 4 | 4 | 4 | 4 | 2 | 2 | 4 | 2 | 2 | 0 | 2 | 2 | 0 |
| Pledged assets | 4 | 4 | 4 | 2 | 4 | 4 | 4 | 4 | 4 | 2 | 2 | 2 | 4 | 0 | 2 |
| Receivables and payables to related parties | 4 | 4 | 2 | 2 | 2 | 4 | 4 | 2 | 4 | 2 | 2 | 2 | 0 | 0 | 2 |
| Contingent assets and liabilities | 4 | 4 | 4 | 4 | 4 | 4 | 4 | 4 | 4 | 4 | 2 | 2 | 0 | 0 | 0 |

(continued)

Exhibit 2 - Continued

| Criteria | Country | | | | | | | | | | | | | | |
|---|---|---|---|---|---|---|---|---|---|---|---|---|---|---|---|
| | U.S. | A | B | C | D | E | F | G | H | I | J | K | L | M | N |
| Statement of changes in financial position | 4 | 4 | 2 | 4 | 2 | 0 | 2 | 2 | 2 | 2 | 4 | 0 | 0 | 2 | 0 |
| Unusual income statement items | 4 | 4 | 4 | 4 | 4 | 4 | 4 | 4 | 4 | 4 | 0 | 0 | 2 | 2 | 2 |
| Changes in accounting policies | 4 | 4 | 4 | 4 | 4 | 4 | 4 | 2 | 4 | 4 | 2 | 2 | 4 | 0 | 0 |
| Research costs | 4 | 4 | 4 | 4 | 4 | 4 | 4 | 4 | 4 | 4 | 2 | 0 | 4 | 2 | 2 |
| Research and development cost disclosures | 4 | 4 | 2 | 2 | 2 | 4 | 2 | 2 | 4 | 0 | 0 | 4 | 0 | 4 | 2 |
| Subsequent events disclosure | 4 | 4 | 4 | 4 | 4 | 4 | 4 | 4 | 4 | 2 | 2 | 2 | 0 | 0 | 0 |
| Long-term contracts | 4 | 2 | 2 | 4 | 2 | 2 | 2 | 2 | 2 | 2 | 2 | 0 | 0 | 2 | 0 |
| Deferred taxes | 4 | 4 | 4 | 4 | 4 | 0 | 0 | 2 | 0 | 2 | 2 | 0 | 0 | 0 | 0 |
| Business segments | 4 | 4 | 4 | 4 | 2 | 0 | 2 | 2 | 2 | 2 | 0 | 0 | 0 | 0 | 0 |
| Leases | 4 | 4 | 4 | 0 | 2 | 0 | 2 | 0 | 0 | 0 | 0 | 0 | 0 | 0 | 0 |
| Pensions | 4 | 4 | 4 | 4 | 4 | 2 | 4 | 4 | 0 | 0 | 2 | 2 | 4 | 0 | 0 |
| Goodwill | 4 | 4 | 2 | 0 | 0 | 4 | 0 | 2 | 0 | 0 | 2 | 4 | 0 | 0 | 0 |
| COMPOSITE TOTAL | 100 | 98 | 88 | 86 | 82 | 76 | 72 | 70 | 66 | 60 | 48 | 48 | 38 | 34 | 28 |

NOTE: Rating was as follows:

4 - required by professional standards and/or found to a high degree in financial statements
2 - applied with a frequency of fifty percent or less in financial statements
0 - not required by professional standards and/or not generally found in financial statements

Exhibit 3

## Basic Auditing Standards and Procedures Chosen as Criteria for Evaluating International Auditing Practices

### Auditing Literature

The professional standards and procedures are codified adequately to provide guidance to the profession.

### Independence (General)

An auditor does not express an opinion on financial statements of an enterprise unless he and his firm are independent with respect to such an enterprise.

### Independence (Actions)

An auditor is not considered independent if, at the time of expressing an opinion on the financial statements of an enterprise, he or any member of his firm

(a) holds any direct or material indirect financial interest in the enterprise;

(b) is connected with the enterprise as an underwriter, director, officer, etc.; or

(c) is a trustee or executor of any trust or estate having any direct or material indirect financial interest in the enterprise.

### Independence (Procedures)

The professional standards of the country require that policies and procedures be established to provide reasonable assurance that persons at all audit organizational levels maintain independence in fact and in appearance.

## Technical Training and Proficiency

Professional standards require that policies and procedures be established to assure that audit work will be performed by persons having the degree of technical training and proficiency required in the circumstances.

## Supervision

Professional standards require that policies and procedures for the conduct and supervision of work at all organizational levels be established to provide reasonable assurance that the work performed meets the country's standards of quality. (Examples include providing direction for the form and content of working papers; developing and using standard audit forms, checklists, and questionnaires; and requiring that working papers, financial statements, and auditors' reports be reviewed by qualified personnel.)

## Professional Development

Adequate continuing professional education and training activities are available to provide personnel with information on current developments, specialized skills, etc.

## Advanced Auditing Techniques

Candidates for entry into the profession are trained and tested in advanced audit techniques such as computer auditing and statistical auditing.

## Confirmation of Receivables

If receivables are material, direct communication by the auditor with debtors is a required auditing procedure.

## Observation of Inventory

If inventories are material, the auditor is present at the time of the inventory count to satisfy himself as to the effectiveness of the methods of inventory-taking and the measure of reliance which may be placed on the client's representations concerning inventories.

## Contingencies and Legal Confirmations

Professional standards provide guidance for the auditor in identifying litigation, claims, uncertainties, etc., and in obtaining opinions from outside counsel.

## Related Party Transactions

The professional standards require review for, identification of, and examination of related party transactions.

## Auditor's Report

(a) The report states whether the financial statements are presented in conformity with generally accepted accounting principles.

(b) The report states whether such principles have been consistently observed in the current period in relation to the preceding period.

(c) Informative disclosures in the financial statements are to be regarded as reasonably adequate unless otherwise stated in the report.

(d) The report contains either an expression of opinion regarding the financial statements, taken as a whole, or an assertion to the effect that an opinion cannot be expressed. When an overall opinion cannot be expressed, the report states the reasons therefor. In all cases where an auditor's name is associated with financial statements, the report contains a clear-cut indication of the character of the auditor's examination, if any, and the degree of responsibility he is taking.

## Interim Financial Statement Reviews

The professional literature provides guidance for limited reviews of financial statement information and for reporting upon such reviews.

## Quality Control Review Program

The professional standards contain guidelines and suggestions for a quality control review of audit firms as a means of self-regulation.

Exhibit 4

INDIVIDUAL COUNTRIES' TREATMENT OF BASIC AUDITING STANDARDS AND PROCEDURES

| Criteria | Country | | | | | | | | | | | | | | |
|---|---|---|---|---|---|---|---|---|---|---|---|---|---|---|---|
| | U.S. | A | C | I | D | B | G | E | K | H | J | M | F | L | N |
| Auditing literature | 5 | 5 | 5 | 5 | 5 | 2.5 | 5 | 5 | 5 | 2.5 | 2.5 | 0 | 0 | 0 | 2.5 |
| Independence | | | | | | | | | | | | | | | |
| - General | 5 | 5 | 5 | 5 | 5 | 5 | 5 | 2.5 | 5 | 5 | 2.5 | 0 | 5 | 0 | 2.5 |
| - Actions | 5 | 5 | 2.5 | 2.5 | 5 | 2.5 | 2.5 | 0 | 5 | 0 | 2.5 | 0 | 0 | 0 | 2.5 |
| - Procedures | 5 | 5 | 5 | 0 | 5 | 0 | 0 | 2.5 | 2.5 | 5 | 0 | 0 | 0 | 0 | 0 |
| Technical training and proficiency | 5 | 5 | 5 | 5 | 5 | 5 | 5 | 5 | 2.5 | 5 | 2.5 | 2.5 | 0 | 0 | 0 |
| Supervision | 5 | 5 | 5 | 5 | 5 | 5 | 5 | 5 | 2.5 | 5 | 2.5 | 2.5 | 0 | 0 | 0 |
| Professional development | 5 | 5 | 5 | 5 | 5 | 5 | 5 | 5 | 0 | 5 | 2.5 | 0 | 2.5 | 0 | 0 |
| Computer auditing | 5 | 5 | 5 | 2.5 | 0 | 5 | 2.5 | 0 | 2.5 | 0 | 0 | 0 | 0 | 0 | 0 |
| Statistical auditing | 5 | 5 | 5 | 2.5 | 0 | 5 | 2.5 | 0 | 0 | 5 | 0 | 0 | 5 | 0 | 0 |
| Confirmation of receivables | 5 | 5 | 2.5 | 2.5 | 5 | 5 | 5 | 5 | 5 | 2.5 | 0 | 2.5 | 0 | 0 | 0 |
| Observation of inventory | 5 | 5 | 5 | 2.5 | 5 | 5 | 5 | 5 | 5 | 2.5 | 5 | 2.5 | 0 | 5 | 0 |

(continued)

Exhibit 4 - Continued

| Criteria | Country | | | | | | | | | | | | | | |
|---|---|---|---|---|---|---|---|---|---|---|---|---|---|---|---|
| | U.S. | A | C | I | D | B | G | E | K | H | J | M | F | L | N |
| Contingencies | | | | | | | | | | | | | | | |
| - General | 5 | 5 | 5 | 5 | 5 | 0 | 0 | 0 | 2.5 | 5 | 2.5 | 2.5 | 0 | 0 | 0 |
| - Legal confirmation | 5 | 2.5 | 5 | 5 | 0 | 0 | 0 | 0 | 2.5 | 0 | 2.5 | 2.5 | 0 | 0 | 0 |
| Related party transactions | 5 | 2.5 | 2.5 | 5 | 0 | 0 | 5 | 5 | 2.5 | 5 | 0 | 2.5 | 0 | 0 | 0 |
| Auditor's Report | | | | | | | | | | | | | | | |
| - Conformity | 5 | 5 | 5 | 5 | 5 | 5 | 5 | 5 | 5 | 0 | 5 | 5 | 5 | 5 | 5 |
| - Consistency | 5 | 5 | 5 | 5 | 5 | 5 | 0 | 5 | 5 | 0 | 5 | 5 | 0 | 5 | 0 |
| - Adequate disclosure | 5 | 5 | 5 | 5 | 5 | 5 | 5 | 5 | 2.5 | 5 | 2.5 | 2.5 | 5 | 5 | 0 |
| - Expression of opinion | 5 | 5 | 5 | 5 | 2.5 | 5 | 5 | 5 | 5 | 5 | 2.5 | 5 | 5 | 2.5 | 5 |
| Interim financial statement reviews | 5 | 0 | 0 | 0 | 0 | 0 | 0 | 0 | 0 | 0 | 0 | 0 | 0 | 0 | 0 |
| Quality control review program | 5 | 0 | 0 | 0 | 0 | 0 | 0 | 0 | 0 | 0 | 0 | 2.5 | 0 | 0 | 0 |
| COMPOSITE TOTAL | 100 | 85 | 82.5 | 72.5 | 67.5 | 65 | 62.5 | 60 | 60 | 57.5 | 40 | 37.5 | 27.5 | 22.5 | 17.5 |

(continued)

Exhibit 4 - Continued

NOTE: Rating was as follows:

5 = required by professional standards and/or found to a high degree in practice

2.5 = professional standards provide little guidance and/or are applied only 50% or less in practice

0 = not required by professional standards and/or not generally found in practice

## References

Chetkovich, Michael N. Testimony in *Accounting and Auditing Practices and Procedures*, Hearings before the Subcommittee on Reports, Accounting and Manangement of the Committee on Governmental Affairs, U.S. Senate, 95th Cong., 1st sess. (April 19, 1977), pp. 97-103.

Einhorn, Hillel J. "Equal Weighting in Multi-Attribute Models: A Rationale, an Example, and Some Extensions." In *Proceedings of the Conference on Topical Research in Accounting*, edited by Michael Schiff and George Sorter, pp. 1-13 (New York: Ross Institute of Accounting Research, New York University, 1976).

Elliott, Robert K., and Walter Schuetze. "Regulation of Accounting: Practitioner's Viewpoint." Round Table Conference on Government Regulation of Accounting and Information, University of Florida (March 30-31, 1979).

Hanson, Walter E. Testimony in *Accounting and Auditing Practices and Procedures*, Hearings before the Subcommittee on Reports, Accounting and Management of the Committee on Governmental Affairs, U.S. Senate, 95th Cong., 1st sess. (May 12, 1977), pp. 862-876.

Hayes, Donald J. "Should the Public Sector Take on the Function of Determining Generally Accepted Accounting Principles? Position *nay*." *The Accounting Journal* (Spring 1977): 124-29.

Kanaga, William S. Testimony in *Accounting and Auditing Practices and Procedures*, Hearings before the Subcommittee on Reports, Accounting and Management of the Committee on Governmental Affairs, U.S. Senate, 95th Cong., 1st sess. (May 24, 1977), pp. 1363-82.

(PMM Study). "A Comparison of International Accounting and Auditing Standards." In Statement of Walter E. Hanson, Senior Partner of Peat, Marwick, Mitchell & Co., in *Accounting and Auditing Practices and Procedures*, Hearings before the Subcommittee on

Reports, Accounting and Management of the Committee on Governmental Affairs, U.S. Senate, 95th Cong., 1st sess. (May 12, 1977), pp. 927-43.

Zeff, Stephen A. Correspondence and Comments. *The Accounting Journal* (Winter 1977-78): 358-59.

# A Reply

Robert K. Elliott and Walter Schuetze

Peat, Marwick, Mitchell & Co.

Zeff's comments pertain to an illustration in our paper drawn from a different paper by a different author. The material is included in our paper solely to illustrate the point that "empirical evidence should take priority over acceptance of critical, unsupported assertions" in determining the extent of government regulation. The illustration shows how empirical evidence might be used to illuminate this issue. To disagree with the particular study is not to disagree with the main point we are making. Nevertheless, we will respond to Zeff's argument in view of the fact that the paper from which the illustration was drawn was authored by our partner.

Zeff questions whether any empirical study can reach valid conclusions as to whether government regulation results in better or worse accounting and auditing standards. The answer to this question must hinge on the definition of "better", a definition supplied by neither Zeff nor Hanson. Following are several candidate elements in a definition of a "better" system of accounting and auditing: one system of accounting and auditing is better than another, *ceterus paribus*, if

1. it leads to improved resource allocation
2. it leads to higher *per capita* wealth
3. it maximizes citizen welfare

4. it is finer
5. it is less biased
6. it leads to lower variability of information errors.

If elements similar to 1-3 constitute the definition, Zeff is correct that it will be impossible to decide which system is better based upon empirical data (owing to the impossibility of aggregating utilities over individuals and similar difficulties). Although Zeff did not define a "better" system, he used words like "economic and social consequences of the standard-setting process," which leads us to believe he would incorporate elements similar to 1-3 in his definition. If we accept this type of definition, then all empirical studies will be useless, not just the Hanson study.

On the other hand, if elements similar to 4-6 constitute the definition, empirical data will be useful in deciding what is a better system. Although Hanson did not define a "better" system, he collected and presented evidence relating to fineness (i.e., the application of specific accounting and reporting features) and bias and variability (i.e., the application of specific auditing procedures). Thus, his definition may be inferred. If this definition is accepted, empirical evidence will be useful in deciding what is a "better" system and, we hope, in making policy decisions.

Assuming empirical evidence to be relevant, the next question is whether the Hanson study reaches valid conclusions. Zeff's criticisms in this regard mostly reduce to questions about the weightings of factors included. The equal-weighting scheme used is extremely robust--i.e., it results in substantially equivalent rank-orderings--if (1) a large number of variables are included (a condition met in the Hanson study) or (2) the variables are not negatively correlated (a condition also met in the Hanson study). Thus, the rank-ordering would not be significantly affected by any of the reweightings Zeff mentions. In fact, the study contains sufficient data for the reader to verify this assertion by eliminating and/or reweighting variables, determining new rank-orderings, and comparing. (Because the countries are not identified by name, it would not, of course, be possible for the reader to add new variables, but we are of the opinion that adding new variables would not have any significant effect.)

We hope that readers will agree with the point we were illustrating, which is that social policy making should be based on empirical evidence rather than unquestioning acquiescence to unsupported, critical assertions.

4

# Would Market Forces Cause Adequate Securities Disclosure Without SEC Mandate?

Homer Kripke

New York University School of Law

As a lawyer, I feel out of place and over my head in a workshop devoted to accounting and economic issues. Nevertheless, as some of you know, I have for many years been concerned with these issues as they relate to securities disclosure.

Many years ago, I became dissatisfied with the SEC's role in securities regulation and with the results. I began to read diligently the new economics of the securities markets and the flood of empirical accounting studies, to understand what their impact should be on securities regulation. Economists ought to play a key role in determining the scope and direction of securities regulation, but they have chosen to forego that role by talking in a new language reserved for scholars, in this case not scholastic Latin but mathematical notation, even when (as frequently happens) the mathematics is not necessary to the discussion, and the notation is not used for the mathematics. Consequently, substantial and useful insights, even wisdom, are neglected by those who do not make the effort to penetrate the learned jargon.

The question here concerns the necessity of mandating the disclosure that the SEC now requires for the securities markets. I have tried to read in the area of economics of information, which seemed to hold promise for my topic, but I have not succeeded in acquiring any wisdom. I can understand the assertions that information is a commodity but that because, unlike other commodities, its scarcity cannot be maintained, it is a public good, and therefore its production is not governed by the ordinary laws of supply and demand. Except for such wide generalizations, the techniques of economics and mathematics have so abstracted the subject that it is meaningless and its applicability to a real world difficult to perceive or to verify. Thus I remain uninformed by reading the economics of information.

I also find little value for my purpose in the more insistent efforts to apply to the financial world the latest fad; the economics of signaling. I elsewhere have paid my unenthusiastic respects to some applications to financial contexts of signaling theory, which were predicated on the assumption that the signal becomes reliable if the signaler accepts a penalty for false signaling. But even these applications lack practical relation to reality and utility to the present inquiry. (Let me make clear that I have no difficulty with the more modest use of a signaling perspective by Professors Nicholas J. Gonedes and Nicholas Dopuch. Their writings from that perspective point to the same conclusions as my own.)

In my discussion I am going to assume a real world, the United States; the time is today, not when the New York Stock Exchange was founded under the Buttonwood tree in the eighteenth century, not even when the securities laws were passed in the 1930s. This means that, unlike my friend George Benston (1973), I do not have to argue whether the securities laws and Securities and Exchange Commission (SEC) were ever necessary, or whether they have done some good in conditioning the financial markets to demand relevant information. My only question is to what extent they are necessary *now,* with the markets in place, the analytic apparatus in place, and a developed concept of adequate disclosure in place.[1] I also am going to assume the continued existence of the securities antifraud laws, including the inhibitions on the use of inside information. I am going to assume the broad securities markets of the U.S., in which an issuer can hope to obtain equity or debt financing, not a country without any broad financial markets like Uganda or Namibia or even most countries of Europe. The question I propose to pursue is whether the insistent detailed disclosure still being mandated and cumulated by the SEC is necessary or whether market forces would cause adequate disclosure in the present U.S. environment.

I am going to talk about disclosure for securities decisions in the two contexts of new fund raising, both private and public, and the trading market.

An active discussion goes on among the academic specialists in the economics of information about whether adequate financial information would be supplied by firms in the absence of compulsion. While Professors Benston (1973) and Lev (1976) argued that it would be supplied, and Professor Beaver (1977) suggested that it might be, the prevailing view seems to be that information is not a commodity subject to the usual laws of supply and demand, because its exclusive possession cannot be guaranteed to a buyer (i.e., it becomes a "public good" and we have a "free rider" problem) and because the securities rules on inside information preclude a buyer from exploiting exclusive information (e.g., Professor Mendelson, 1978). Thus, it is argued, neither the companies themselves nor private persons would have the economic motives for discovering or assembling the information if it were not for the compulsion of the reporting system.

But these views limited by ordinary demand and supply concepts do not take into account the simple fact that an issuer must supply the information demands of the buyers to whom the issuer proposes to issue its securities, whether they be private placees or underwriters, and firms desiring an active trading market in their securities must supply information sufficient to attract buyer interest and to satisfy the needs of recommending brokers and analysts. The whole academic argument is irrelevant because it deals with information unilaterally produced in some kind of empty state of the world instead of negotiated disclosure in connection with securities issuance or trading, where the recipient has some bargaining chips and uses them. Thus the economics *of this kind of information* cannot be abstracted from the economics of the capital markets any more than the economics of producing automobile doors could be abstracted from the economics of producing automobiles.

### Why Issuers Will Furnish the Information Desired by the Market

Whether a disclosure must be mandated or whether it will be supplied voluntarily by issuers interested in the capital markets depends on whether there is a consensus among suppliers of capital or other transactors in the capital markets that this kind of information is necessary for lending and investment decisions. If there is such a consensus, issuers will supply it rather than forego access to the capital markets.[2] If not (i.e., if it is material only under SEC conceptions), SEC must mandate it.

The question should not be put in terms of whether voluntary disclosure would replicate SEC-mandated disclosure, because few would agree that SEC disclosure represents the optimum. For 40 years it was hidebound in the interest of protecting the SEC staff from being criticized for permitting anything that was not objective and verifiable and protecting the public from deception thereby. Thus it limited disclosure to historical cost financial statements, excluding projections, appraisals, and all "soft" or optimistic information. My 1970 article was the first substantial attack on this approach. SEC is only slowly moving away from it.

Moreover, we have recently witnessed explosive and questionable revisions of SEC concepts of materiality. First, there have been those related to "quality of management," regardless of amounts involved, e.g., "questionable payments," "perks," "sweetheart loans," and "integrity of the books." Second, there are those designed to effect changes in corporate governance but included also in the financial disclosure forms, e.g., disclosing directors' affiliations, increasing details of disclosure of officers' direct and indirect compensation, and so on.

Thus, the answer to my question today is obvious: those parts of the SEC system that are recognized by lenders and investors as being material to their decisions, and any other information deemed by them to be material, would be required by them under free market conditions and, subject to expense constraints, would be furnished by issuers. Other parts would not be required. It is as simple as that. Which system would be optimal depends on your judgment of SEC wisdom.

Private New Issue Placements

Alongside the Securities Act disclosure system for public offerings are the systems of private placement for debt securities of institutional quality and for "venture capital" equity securities, operating under the private placement (Section 4(2)) exemption. In both of these types of situations, investors and issuers freely negotiated for 40 years the information to be furnished by the issuer to the prospective investor. I show a comparison between information obtained in private placements and the commission's typical required disclosures.[3] It shows that private transactors in the capital markets have the ability to obtain the information they require, and the fact that the information that they require does not coincide with mandated information is not to the former's discredit.

This private system worked well, without significant complaint. No doubt there must have been substantial losses in some cases because of the risks of promotional ventures, but before the advent of Rule 146 there were few reports of litigation by disgruntled investors in private placement situations even in this litigious era. For this reason, the SEC's intervention in the area through Rule 146, attempting to enforce its own views of disclosure on types of private negotiation that were proceeding satisfactorily, was in my view a great mistake (Kripke, 1974). The SEC's own disclosure requirements have had no great success in the venture capital fields.

When there are market--i.e., negotiated--systems of disclosure side by side with the mandatory system, one would think that the governmentally mandated system would have been carefully and frequently checked to see how it compares with the disclosure negotiated from issuers by investors who were free to contract for what they wanted without governmental constraint. If the SEC really wanted to know what information investors demand and use and how securities decisions are made, and to what extent a mandatory system was necessary, it could have done no better than to study some of these private placements. And yet a leading SEC official said in 1975 that the SEC had never done so.

Nor did it do so when it adopted Rule 146 and did its best to destroy the privately negotiated system by forcing on the parties its own concept of disclosure (see Kripke, 1974).

### Market Disclosure on Public Issues

The information obtained from the issuer in the private placements discussed above was obtained by persons strong enough to negotiate. What about the small investor? This takes us back to the economic view that when the negotiation or transaction cost would be too high, government many reasonably step in and try to achieve approximately the same result as negotiation. The average small investor could not negotiate effectively for information, and it might be argued that the mandated system is therefore necessary. But the underwriters of a public issue have the same negotiating strength as the large institutional investors in an institutional private placement or the group of venturers in a venture capital private placement. Underwriters have every reason to obtain and to furnish correct information, because they have their reputations on the line. As the Advisory Committee Report (p. 426) points out, they have an "adversary" relationship with the issuer. They are liable for negligence under Section 12(2) of the Securities Act, even in an unregistered issue.

The antifraud provisions of the acts would also operate to compel underwriters or persons organizing private placement to procure adequate disclosure.

### Market Disclosure in the Trading Market

The problem of disclosure under the continuous information system of the Securities Exchange Act for the trading market is different. The issuer does not participate in the trading market and, in contrast to the case of a distribution, seemingly does not want anything from that market. There is no clearly identified group of prospective buyers with whom to bargain concerning disclosures.

But the issuer does want something. The market price of the stock is important to a company and its management. The market appraisal of the equity is considered by most analysts to be a far better indication of that equity than the accountants' computation. The size of that equity can significantly affect the company's borrowing power, the interest rate it pays on it borrowings, and the value of its "paper" in mergers and acquisitions.

The market value of the stock is also important to the management for personal reasons. The management typically has stock, stock options, phantom stock, or stock appreciation rights. If the corporation has satisfied stockholders, management can more easily award to itself generous salaries and fringe benefits.

The market for the company's equity securities depends not only on the company's performance, past and future, but on the demand for the company's securities.

For most major companies, the dividend yield to stockholders is less than the going rate on corporate bonds, even without weighing comparative risk. The willingness of investors to hold stocks for investment depends on their expectation that the dividend return will increase and be supplemented by capital gain from a rise in market price. In short, the stock must have a "following," which does not materialize from thin air but consists of investors who have been interested in the stock by sponsorship by brokers and dealers making recommendations to institutions and individuals. These groups are advised by financial analysts, and companies which will not furnish adequate information conforming generally to the disclosure standards of other companies will lose their following. Those whose results do not conform to what they have given the professionals reason to expect learn that "analysts do not like surprises."[4] The signaling perspective tells us that issuers (and underwriters) who would be believed have to keep their track records clear.

The SEC has built up a series of monitors who, for their own self-protection, will demand adequate and truthful disclosure. First, of course, are the public accountants, who regularly audit the annual reports and whom the SEC has caused to become "associated" with quarterly reports (ASR 177). Behind them are two new features of the financial landscape, audit committees composed of independent directors and boards composed heavily of independent directors. The SEC is now also pointing the finger at internal auditors, internal counsel, and, of course, external counsel. All of these are learning that display of a sense of public responsibility on disclosure is also self-protective.[5]

The bottom line, in Commissioner Sommer's opinion (Sommer, 1975, p. 7), is that "an overwhelming number of companies in this country realize the value of the disclosure system and cooperate fully in the effort to procure for investors the fullest possible information which may bear upon investment decisions."[6]

## What Would Happen to Financial Accounting in the Absence of Regulation?

This question assumes, of course, that financial accounting is presently regulated. Current rhetoric about the preservation of our system of determining accounting principles in "the private sector" merely obscures the fact that the FASB's powers are delegated by the SEC and their force comes from SEC mandate (Horngren, 1972).

If we could conceive a world without mandate in this field, I would expect the general principles urged above to apply in this special field.

First, there would continue to be adequate accounting disclosure, as issuers negotiated with lenders, investors, and underwriters in the new issue market and felt the pressure of analysts in the trading market.

Second, the accounting would be less uniform than it is now, because vast differences in views as to the appropriate interpretation and abstraction of events are concealed by the mandated system. But the pressures would be such that the disclosure would be adequate to enable the reader to make his own adjustments. The accounting would thus tend to conform to the pattern suggested by Professor Beaver (1973). His pattern has not prevailed, and I confess that I see a great economy if the abstraction of financial events is done as uniformly as possible.

## Consideration of the SEC's Opposing Arguments

The SEC is and for many years has been among the better government agencies. But it has reacted in defensive bureaucratic fashion to suggestions that financial disclosure might somehow be turned back to the marketplace.

The SEC's first point is that only about 1,000 out of 10,000 reporting companies are followed by analysts (Advisory Committee Report, p. xviii) and that therefore the others have little incentive to disclose except for the SEC mandate (pp. 91, 92).

These figures probably present a somewhat misleading picture of the limited number of companies followed by analysts. The study by the Financial Analysts Federation relied on for this information was made when the brokerage industry was disrupted by the recent termination of fixed commissions, by the disspirited market, and by the wave of mergers of brokerage companies, all resulting in decreased employment on Wall Street. The FAF Report itself (Advisory Committee Report, Appendix II-B, p. A-52) shows that there were expectations that the employment of analysts would increase. It also shows a rising recognition that in the case of larger capitalization companies, the market was too efficient to make analytic work profitable, while more opportunities existed with respect to smaller capitalization companies. This insight has been followed by sales campaigns based on the opportunity for gain in the case of the less followed companies,[7] and this will certainly result in some analyst attention being turned to them.

As smaller companies approach the stage at which they need and have hopes for obtaining additional equity capital and for tapping the bond or private placement debt markets, they have every reason to try to create a "following" and to attract brokerage and analyst interest by being forthcoming with information.

Nevertheless, there will remain a residue of "minimum 12(g) companies," i.e., those required to report under the 1934 Act but which have close to the minimum of 500 stockholders and $1 million of assets and which have no hopes of attracting analyst interest in the near future. About these companies, one may ask a series of questions.

Is there really a public market for their securities? If so, is the function of analysts in these cases being performed by market makers, to whom the company will be forthcoming with disclosure to maintain that market? If there is no public market, the facts seem to indicate that the company really ought not to be a reporting company under the requirements of the 1934 Act and that the statutory threshold for reporting is too low.

If, finally, it is true that some companies do not issue the steady stream of informal information so frequently referred to in the Advisory Report but only the formal filed information, one must ask, "What good is filed information to an ordinary investor?"

The Introduction to the Advisory Committee Report has an answer (pp. xxxv-xxxvi):

> (F)ew, if any, believe that satisfactory investment decisions. . .can be made solely on the basis of information that is contained in documents filed by issuers with the SEC, or for that matter, can be made on the basis only of company-originated information. Experienced analysts universally equip themselves not only with company-originated information, but with extensive information as well concerning other components of the industry. . .and a host of other data. To the extent that the criticism of the Commission is justified that it has administered the securities laws as if filed information were sufficient for investment decision-making, the Committee strongly urges the Commission to take steps to clarify the limitations of information filed with it.

As Professor Beaver points out, in ordinary settings investors can use financial intermediaries or information intermediaries. "There is an implicit reliance on the functioning of the professional investment community in order to justify the current system as an effective mechanism for disclosure" (Report, pp. 619-21). But here, by assumption, the professional investment community is not functioning with respect to the particular issuer.

Without the informal supplement, the mandated disclosure accomplishes little for anyone. The commission document is lifeless, unable to produce a sophisticated securities decision until it is combined in the market with information about the macroeconomy, the industry, the judgment of peers on management, and the future. When a company is unable to attract the attention of analysts and disseminators, there is no justification for the commission's mandated disclosure.

Beyond the argument resting on the absence of analyst interest in most reporting companies, the SEC constantly cites four types of examples in support of its assertion that market incentives would not produce adequate disclosure. Of these the first two touch areas in which the SEC has recently expanded or wants to expand its jurisdiction.

*Segmented Disclosure*

The Advisory Committee Report refers several times to the fact that the market did not produce adequate segmented information without compulsion (pp. xi, xxi). But this was a case of real contention between analysts and issuers who were concerned about giving competition an advantage by disclosure as well as substantial issues of expenses and the value of the information.

Issuers told the Advisory Committee staff that "the Commission responds too readily to the demands of professional securities analysts, who are viewed as possessing an almost insatiable desire for information." The result of the Commission's catering to this demand is perceived as being bulky and complex (Report, p. 19). At the time of the staff survey, FASB Standard No. 14 had just been adopted and the Advisory Committee was considering extension of segmented information to disclosures other than the financial statements. Segmented information must have been one of the key points that issuers had in mind with these remarks.

Dan Goldwasser, a lawyer who has done much work on accounting related problems, summarizes the situation comprehensively:

In the final analysis, the most important imponderable is whether the data that industry is being asked to produce is cost effective. Is it so useful as to justify the additional cost to generate it? To answer this question I think you have to look at who will be using the data and what this data is likely to reveal. One of the benefits of segment data is that you will be able to analyze trends within the industry segment. You will also be able to tell whether a single product line is actually increasing in profitability or whether it is decreasing in profitability. You will not, however, be able to compare one company's operation within a given business segment with that of another company; i.e., you will not be able to compare IBM's typewriter operations with those of Xerox. The data will just not be comparable. There are too many judgment decisions which must be made "on a reasonable basis" which will prevent the comparison of data of one segment of a business enterprise with a similar segment of another business enterprise. Therefore, I do not believe that segment reports are going to be useful in this respect.

I suspect that the person who is going to be able to use segment data the least is the average investor. If financial reports adhere to the forms suggested by the FASB and the SEC, they are probably going to increase from roughly 15 pages to somewhere in the vicinity of 25 to 30 pages. Thus, the average investor is going to be overwhelmed when he looks at a set of financial statements. What will be even more overwhelming is the thought that he is going to have to pay for this data.

Bank creditors may get some use out of segment reports; however, I think that use will

> be marginal. Trade creditors will get almost no use out of them, and the only persons which are likely to get any significant benefit from the segment data are the security analysts, who will be able to better evaluate the weaknesses in any given industry ....
>
> Despite these advantages, I think the price of the data is going to far outweigh its marginal utility. Nobody in the accounting profession has been able to give me any sort of clear indication as to what is going to be the additional cost. I think the initial costs of having to go back and reformulate accounting systems so as to develop this data are going to be significant, both in terms of diverted management efforts as well as increased audit costs. The continuing auditing process may also be significantly more costly if the standard of materiality is altered. If the standard of materiality is not adjusted, then auditing costs, once the system has been implemented, may not be significantly increased.
>
> On balance though, I think that the average shareholder, the equity owners of public corporations, are going to end up paying a lot more for data which may or may not have any significant marginal utility...(1978, pp. 2489-90).

Goldwasser asserts (p. 2483) that the SEC and the Financial Analysts Federation "pressured the FASB to adopt Statement No. 14" and that the SEC, on the recommendation of the Advisory Committee, then used that adoption as a reason for making conforming amendments to the nonfinancial portions of its forms.

Mr. Robert Malin, an executive vice-president of First Boston Corporation and a member of the Advisory Committee, objected to its recommendation. He saw the issue in this way:

> "(I)f investors require furthur segment information, their market power can produce it. That sell-side analysts must continually press for increased SEC requirements in this area offers proof that the market won't voluntarily pay for it" (Report, p. D-57 at D-59).

Would not the market--the forces of analysts' pressure--have forced the issuers into conformity if there was a broad consensus among analysts? The market's failure to force the issuers shows that the market issue was not clear. The incident raises a question whether it was the function of government and the FASB to resolve this issue in favor of some analysts and against the issuers and other analysts.

*Municipal Disclosure*

The inadequacy of municipal disclosure in the past is pointed to by the SEC. Here the SEC or some persons in it are clearly waging a campaign for regulatory authority over disclosure in the municipal field, while the private parties involved and municipal authorities are fighting for development of a disclosure system not governmentally mandated.

The municipal securities case presents several unusual features. First, experience for many years before the New York City bond crisis had led people to believe that there was no real danger of default and hence little real need for disclosure. Second, enormous reliance was placed on the rating agencies, to the virtual exclusion of private analysis, and therefore there was little development of thinking on the essentials of the credit-worthiness of a municipality and the nature of appropriate disclosures. Third, because of the marketing techniques used, the roles and responsibilities of municipal bond underwriters and bond counsel were ambiguous. After the New York City and Yonkers events, and after several suits by the SEC applying antifraud laws, privately negotiated disclosure in municipal offering circulars improved tremendously and is in the process of further improvement--all without the benefit of any detailed disclosure manual from the SEC. The Municipal Finance Officers' Association continues to work on the problem of encouraging better disclosure in municipal financing.

Thus there is no reason to think that municipal issuers failed from the 1930s to the 1970s to respond to the demands of investors for disclosure or indeed that the objective facts show that investors should have demanded better disclosure. I suggest that on a cost/benefit basis it would be hard even now to justify a vast new mandatory apparatus of disclosure in the municipal field.

*Examples of Inadequate Disclosure in the Past*

It is easy to cite examples of inadequate disclosure in the past and thus draw the conclusion that mandated disclosure is necessary. But the justification for the conclusion has to be examined with some care.

The Introduction to the Advisory Committee Report says, "There have been many instances known to members of the Committee which demonstrate that falsified financial statements and other abuses of the disclosure process have endured for a long time without market forces in any way bringing about sufficient, reliable or timely disclosure" (p. xxii).

But we need not depend only on the special knowledge of the members of the committee. Any member of the public can add to the list: Equity Funding, Penn Central, Stirling Homex, and many others. The point is *that these instances of inadequate or fraudulent disclosure occurred in cases to which the SEC's mandated disclosure system applied, "without...in any way bringing about sufficient, reliable or timely disclosure."* The quotation continues, "[i]n these cases, the remedy usually lay not in the market but in intervention by the Securities and Exchange Commission."

This claim simply cannot be substantiated. The typical pattern is to the contrary. Generally the *market* rejected the company and cut off its credit. The frauds were discovered only on the occurrence of bankruptcy or some other debacle, with the SEC as a Johnny-come-lately, not one who prevented the fraud.

If the frauds occur despite the mandated disclosure system, the system cannot be justified as necessary because frauds occur.

*The Comparison between Stockholder Reports and Forms 10-K*

Finally, the supporters of mandated disclosure point to the differences in disclosure shown in a review of the mandated Form 10-K Reports and the unfiled Annual Reports to Stockholders (Introduction to Report, pp. xxviii).

It is difficult to evaluate this claim. Form 10-K is, of course, the mandated disclosure and presumably meets all statutory requirements of disclosure to the marketplace. The commission's Rule 14a-3(b) (9) requires the issuer to send to each stockholder of record or beneficial owner on request and without charge a copy of the Form 10-K. If all of this has been done, is the commission in a position to argue that it has not served its purpose, and that some more disclosure is required?

The commission does require more. To aid the stockholders in the exercise of their rights of corporate suffrage, the commission by nine paragraphs of Rule 14a-3(b) specifies the financial information that must be contained in an annual report to stockholders, which must precede or accompany the proxy statement for the annual meeting. Rules 14a-3(b) (2) and 14a-9 make clear that this material must not contain any misleading statements or omissions. But why does the commission specify nine paragraphs of detail for an annual report to stockholders that differs from the annual report on Form 10-K? Why not require that the Form 10-K be *sent* to all stockholders instead of being merely *offered* free?

The answer is that the commission for some years recognized that Form 10-K's were "compliance" documents (Advisory Committee Report, p. 10), too lawyerlike in tone and with too much detail for the average stockholder. The commission toyed for a while with a concept of differential disclosure (Release No. 33-5427 (1973)): full detail to professionals, less to stockholders. The less restrictive annual report to stockholders is a survival of the commission's differential disclosure thinking.[8]

Both forms of annual report are controlled by the commission, and the commission intended the difference in detail. The commission opted for readability of annual reports to stockholders, and it relied on the fact that, as stated in Release No. 33-5427, "By being included in financial statements filed with the Commission ... data will become data of public record and, hence, available to all." If the absence of Form 10-K details in an annual report to stockholders proves to have been significant in some case, that is simply a normal consequence of the process of trade-off between the inconsistent goals of readability and completeness.

Mandated reporting becomes more cumbersome as the commission continues its practice of imposing disclosure requirements on all issuers because of perceived abuses in a few cases (Advisory Committee Report, p. 20). Recent rules on management compensation are a conspicuous example. Adding mandated details has passed the point of diminishing returns. It is time to give our vaunted capital markets a chance to work out freely the part that disclosure should properly play. There are good reasons to assume that voluntary disclosure will have a high quota of reliability.[9] If it does not coincide with the commission's views of necessary disclosure, that fact will not establish that it is inadequate.

## Notes

[1]Professor Barefield challenges my remark about a developed concept of adequate disclosure. He is, of course, right that there is no agreed on concept of what constitutes adequate disclosure, and I confess that my phrase is ambiguous. I meant to say that there is a developed recognition that issuers owe a duty to make adequate disclosure.

[2]Gonedes, Dopuch, and Penman (1976) present an interesting discussion of the existence of externalities in the supply of information by issuers, the problem of effective competition for the production and furnishing of the information, and the possibility of cooperation by users in obtaining and supplying it. I have no quarrel with their exploration of these possibilities, but the points are outside my immediate range of discussion.

[3]In the absence of an organized study, any assertions about the information supplied in private placements must be very tentative, but the following contrasts with SEC-mandated disclosure are offered:

1. The accounting disclosure is far more penetratingly pursued as to discrepancies in amounts or ratios from year to year.

2. Considerably more emphasis is placed on values, in the case of oil, gas, minerals, and real estate. (The SEC has only recently proposed to require disclosure of values of oil and gas reserves.)

3. Considerably more emphasis is placed on the future than was true of reporting to the SEC up to the time of the Advisory Committee recommendations--i.e., as to plans and budgets for the future, expected sources of funds, earnings forecasts, and so on.

4. In the case of venture capital offerings, there is a frank discussion of risks, far more

realistic than in commission documents, and less in the form of the SEC-compelled standard litany: "There can be no assurance that" any particular expectation can be achieved.

5. There is a far greater effort to explore the workings of the issuer's business, as to patent and technical position and so on.

6. While lists of officers and directors are given, it is recognized that meaningful judgments as to their qualifications and competence must come from confidential inquiry among their peers and cannot be expected to come from the issuer itself.

7. It is recognized that a meaningful picture as to the issuer's competitive position must come from outside inquiry, not from the issuer itself.

[4]The issuers are interested enough in favorable reporting by brokers and analysts that they devote considerable time and attention to supplying information to the analysts, holding meetings with them and answering their questions. Thus it is reported that J. C. Penney & Co. holds over 1,000 meetings with analysts per year (Axelson, 1975). A whole new profession of financial public relations experts is evolving to deal with these tendencies. This kind of activity would be even greater and the companies would be even more forthcoming with information were it not for the inside information problem.

[5]Whether these SEC pressures are appropriate is a subject for another time.

[6]Professor Barefield senses an ambiguity on the question whether I advocate merely an end to the proliferation of mandated disclosure or an end to mandated disclosure altogether. Again I admit the ambiguity. Theoretically we could end the mandated disclosure altogether, but we know that this is not going to happen, and I therefore do not have to face the question whether I

would really recommend trying it.

[7]See David A. Baker, Drexel Burnham Lambert, Inc., Investment Overview: "An Inefficient Market Hypothesis," Aug. 5, 1977; "Research Concentration and the All-America Team," Oct. 28, 1977; "Research Concentration and Performance," Jan. 9, 1978; "Think Small," March 10, 1978.

[8]The Advisory Committee recommended that the commission encourage the use of stockholder reports as compliance with the Form 10-K and 10-Q requirements (Report, pp. 470-81). It was recognized that this might upgrade the stockholder report (p. 478). The commission implemented this recommendation by Guide 4 to the 1934 Act filings (Release No. 34-13639 (1977)).

[9]Nothing that I have said implies any naive failure to recognize that when the going gets tough, issuers may front-load the income or even falsify the accounting records altogether. But there are many instances to show that this may happen in filed as well as nonfiled reports. For example, SEC contributed usefully to the development of accounting principles with Accounting Series Release No. 95 (1962) restricting the reporting of income based on land sales without arms'-length bargaining or represented by without-recourse mortgage notes. But that did not preclude Penn Central, its subsidiary Great Southwest, and their independent public accountants from creating income in filed reports by deals of the type condemned by Release No. 95, all as described in Accounting Series Release No. 173 (1975).

## References

Axelson, Kenneth. 1975. A Businessman's View of Disclosure. J. Accountancy 42 (July).

Beaver, William H. 1973. What Should be the FASB's Objectives? J. Accountancy (August).

---. 1977. The Nature of Mandated Disclosure, Chap. 22 of Report of SEC Advisory Committee on Corporate Disclosure.

---. 1978. Future Disclosure Requirements May Give Greater Recognition to the Professional Community. J. Accountancy 44 (January).

Benston, George J. 1973. Required Disclosure and the Stock Market: An Evaluation of the Securities Exchange Act of 1934. 53 Am. Econ. Rev. 132 (March).

Fama, Eugene, and Laffer, Arthur B. 1971. Information and Capital Markets. 44 J. Bus. 289.

Goldwasser, Dan. 1978. Reports for Segments of a Business Enterprise. 33 Bus. Lawyer 2481.

Gonedes, N. J.; Dopuch, N.; and Penman, S. H. 1976. Disclosure Rules, Information-Production, and Capital Market Equilibrium: The Case of Forecast Disclosure Rules. J. Accounting Research 89.

Hirshleifer, Jack. 1971. The Private and Social Value of Information and the Reward to Inventive Activity. 61 Am. Econ. Rev. 561.

Horngren, C. T. 1972. Accounting Principles: Private or Public Sector. J. Accountancy (May).

Kripke, Homer. 1970. The SEC, the Accountants, Some Myths and Some Realities. 45 N.Y.U. L. Rev. 1153.

---. 1974. SEC Rule 146: A Major Blunder. N.Y. Law Journal (July 5).

Lev, Baruch. 1976. On the Adequacy of Publicly Available Financial Information for Security Analysis. In Duke Second Accounting Symposium, p. 123.

Mendelson, Morris. 1978. Economics and the Assessment of Disclosure Requirements. 1 J. Comp. Corp. L. &

Secur. Reg. 49.

Ross, Sidney. 1977. The Determination of Financial Structure: The Incentive Signalling Approach. 8 Bell J. Econ. 23.

Securities and Exchange Commission. 1977. Report of Advisory Committee on Corporate Disclosure, House Committee Print 95-29 and 95-30, 95th Cong., 1st sess.

Sommer, A. A., Jr. 1975. Can the SEC Help the Capital Crunch? Address before the National Investor Relations Institute, Washington, D.C., September 29.

# A Comment on Homer Kripke's "Would Market Forces Cause Adequate Securities Disclosure Without SEC Mandate"

Russell M. Barefield

University of Arizona

I find Professor Kripke's paper a difficult one to critique. While philosophically in agreement with the spirit of his conclusions, I don't find his analysis particularly persuasive. I suspect the very complexity of the phenomena causes the problem. An author who deals with the subject in a methodologically rigorous fashion is going to have the language or communication problem Professor Kripke attributes to economists and their mathematical notation.[1] On the other hand, to make concrete recommendations about policy frequently requires one to leave the safety of a methodologically sound model.

However, let me address some of my methodological concerns. First, I'm not sure I understand Professor Kripke's research question; second, I don't agree with one of the premises of his analysis; and third, I find the primary conclusion difficult to interpret and somewhat narrow in its coverage.

## The Research Question

Professor Kripke says, "The question I propose to pursue is whether the insistent detailed disclosure still being mandated and cumulated by the SEC is necessary or whether market forces would cause adequate disclosure in the present United States environment." It is not clear to me if he wishes to consider two extreme alternatives, that is, to release all disclosure matters to the market or to leave the present SEC process intact. Other alternatives exist, including changing the SEC process, and elsewhere Professor Kripke has objected to consideration of extreme alternatives. In particular, in his dissent to the Report of the Advisory Committee on Corporate Disclosure to the Securities and Exchange Commission, he says:

> In a series of memos to Chairman Sommer and to the Committee. . ., I tried to indicate that a black-or-white, all-or-none approach to the evaluation of mandated disclosure was inadequate (p. D-49).
>
> . . . .
>
> Then the Committee never went beyond the conclusion that some mandatory disclosure was needed, to the question, "how much?" (p. D-50).

This confusion as to the objective of the paper makes it difficult for me to appraise its conclusions.

## Premises

Professor Kripke places his analysis within a contemporary setting by assuming these premises: (1) broad financial markets are in place; (2) the analytic apparatus is in place; (3) the securities and antifraud law continue to exist, including the inhibition on the use of inside information; and (4) a developed concept of adequate disclosure is in place. I have no quarrel with the first three premises; I do have doubts about the fourth. In fact, I believe it is our lack of understanding of the relevance of disclosure items to decision-making in the financial markets that causes many of the problems we perceive in the current disclosure system. When we don't understand cause and effect relationships, political rather than analytical processes are likely to settle debates. More precisely, if it is not clear how a particular disclosure will serve investor decision-making, analytical arguments fail and the SEC is free to act "in defensive bureaucratic fashion," CPAs are free to lobby in their self-interest, and congressional desires to slow the conglomerate movement of the mid-1960s are all likely to be a part of a decision to adopt a disclosure requirement. In summary, I doubt if we have a "developed concept of adequate disclosure," and, in fact, the term adequate itself conflicts with the cost-benefit framework typically adopted in discussions of information.

## Conclusions

Professor Kripke presents the heart of his argument when he says: "Whether a disclosure must be mandated or whether it will be supplied voluntarily by issuers interested in the capital market depends on whether there is a consensus among suppliers of capital or other transactors in the capital markets that this kind of information is necessary for lending and investment decisions. If there is such a consensus, issuers will supply it rather than forego access to the capital markets. If not (i.e., if it is material only under SEC conceptions), SEC must mandate it."

In examining this argument, let's first look at the prior conditions. Two mutually exclusive sets of conditions are specified. Professor Kripke first covers the case where there is *consensus* that information is *necessary*. Earlier, I objected to his assumption of a developed concept of adequate disclosure, and here I would simply say that "consensus" is not likely to cover many disclosure items and that "necessary" has an enabling connotation that is incompatible with business decision settings. The word implies that lending and investing would not proceed without the subject information. However, when one sees a bank make a small business loan without requiring an audit or without requiring financial statements, one quickly realizes that the cost in dollars and time to obtain a particular bit of information varies across settings and that very little is "necessary" in an enabling sense to lending and investing decisions.

The last sentence of the quotation presents the only other prior condition, but I don't believe Professor Kripke's *id est* part of this statement is proper. Is it fair to say that when consensus does not exist, the disclosure is material "only under SEC conceptions?" I believe only modest numbers of disclosure issues are covered by the consensus case. If Professor Kripke intends to put all other cases in his second set of prior conditions, he leaves a substantial role for the SEC to play.

In elaborating on his argument, Professor Kripke discusses private placements and open market trading in turn. He discusses the incentives of parties to these transactions and makes observations with respect to disclosures in private placements. This subject of incentives is quite complex. Management does have incentives to be open and truthful in their dealings with the investment community. These incentives weaken when severe problems give managers very short time horizons. Thus, the observation that "analysts do not like surprises" can be irrelevant just at the time one would hope management would take the longer view. This problem is acknowledged by Professor Kripke in his footnote 9, but he discounts the problem by saying that a mandatory disclosure system can't deal with the problem either. Perhaps the real issue is whether we as individuals are lulled to sleep when "protected" by a regulatory agency but remain alert when left alone.

Similarly, financial intermediaries do have incentives to procure information. However, they also compete among themselves for business, and they must deal with a legal system (again in a dynamic environment where I argue there is not a developed concept of adequate disclosure) that perhaps provides an incentive to gather information simply in anticipation of defending one's actions as in the medical area where excessive numbers of laboratory tests are probably conducted simply as a guard against legal proceedings inclined to use hindsight to evaluate profession judgements). Perhaps this is the appropriate place to discuss the municipal sector. Did the market work properly here? Professor Kripke states that "enormous reliance was placed on the rating agencies, to the virtual exclusion of private analysis, and, therefore, there was little development of thinking on the essentials of the credit-worthiness of a municipality and the nature of appropriate disclosures. . .because of the marketing techniques used, the roles and responsibilities of municipal bond underwriters and bond counsel were ambiguous. After the New York City and Yonkers events, and after several suits by the SEC applying antifraud laws, privately negotiated disclosure in municipal offerring circulars improved tremendously and is in the process of further improvement. . . ."

What happened here to our "developed concept of adequate disclosure?" Similarly, did the lawsuits define general responsibilities or are we observing an undesirable overreaction to "abuses in a few cases?" Professor Kripke puts an unfavorable light on the SEC system that imposes "disclosure requirements on all issuers because of perceived abuses in a few cases." Can't our legal system do the same?

Finally, Professor Kripke continues on the municipal subject by arguing that the market is working. One bit of evidence is that the MFOA "continues to work on the problem of encouraging better disclosure in municipal financing." Are they so working to serve analyst and investor needs (and thereby serve the municipalities) or are they acting in fear of SEC action? Overall, I'm simply questioning the degree to which events in the municipal sector clearly support Professor Kripke's arguments. Couldn't some of the developments in the municipal sector instead be used to cast unfavorable light on the market or on the legal system?

In closing, I would like to make a personal observation with respect to segment reporting. This observation corresponds to Professor Kripke's views in this area. Professor Kripke points out that supporters of mandatory disclosure argue that market pressures "did not produce adequate segmented information without compulsion." He disagrees with the word "adequate", and he simply argues that the market did not judge the information sufficiently valuable to press for its release. I believe the continuing expressions of dissatisfaction with segment data and the accompanying arguments for more information support Professor Kripke's position. For example, David Norr, in his separate statement as a member of the SEC Advisory Committee on Corporate Disclosure, expressed dissatisfaction with existing segment reporting. He said, "No subject is more important to investors than segment reporting. But 10 years after the SEC first issued a call for this method of disclosure conspicuous gaps persist in the information available to investors" (p. D-62). He went on to endorse the Advisory Committee's recommendations that segment data be included in interim reports and to say that other reforms are necessary.

I accept the assessment that "conspicuous gaps" exist. However, I object to the accompanying conclusion that more disclosure is needed. Why don't we conclude that the original opponents of segment reporting were right when they argued that segment data would not be as useful as hoped? Perhaps the better solution is to drop the requirement. At least, when "no subject is more important to investors" we could expect the analyst community to show us precisely how they use or would propose to use segment data.

## Note

[1]Professor Kripke's paper contains an occasional interpretation of the economics literature. His view that information as a commodity is not subject to the ordinary laws of supply and demand is a misinterpretation. To the contrary, the fact that the laws work in a setting where "free riders" exist is the source of the problem.

# A Comment on Homer Kripke's "Would Market Forces Cause Adequate Securities Disclosure Without SEC Mandate?"

Felix Pomeranz

Coopers & Lybrand

As I understand it, Professor Kripke raises two questions: Is the insistent detailed disclosure still being mandated and cumulated by the SEC necessary, and would market forces cause adequate disclosure in the present environment?

He answers the first question with a "no," based on a "yes" to the second. I would answer the first question with a qualified "no," although for different reasons, and the second with another "no" based on lack of hard evidence to the contrary. At first blush these disharmonious views appear to represent a tribute to our admired chairman's pairing of papers and discussants. However, I would add that there are as many points of agreement as of disagreement.

To establish my understanding, I would like to recapitulate those of Professor Kripke's points that I have chosen for comment. I hope that I have not engaged in transmogrifications; the sequencing and numbering were supplied by me.

## A Capsule Summation

(1) Markets are in place, the analytic apparatus is in place, and a developed concept of adequate disclosure

is in place.

(2) SEC disclosure does not represent the optimum. The SEC is only slowly moving away from historical cost related disclosures. (Presumably Professor Kripke would prefer cessation of this activity to its speed-up.)

(3) We have witnessed explosive and questionable revisions of SEC concepts of materiality.

(4) The SEC should study some private placements to determine those parts of the SEC system that are recognized as material to lending and investment decisions.

(5) Information will be forthcoming when there is a consensus among suppliers of capital that the data is necessary for lending and investment decisions. An issuer must meet the information demands of buyers to whom he proposes to issue securities; likewise, firms desiring an active market for their emissions of securities must supply information.

(6) Companies which will not furnish information deemed adequate by analysts, and which conforms generally to disclosure standards of other companies, will lose their following.

(7) The market's failure to force issuers to disclose segment information shows that the market issue was not clear.

(8) Formerly, the roles and responsibilities of municipal bond underwriters and bond counsel were ambiguous. Privately negotiated disclosure has improved tremendously and is in process of further improvement. It would be hard to justify a vast new mandatory apparatus of disclosure.

## The Answer to Question 1 is "No"

My reason for the answer is based on the doubtful merit of some disclosures presently required, as much as on a paucity of important disclosures, such as:

- Information as to capital budgeting plans. (This element is particularly important for companies caught in a vise formed by environmental expenditure needs accompanied by a cash shortage.)

- Disclosure of cash flow received historically from investment assets. Professor Yuji Ijiri described the significance of this measure in testimony before the Financial Accounting Standards Board. (Perhaps, *historic* cash flow might be of greater interest now that discounting of *future* cash flows is so definitely "in.")[1]
- Disclosure of corporate programs and of their effectiveness. Program effectiveness evaluation, pioneered by the United States General Accounting Office, has applicability in the private sector and merits experimentation. Quantification of program effectiveness is now feasible; the technology is in place.
- Disclosure of a company's and its officers' records of significant citations by regulatory bodies to the extent that consents, guilty pleas, or nolo contenderes have resulted. I am aware of the fashionable view that a second (or third, or fourth) chance should be given to offenders. However, I suspect that recidivism afflicts many once they have run afoul of the securities laws.
- Disclosure of the "floating" supply of a stock and its position within its own cycle and relative to the market.

Some have produced evidence that the existing disclosures bear only tangentially on investment decisions.

(Our host has coauthored an outstanding paper dealing with this issue.) However, I don't believe that the evidence is sufficient to suggest scrapping the system. Rather, I would seek to strengthen it by weeding out disclosures that are least effective relative to cost and by considering the introduction of more meaningful measures.

I agree with Professor Kripke that the "commission document is lifeless. . .until it is combined in the market with information about the macroeconomy, the industry, the judgment of peers on management, and the future." However, that means that there is no possibility, except by chance, that a "small" investor can "score" in the market. Nonetheless, it is better to bring more candles than to curse the darkness. The only viable alternative that I see to banning small-time investors is to make more meaningful *micro*economic information available.

Professor Kripke's first "no" answer is premised on the existence of an *analytic* apparatus cum *adequate* disclosures. The operative words are "analytic" and "adequate." Analysis implies separation of a thing into its parts to find out its essential features; in a philosophical context, analysis breaks a concept into its constituent elements to reveal concealed content.

Presumably the word "adequate" equates with "sufficient." Now, as Humpty Dumpty said in "Through the Looking Glass," "When I use a word it means just what I choose it to mean, it means neither more or less." In my view, the apparatus in place does not provide all of the data needed for meaningful analysis, and the disclosures are not entirely adequate. (In the absence of meaningful research one can speculate on the reasons for the celebrated failures of the last decade and on those disclosures that might have resulted in more realistic valuations of securities.)

Present disclosure approaches are--and must remain--fundamentally incongruous. The SEC engages in rulemaking presumably to protect the "users." This dichotomy contrasts with other countries wherein the government acts as both user and rulemaker. (This issue has been explored by Professor Dhia AlHashim in his writing on purposive accounting.)[2] While I certainly favor our system it is clear that our regulator places himself in loco parentis and determines what is best for any and all users. This undertaking appears almost impossible because of the different goals of users. I should think that a differential disclosure approach *based on user objectives* might be worthy of experimentation.

While I have feelings of apprehension over the soft data approach, I'm not as ready as Professor Kripke to criticize "objective and verifiable" data. Round Table persons, we've been there! As George O. May said, "It is only in the light of later developments and on the basis of new modes of thought, that [writeups] can be indiscriminately condemned. . .the depression. . .created new conditions favoring close adherence to cost. . . ."[3]

I disagree that the SEC's "revisions of the concept of materiality" have been "questionable." True, the commission's emphasis on corporate governance has an ethereal quality. However, I believe that "materiality" cannot be applied to such matters as patterns of bribes. A little bribery may be just as significant as a little pregnancy. The issue of bribes is on target when one compares the business morality of one company vis-à-vis another. And, if that is not of interest to potential investors, I can think of little that would be.

## The Answer to Question 2 is Also "No"

Professor Kripke assumes that information will be made available if the suppliers of capital are convinced of its usefulness. By implication, he assumes that the interests of the underwriter, the analyst and the investor coincide. There is certainly *some* commonality of interest; however, there are pervasive dissimilarities. The underwriter is interested in collecting his commission, in not being stuck with inventory subject to markdowns, and in protection from liability. The analyst is interested in adding to his reputation as a man of prescience. The investor may be interested in a security to accomplish a variety of goals. While the underwriter's risk tends to be relatively short-term, that of an investor may be long-term.

An important distinction involves the diverse risk preferences of the underwriter, analyst, and investor. "If stochastic dominance has not determined the best alternative, [we] must turn to the question of risk preference. To demonstrate that most individuals are averse to risk, it is only necessary to note that few, if any, are willing to toss a coin, double or nothing, for a year's salary. Organizations typically act in the same way. A realistic analysis of decisions requires capturing this aversion to risk. . . ."[4] There is no practical way of determining whether the risk aversions of the named parties coincide.

Moreover, decision theory indicates that resources will be devoted to the gathering of additional information, as long as that incremental information bears on the decision. However, in the case of securities, the cost of the information would be absorbed by the issuer, while its value would be different for each of the parties. Thus, the incremental information cost/value relationship may not apply.

## Private Placements are Different

I will give a brief example of a private placement. In private placement, among other things, the investor obtains data relative to the five disclosures proposed earlier. He would also:

- Determine the objectives of the acquisition. (In my example, it was desired to buy a "stable of advanced science talent.")
- Rank the risks confronting the acquiree; see whether one wanted to

ignore risk, shift it to others, or control it.

- Select a competent team of reviewers. (In my example, four of five team members were Nobel Laureates.)
- Conduct the evaluation, largely using in-depth interviews; review related papers; examine forecasts and projections and supporting documentation.
- Analyze the backgrounds of the company officers and of their principal associates, supplemented by special investigatory approaches.
- Read the financial statements to see whether the company's auditors had ferreted out any information not already discovered.

While the case is specialized and not comprehensive, it directs attention to the obstacles confronted by a potential investor in analyzing a company of the type described. (Some of the techniques mentioned by Professor Kripke would have muddled a small investor: Ratio analysis--dynamic? Regression--multiple? Values--entry?)

## Does Disclosure Aid Values?

To the extent that information is available as to the relationship of market values to "performances" before analysts, there is some indication that the performance results in a short-term hypo, at times presaging a long-term decline. (I should think that a "post audit" of claims made to analysts would be revealing.) In any event I question that there is sufficient evidence that aggressive "disclosing" before analysts buoys values permanently.

## The Segment Parallel Seems Inappropriate

Management's reluctance to make segment information available may or may not have had much to do with the risk of leaking data to competitors. I know of one industry--typical in its opposition to segment information--which provided copies of customer invoices to the trade association for planning purposes. Although this information was coded, a knowledgeable analyst would have had little difficulty in attributing the data to particular companies. In at least some instances, the reasons for the opposition to segment reporting lay elsewhere.

For example, one concern made an unfortunate acquisition at an exorbitant price. When the market bottomed for the products of the investee, and the acquired company reported losses, the investor still had to show a disturbingly large amount of goodwill. The investor petitioned the SEC to allow the transaction to be handled as a retroactive pooling. The SEC demurred--on the grounds that too much time had elapsed since the purchase to permit retroactive pooling.

Goodwill is now being amortized over forty years, courtesy of the Accounting Principles Board; thus, time eventually would have washed away evidence of management's ineptness in my example. (On a segment reporting basis, the performance of the new product line might have been spelled out for all to see.)

## The State and Local Entity Issue

Professor Kripke notes that it would be hard to establish on a cost/benefit basis that a vast new mandatory apparatus of disclosure in the municipal field is justified. I couldn't agree more.

Public entity accounting and auditing differ fundamentally from private entity accounting and auditing. As stated by Professor Abraham Simon: "There has been a tendency for accountants to use commercial accounting as a frame of reference against which to assess the state of the art in public sector accounting. Such an approach provides at best only a partial standard of reference."[5] While it is possible that availability of private sector disclosures will lead to benefits to issuers of securities (or to purchasers for that matter), I suggest further research before costly new requirements are introduced.

## Summary

The present disclosure system should be revised to add to its meaning and to reduce its cost. There is insufficient evidence that the marketplace is in a position to identify disclosures that will adequately protect all parties at interest. The actions of a tiny minority of the business community will offer excuses for continued government concern. While I don't subscribe to the implied accusation, I would like to quote Johannes Schroeder, retired president of West Germany's Federal Office of Finance: "The government is obligated to see that no citizen loses his life savings as a result of the actions of institutions with branches in the Grand Cayman Islands."

## Notes

[1]Yuji Ijiri, "Cash Flow Accounting and Its Structure," *Journal of Accounting, Auditing and Finance* (Summer 1978), pp. 331-348.

[2]Dhia AlHashim, "Accounting Control Through Purposive Uniformity: An International Perspective," *International Journal of Accounting, Education and Research* 8 (Spring 1973), pp. 21-32.

[3]George O. May, *Financial Accounting* (New York: MacMillan, 1946), p. 46.

[4]J.E. Matheson and R.A. Howard, *An Introduction to Decision Analysis* (Stanford Research Institute, 1968), p. 20.

[5]Abraham J. Simon, "Fiscal Accountability and Principles and Mechanisms of Disclosure for Major Local and State Governments in a Democratic Society," *Collected Papers of the American Accounting Association's Annual Meeting* (August 1978), p. 794 ff.

5

# The Effect of State Accounting and Auditing Regulations on Municipal Borrowing Costs and Bond Ratings

Wanda A. Wallace

University of Rochester

## 1. The "Rationale" for Federal Legislation to Extend Municipal Financial Disclosure

Federal legislation has been introduced to extend the Securities Laws to municipalities ("Williams," p. 3). The bill (S 2339) under consideration provides for uniform accounting methods and audited financial statements. The bill's stated rationale includes the protection of investors and the assurance of available money at reasonable rates. Senator Thomas Eagleton, active in promoting the "Williams" bill, claimed that mandatory audits would have the following effect: "The many well-run states and communities could more easily demonstrate their soundness and the deservedness of their high credit ratings and low interest rates. At the same time, any bond issuer which has been manipulating figures to show a balanced budget would be exposed. Good issues could be more easily differentiated from bad issues, and financially responsible units of government might then see their prudence rewarded by lower interest rates and more competitive bidding" (U.S. Senate, pp. 15-16).

Similar assertions regarding the effects of accounting and auditing practices of municipalities are common in the financial literature. Davidson et al. report, "State and local governmental units may be paying a substantial price in higher interest costs for their failure to provide financial statements that are meaningful. . ." (p. 13). The financial press repeatedly reports similar effects: "The few municipalities that won't or can't meet all the new disclosure requirements find they sometimes pay a steep price" (Klapper). Descriptions of the bill typically include reference to the following presumed effect: "Among the benefits that are likely to be identified (in discussing Federal influence on reporting practices) are: . . .reduction of borrowing costs" (Alexander Grant & Co.).

The bill closely parallels existing state legislation, including the bureaucrats' claims that favorable market effects result from their legislation: "The more comprehensive the disclosure, the more marketable the bonds may become, resulting in favorable interest bids" (Oregon Statute 287.018, clarified by the Municipal Debt Advisory Commission). Yet the market effect rationale for state and federal regulation of the municipal market has not been examined carefully.[1]

The objective of this research effort is to provide empirical evidence as to the likely effect of federal regulation of municipal disclosure. The approach will be to examine the impact of state regulation of municipal disclosure. In particular, the study asks what impact state legislation that mandates audits has had on municipal borrowing costs and bond ratings. Obviously, the observance of a positive (lowering of interest cost and raising of bond rating) effect of state legislation does not necessarily mean similar federal legislation would have the same effect. However, if no effect or a negative effect of mandated state audits is found, the burden of proof falls on supporters of federal legislation to further justify their proposals. If a decline in municipal borrowing costs is observed, proponents must then argue that a net marginal benefit accrues from federal legislation that does not now result from similar state legislation with respect to the claimed market effect.

The methodology for testing for an effect of the enactment of state regulations is discussed in section 2.

Section 3 reports the results of cross-sectional tests using municipal bonds issued in 46 of the 50 states for 1975 and 1976. Existing forms of state legislation are described. State demographic and finance characteristics have been controlled while testing for the association between interest cost and presence of audit legislation, including differing features of the legislation, i.e., who performs the mandated audit, how frequently, and for which municipalities.

Four states were selected for further study. Two states have extensive state regulation of audit practices and two have less comprehensive audit practices relative to other states on average. Section 4 reports a comparison of these four states' interest cost and the number of bids submitted for all general obligation and revenue bonds issued in 1976. The variables of issue size, type of issuer (state, county, or other municipality), and the market index have been controlled to determine if differences appear to exist between the four states' market measures.

Sections 3 and 4 report on the cross-sectional association between interest cost and audit legislation. A time series analysis for the State of Florida, drawing paired samples from 1966 to 1976 data on either side of key legislation dates, is presented in section 5. Bids, interest cost, and bond ratings are compared. As additional time series evidence, the bond rating of Tennessee issues pre- and postmandatory audit legislation are compared. Similarly the interest cost of Michigan issues before and after legislation are compared. Tennessee and Michigan evidence is also presented in section 5. The clear advantage of investigating the effect of state legislation is that more than one piece of legislation is available for testing. Comparison of the different state results provides validation of the findings.

The evidence presented in sections 3 through 5 is consistent; higher interest cost is associated with mandatory audit legislation. Similarly, no significant increase in the number of bids submitted is observed when mandatory audit legislation is present. Higher bond ratings are associated with audit legislation; however, when a control sample is examined, there appears to have been a shift upwards in the average bond rating for the municipal market over the time periods analyzed.

The implications of these findings and the author's conclusions are presented in section 6.

## 2. Testing for the Effect of State Accounting and Auditing Regulations

Existing state legislation mandating audits is similar to proposed federal legislation with respect to the requirements that have been mandated and the rationale for the regulations offered by bureaucrats. Therefore, a means of predicting the likely effect of proposed federal regulation of municipal disclosure is provided by existing state legislation. Of course, the ideal means of analyzing federal legislation effects via states' experience would be to apply randomly the treatment to the states, i.e., the type of audit and disclosures required. However, such controlled experiments are rare in the social sciences. In an attempt to gain as much control as feasible, theories identifying relevant variables for a given research question are first formulated and then tested. It then is possible to measure the impact of a single variable by holding constant the other variables in the model.

One obstacle to such an analysis is the lack of a theory of political process. Without such an empirically tested theory, it is difficult to separate the effect of state disclosure legislation from other economic and political events, and the effect of the accounting and audit requirements from other provisions of the state legislation.

The application of cross-sectional tests may be inappropriate due to simultaneity of the relation between market measures and accounting and audit practices. For example, a self-selection bias may exist; are high-cost states more prone to mandate audits? Since a well-defined theory of audit selection, particularly in the municipal area, has not been developed as yet, it is difficult to preclude such possibilities.

Similarly, state legislation of municipal auditing and accounting practices may well be only one component of some larger variable such as "state control over municipalities." Therefore, even if the presence of audit legislation is associated with a lower net interest cost, it is possible that the legislation does not *cause* the lower cost but that both are effects of the state control over municipalities.

However, what can be discovered by the study undertaken is whether claimed market effects are observed when audit legislation is present. Such evidence on the basic validity of the rationale for disclosure legislation offered by proponents is important in evaluating whether there is a basis for the legislation.

Federal legislators will not wait until a theory of political process develops before deciding on the merits of the pending "Williams" bill. In fact, this analysis is particularly timely in light of federal bureaucrats' recent action which increased the accounting and auditing requirements of municipalities receiving $25,000 or more of revenue sharing funds (Local Fiscal Assistance Amendments of 1976). There is a definite shift by federal bureaucrats toward increasing municipal market regulation. The economic rationale for such legislation should be examined carefully before additional legislation is passed.

Expectations

The economic/finance literature provides a rationale for anticipating that voluntary audits by municipal officers are associated with lower interest cost. Jensen and Meckling, and Watts, point out that an incentive exists for economic entities to provide financial statements which have been audited by an external accounting firm if the increase in the market value of the bonds is greater than the present value of the auditing fees (net of any other benefits that accrue from the audit). The increase in the market value is expected because the audit fees incurred by a municipality reduce the monitoring costs of debtholders.

*Voluntary Audits*

Attributing this monitoring cost advantage of the audit to mandatory legislation is fallacious because it ignores the voluntary contracting with CPAs by municipal units prior to the regulation. In fact, audits of municipalities have been commonplace since the 1950s prior to most existing state legislation which mandates an audit.[2]

*Limitations of the Audit as a Monitoring Device*

While the audit decreases monitoring costs, it does not eliminate them. Although Senator Eagleton and others sharing his view state that mandatory audits will expose fraud and protect investors, it is clear from the Securities and Exchange Commission (SEC) regulated corporate sector's National Student Marketing, Equity Funding, and Home Stake Production fraud cases that federal regulation guarantees neither. If investors desire protection from fraud, the purchase of Municipal Bond Insurance (MBIA) coverage is a direct means of obtaining financial security. If fraud is suspected, CPAs or others can be contracted to search specifically for defalcations, but the normal audit does not include an explicit investigation for fraud.

It has been suggested that the New York City experience was the impetus for the "Williams" bill and that if an audit had been conducted, the New York City problem might have been prevented. The role of the auditor is to attest to compliance with Governmental Accounting, Auditing, and Financial Reporting (GAAFR). The dominance of cash accounting in the municipal sector, the relative acceptability of direct and/or indirect transfers between funds, and the ability of some political bodies to alter the budget and fund balances with relative ease all contribute toward a lack of accountability by municipalities which will not be corrected by mandating audits or by mandating compliance with GAAFR. New York City highlighted questions concerning the adequacy of accounting procedures used by governments (Sommer, p. 26), and these questions are being addressed by the private sector via a revision of GAAFR and increased interest by the Financial Accounting Standards Board (FASB) in the financial reporting concepts for government (*Wall Street Journal*).

Existing fund accounting provides some inherent protection, particularly if the "integrity of funds" is maintained effectively. Bondholders can negotiate for protective covenants which preclude or at least limit the amount of funds that can be transferred from a facility for which revenue bonds are issued, e.g., an electric utility. Due to the penalties related to noncompliance, such requirements are likely to be met. In light of the availability of these and other alternate monitoring devices, including voluntary audits, and in light of the fact that an audit is *not* intended to reveal fraud as Senator Eagleton believes, a lowering of interest cost by mandatory audit legislation is unlikely.

### *Mandatory Audits*

Since audit legislation mandates an activity not voluntarily undertaken by municipal managers, such legislation can affect the default costs of the bondholders. Assuming efficient markets and municipal managers who minimize interest costs, we can expect that any increase in market value of the bonds to a mandated audit will be less than the auditing fees. Unless other benefits offset the cost of the audit, this implies a decrease in the asset value and coverage of outstanding debt.

*Regulation Costs*

Audit legislation has related costs of regulation, including those of operating the regulatory agencies [3] and of compliance by issuers, the underwriters, and others involved in the issuance and trade of municipal securities. The cost of compliance with mandatory audit legislation and its accounting guidelines will decrease the total asset level and the related bond coverage provided to bondholders.

*Constrained Decision-Making*

Audit legislation may be symptomatic of increased state control in general, with concomitant legislation and other costs imposed on municipalities. This would suggest less taxing power on the municipal level and consequently a greater default risk.[4]

*Divergence of Utility Maximization and Interest Cost Minimization*

If municipal officials are acting in their constituencies' interests already, they will be minimizing the total costs of the municipality. The amount of auditing that is optimal at the point of minimum total costs may not coincide with the amount of auditing that minimizes net interest cost. Hence, even in the presence of voluntary audits, legislation could favorably affect interest cost.

*An Empirical Question*

Expectations concerning the effect of audit legislation are mixed, in light of the above arguments. This can be illustrated by describing bondholders' demanded rate of interest ($R_e$) (net interest cost in this study) as a reflection of the risk-free interest rate ($R_f$) and the level of monitoring costs (MC) and default costs (DC) associated with a particular investment

$$R_e = R_f + MC\ (A,\ldots) + DC\ (A,\ldots),$$

where A = audit legislation.

(a) $\frac{\partial MC}{\partial A} < 0$ • to the degree that audits were not already being performed, and if performed, replaced other monitoring costs.

(b) $\frac{\partial DC}{\partial A} > 0$ • due to the excess of the present value of audit fees over the increase in market value of the bonds and other benefits that accrue from the audit.

• due to regulation costs.

• due to constrained decision-making.

(c) $\frac{\partial R_e}{\partial A} < 0$ • due to divergence in total cost and interest cost minimization policies.

It is clear that the effect of audit legislation on borrowing costs while asserted to be favorable by legislative proponents, may be unfavorable or nonexistent. The assertion cannot be theoretically deduced; it is an empirical question.

Methodology

As a means of providing empirical evidence as to the market effects of differential audit requirements, different samples were examined.

### *Forty-six-State Sample*

States with disclosure legislation should be incurring lower interest costs relative to states not enacting such legislation, if the proponents' claims are correct, and a cross-sectional multiple regression technique was utilized to test for any such association between audit legislation and interest cost. Like bonds from each of the issuing states were included in the analysis, and demographic and finance statistics were used to control for other effects.

### *Four-State Sample*

Four states were selected for further study to permit an analysis of disclosure legislation's association with market measures for different types of bond issues. These market measures include interest cost and the number of bids submitted. Additional data were collected for each state (e.g., average bond sales from 1974-76 and revenue sharing) and for each issue (e.g., the size of each issue). Controlling for variation in these attributes, multiple regression analysis was used to see if the two states with extensive audit legislation currently experience lower interest costs and a higher number of bids in relation to the other two states which have less extensive audit practices.

### *Time Series Tests*

The tests on all forty-six states and the more detailed consideration of four states with diverse legislation examine the cross-sectional association between market measures and audit legislation. A time series analysis on data obtained before and after state audit legislation passed in Florida, Michigan, and Tennessee provides more causal evidence on the likely effect of federal audit regulation. Paired samples were drawn per state as a means of reducing extraneous influences on the variables being measured. Multiple regression analysis and paired sample t-tests of significance then were computed to determine whether a difference exists between each market measure before and after the applicable state legislation.

Comparison of the tests described in this section provides a measure of the validity of the conclusions drawn in section 6. By combining tests, it is possible to observe the association of audit legislation and market measures (interest cost, bond rating, and the number of bids submitted) both cross-sectionally and through time. This descriptive evidence, as reported in sections 3 through 5, suggests that the presence of state mandatory audit legislation is not accompanied by favorable changes in market measures or by favorable market measures relative to states without audit legislation. Federal legislation proponents need to explain this phenomenon or to provide an alternative rationale for federal regulation of the municipal market.

## 3. The Association of State Audit Legislation and Municipal Borrowing Costs

The wide cross-sectional variation in attributes of state audit legislation provides the opportunity to test for the association of these attributes with the market measures claimed to be affected by audit regulations.

Members of the investment community are quick to point out that legal conditions within each state make each state's bonds unique. Variation of state income tax laws, supply conditions, state bank pledging requirements, and differing policies on voter referendum per class of bond may all affect interest cost and affect cross-sectional test results. As one means of minimizing such effects, I selected a single class of bond issues, namely tax-exempt hospital and medical care facility financing issues, as reported by *The Bond Buyer's Statistics* for 1975 and 1976. But to guard against the possibility of results unique to hospital financing, the same tests were performed for all tax-exempt industrial pollution control financing issues in the same years, also reported by *The Bond Buyer's Statistics*.

Studying the price reaction of municipal bonds to unexpected changes in accounting and auditing legislation would be a preferred methodology; however, the data are unavailable.[5] Largely due to the lack of secondary market data, the focus in this study will be on new bond issues and the impact of legislation on the cost of debt *to the municipality*. Since the rationale for federal legislation discussed in section 1 is phrased in terms of interest cost to the municipality, this appears to be an appropriate market measure to analyze.

Dependent Variable

This study utilizes net interest cost (NIC), a commonly reported statistic in the municipal trade as the market measure of interest. The formula for NIC is[6]

$$\text{NIC\%} = \frac{\text{total coupon interest payments* } + \text{ bid discount (or - bid premium)}}{\text{number of bond year dollars**}}$$

$$* \ \Sigma \left[ \begin{matrix}\text{coupon rate} \\ \text{on each maturity}\end{matrix} \times \begin{matrix}\text{par amount} \\ \text{in each maturity}\end{matrix} \times \begin{matrix}\text{number of yrs} \\ \text{to maturity}\end{matrix} \right]$$

** bond year dollars = sum of the product of the par values of each bond and the number of years to its maturity, i.e.,

$$\Sigma \left[ \begin{matrix}\text{par amount} \\ \text{in each maturity}\end{matrix} \times \begin{matrix}\text{number of} \\ \text{years to maturity}\end{matrix} \right]$$

NIC assigns a zero time value of money and therefore only measures the actual interest cost if the issuer or its taxpayers had no alternative use of funds and if the timing of tax payments was of no importance. However, the present worth basis (PW),[7] a more complex calculation, is not commonly used by issuers in awarding municipal bonds.[8]

There are two basic reasons for not expecting NIC to affect seriously the validity of the empirical evidence presented. First, an empirical study by Kidwell, comparing regression results based on a NIC dependent variable relative to a PW dependent variable found no significant difference. Second, an issuer awarding issues by the lowest NIC bid can prevent most of the excess interest costs possible by not utilizing a PW criterion but specifying appropriate coupon constraints. The primary source of excess interest costs arises from the frontloading of interest payments, i.e., higher early debt service payments. For most bond issues this can be largely prevented by some form of nondescending order coupon constraint (it should be noted that constraints are intended to restrict underwriters to produce low PW bids; the type of constraint depends on the effective maturity structure). Since such constraints are commonly applied, the NIC measures should be suitable proxies for PW in evaluating the cost of debt to the municipality (Center for Capital Market Research).

With NIC% as the dependent variable, cross-sectional multiple regression analysis was utilized to test for the association of audit legislation.

## Independent Variables

In order to compare the association between market measures and audit legislation, it is necessary to identify the primary differences in existing requirements and related finance and demographic characteristics which may need to be controlled. First, the nature of existing state auditing requirements is discussed; then the demographic variables that will be controlled are briefly described.

*Independent Variables--Audits*

As of October 1977, "all but five states require that there be audits of local units" (Petersen et al., p. 27) and of these, 37 require use of generally accepted audit standards (Peat, Marwick). However, the requirements vary greatly in terms of (1) who performs the audit--certified public accountant, public accountant, state, county, or municipal employee, or nonlicensed accountant; (2) how often the audit is performed--annually, every two to five years, or waived indefinitely due to staffing capabilities of a state audit department; and (3) which governmental units must be audited--distinctions are often made based on political form (e.g., counties versus cities) and population.

These three major attributes of state legislation are identified for each state having mandatory audit requirements by utilizing the results of a 1975-76 survey by the National Conference of State Legislatures and the Municipal Finance Officers Association (Petersen et al.). The relationship between net interest cost and each of these attributes, as well as the association between the number of bids submitted per bond issue and these three attributes, will be tested with a cross-sectional multiple regression analysis.

*Independent Variables--Demographics*

In an attempt to minimize the omitted variables problem for state demographic or financial characteristics, several demographic and finance statistics per state will be controlled. The following statistics are commonly circulated in municipal market publications: average bond sales per year, dollars and number of displacements per year,[9] total debt outstanding with a state and local debt subtotal provided, per capita debt, rank among the states in terms of tax burden per capita, revenue from the state, revenue from the localities, property tax revenue, revenue sharing,[10] population, and personal income (total and per capita). Since several of these measures are highly correlated, various regressions are run to examine the association of the market measures of interest and the audit legislation attributes while controlling various subsets of the statistics described.

In addition to controlling for the state level statistics in 1975-76, finance statistics related to particular issues were obtained and controlled in the cross-sectional regression analysis. The Bond Buyer's 20-Bond Index[11] on the day of the issue, the dollar size of each issue, and the issue's classification as a revenue[12] or general obligation[13] bond were controlled variables.

## Results

In appendix table 5.A, a subset of the regression models examined is presented. Variations of the models presented were tested and found to have no effect on the sign or significance of the audit legislation coefficients. Table 5.1 presents the coefficients and related F statistic for the audit legislation attributes and the type of accounting system legislation that exists, since these are the variables of interest in this study. Readers desiring more detail with respect to the coefficients and significance of the demographic and finance statistics may refer to the appendix.

Since some of the accounting and auditing legislation variables are correlated, three alternative combinations of the attributes are presented in Table 5.1. The regression results for hospital issues suggest that higher net interest cost in percentage terms (NIC%) is significantly associated with the presence of mandatory audit legislation requiring the use of private CPAs by governmental units and legislation that specifies the use of both private and state auditors (e.g., counties may be audited by the state while other governmental units are audited by private CPAs). However, the significance of the positive coefficient for the use of both private and state auditors is affected by which demographic variables (reported in appendix, table 5.A) are controlled.

If the bureaucrats are correct in asserting that lower NIC is observed in the presence of mandatory audit legislation, what is the probability of getting these reported empirical results? By attributing a 95 percent confidence level to the bureaucrats, i.e., 95 times out of 100 lower NIC results from mandatory audit legislation,[14] it is possible to quantify

$$Pr[b_0 \geq .7479 \mid \beta_0 = -.3093]$$

where

$Pr$ = probability of the occurrence,[15]

$b_0$ = observed coefficient (mandatory use of private CPA),

$\beta_0$ = bureaucrats' claimed coefficient, assuming a 95 percent confidence level and a standard error equal to the observed standard error (i.e., .188 for mandatory use of private CPA).

This probability is .0005, i.e., only five times out of 10,000 samples will a positive coefficient of this magnitude or larger be observed, if the true relationship of NIC and a mandatory audit by a private CPA were a negative coefficient, significant at a .05 level. Similarly, $Pr[b_0 \geq .9536 \mid \beta_0 = -.4211]$ is .0005, suggesting it is highly unlikely that higher NIC could be observed to be related to the mandatory use of both private and state auditors if the true relationship was with lower NIC.

The other hospital regression result of primary interest is the coefficient for the absence of audit legislation variable. The $Pr[b_0 \leq -.1353 \mid \beta_0 = .4425]$ is .017. Again, the probability of observing lower NIC in the absence of mandatory audit legislation, if it were true that higher NIC was related to the lack of such legislation, is extremely low.

The variables representing the frequency of the audit, the percent of units audited, and the presence of a state mandatory accounting system or state guidelines are included in the regressions primarily to control for these variations in legislation[16] while identifying the relationship of NIC and the presence of any form of mandatory audit legislation. Due to the high correlation of mandatory use of a private CPA and mandatory use of a state auditor, these variables were run separately. Although the state audit variable is significantly related to lower NIC, the relationship between higher NIC and the use of both private CPAs and state auditors persists with a related $Pr[b_0 \geq .2266 \mid \beta_0 = -.3142]$ of .0034. In light of the dominant specification of private CPAs or a mixture of private CPAs and state auditors in state legislation, there does not appear to be an overall market reward for audit legislation as claimed by proponents of mandatory audits.

The regression results for the pollution issues (also reported in table 5.1) indicate no significant association with NIC, with the exception of the absence of state legislation which has a significant negative association with NIC. The $Pr[b_0 \leq -.3640 \mid \beta_0 = .3060]$ is .0005; it is highly unlikely that such a relationship could be observed if the bureaucrats' assertion was true at a .05 level of significance.

The mandatory use of a private CPA variable has a .05 probability, the use of only a state auditor has a .0045 probability, and the use of both private and state auditors has a .10 probability of having the observed coefficient were there actually a significant (i.e., .05 level) relation between lower NIC and each of these variables. Hence, the regression analysis of the pollution issues reinforces the hospital issue results. It is highly unlikely that there is an overall market reward for audit legislation as claimed by proponents of mandatory audits, in light of these cross-sectional results.

One further test was performed on the hospital data

for the 46 states: a t-test to identify whether a significant difference in NIC adjusted for the Bond Buyer's 20-Bond Index (BB) exists between issues subject to 100 percent audit legislation and those subject to no regulation. The NIC-BB was significantly higher for states with 100 percent audit legislation; the related t-value is 2.04, with a 2-tail probability of .043. Hence, prima facie evidence is not available to substantiate bureaucrats' claims that issuers subject to state audit regulation realize lower NIC. And when demographic and finance statistics are controlled, the overall implication is that higher NIC is observed to be related to several legislative attributes, including the overall presence of state audit regulations.

## 4. A Comparison of Four States' Market Measures

To permit an analysis of disclosure legislation's association with market measures for types of bond issues other than hospital and pollution financing, (and based on discussions with a bureaucrat active in municipal research for the Securities and Exchange Commission,) four states were selected for further study. Illinois and Michigan have very extensive audit legislation, and Ohio and Washington have less extensive audit practices relative to other states.

The statutes of each of the four states were reviewed. The primary differences in the states' audit legislation rest upon who performs the audit and how frequently it is performed. Illinois and Michigan utilize independent CPAs as auditors annually. Ohio and Washington utilize state auditors, and while the legislation provides for at least biannual audits, staffing difficulties often lead to delays and indefinite waivers of audits.[17] Direct correspondence with Washington municipalities frequently indicated interim periods between examinations of three years or more.

Data were collected for all general obligation, and

revenue bonds issued in 1976 by the four states, as reported in the *Bond Buyers' Statistics*. Those issues for which NIC was available were analyzed utilizing multiple regression analysis.

Table 5.2 shows multiple regression results for the four-state sample. The demographic variables identified as having a significant association with NIC in appendix table 5.A for the 46-state sample were controlled in the four-state regressions; only average bond sales and revenue sharing were significantly associated with NIC or the number of bids submitted for the four-state sample. Since the deletion of the insignificant demographic variables had no effect on the sign or significance of the "extent of legislation" variable, table 5.2 presents the more parsimonious regression. Finance characteristics per issue are also controlled in the regression analysis: specifically, the Bond Buyer's 20-Bond Index, the issue size, the type of issuer (state and counties versus other municipalities), and the number of bids submitted.

The variable of primary interest is "states with more extensive legislation = 1," i.e., a dummy variable with 1 referring to the states of Illinois and Michigan. With NIC as the dependent variable, this dummy variable has a positive sign and approaches significance. This implies that states with more extensive legislation are associated with higher NIC. The $\Pr[b_0 \geq .1556 \mid \beta_0 = -.2221]$ is .0034, which means that it is extremely unlikely that the positive coefficient of the dummy variable would be observed if states with more extensive legislation actually experienced lower NIC.

To examine the relative marketability of municipal bond issues in states with different audit legislation, as measured by the number of bids submitted per issue, this dependent variable was substituted for NIC and NIC was controlled as an independent variable. Table 5.2 suggests that states with more extensive legislation are associated with a lower number of bids. The $\Pr[b_0 \leq -.1708 \mid \beta_0 =$

.7929] is .026, suggesting the observation of a negative relationship is a rather rare occurrence if the assertion of bureaucrats is true at a .05 level. Clearly, there is no support of the legislative rationale that states with more extensive audit legislation have greater marketability; in fact, the analysis implies that states with extensive legislation have a lower number of bids submitted per issue.

This analysis is consistent with the section 3 finding that two states with extensive audit legislation do not currently experience lower interest costs or a higher number of bids in relation to two states with less extensive audit practices despite the rationale for legislation discussed in section 1. In addition, the consistency of the findings make it even more difficult to attribute the results to a nonrepresentative sampling effect. The extremely low probability of observing the coefficients that are contrary to bureaucrats' assertions is persuasive evidence that the bureaucrats' claims are invalid.

## 5. Time Series Tests of Audit Legislation and Municipal Borrowing Costs and Bond Ratings

The empirical evidence presented to this point reports on the cross-sectional association between interest cost and mandated audits. This section presents a time series analysis for three states.

### Florida

Data were collected for all Florida bond issues from 1966 to 1976. The legislative history of audit-related regulations at the state level was obtained, and representatives of the State Auditor General's Office, the Florida League of Cities, the Comptroller's Office, and the Advisory Council on Intergovernmental Relations were contacted to verify the timing of such legislation.

Prior to 1971 no state audit legislation existed.

However, many bureaucrats claim that the reason for the legislation dates back to 1969, suggesting that expectations concerning the likely state mandate of audits may have been formed that early. Before 1969, Florida could not share state revenue with local governmental units. In that year a new constitution was adopted which gave the state more flexibility in its use of revenue. In 1970 a $200 million revenue-sharing program was announced, and there were suggestions that a "need" for uniform reporting existed. It took approximately two years for the money to reach the cities.

In 1971, Chapter 71-218 of the Florida Statutes (167.611) was passed, requiring municipalities with total budgets of $50,000 or more to retain and pay for an independent audit, with the exception of counties, which would be audited by the Auditor General's Office (the act was approved by the governor on June 18, 1971). Committees associated with this legislation had meetings back to December 1970, but the bill was actually introduced to the senate in April 1971.

In 1973, law 73-219 of Florida repealed 167.611 of the 1971 Florida Statutes. The primary differences in this bill and the 1973 legislation include (1) the designation of generally accepted accounting principles as those which should be utilized by municipalities and the citing of *Governmental Accounting, Auditing, and Financial Reporting (GAAFR)* as a useful guide; (2) the requirement that a copy of postaudit reports be filed at the Auditor General's Office; and (3) the requirement that municipalities respond to the auditor's management letter and that they file the comments at the Auditor General's Office. Action on this bill occurred from April 1973 to the approval date by the governor, June 7, 1973.

This legislative history suggests that 1969-73 is a critical transition period for Florida municipalities. Each legislative change within this time span may have affected expectations concerning the mandated audit of governmental units. Despite the 1971 legislation, there was not an effective enforcement technique until the state's required filing threatened a penalty of withheld revenue-sharing funds for municipalities not meeting reporting requirements. This threat was clear by 1974, and audit reports began to be routinely filed with the auditor general in 1973-74.

Key events in Florida's legislative history that either raised an expectation of reporting requirements and mandated audit requirements, or assured the enforcement of such requirements were identified. If a market reward to municipalities exists due to mandatory audits as proponents of legislation suggest, the critical transition period 1969-73 should reflect this reward. All Florida municipalities who issued bonds in the periods 1966-68 and 1974-76 were identified. A paired sample per issuer was formed for the critical event period, i.e., each municipality's issue preceding but as close as possible to 12/31/68 and the same municipality's issue following but as close as possible to 12/31/73 were selected. The use of these paired samples, as discussed in section 2, controls for extraneous influences and facilitates testing for the association of the aggregate change in expectations related to the legislative events and changes in market measures.

Table 5.3 presents the multiple regression results for Florida paired samples relative to the critical transition period 1969-73. The first line reports the average difference in net interest cost (NIC) between paired issues for the 22 Florida municipalities having issues in both the 1966-68 and 1974-76 time periods. The independent variables include the difference in the number of bids submitted, the difference in bond rating, the difference in the Bond Buyer's 20-Bond Index, the change from a general obligation to a revenue issue, or the change from a revenue to a general obligation issue from pre-1969 to post-1973, and whether the issue was by a county or other municipality. By controlling for these independent variables and by reducing extraneous influences with the use of paired samples on either side of the critical transition period, the constant term of the regression is made to reflect only the relationship of the mandatory legislation expectation and implementation period and NIC.

The negative constant term (which is significant at a .05 level) suggests that NIC was higher in the post-1973 period than the pre-1969 period. This finding is contrary to bureaucrats' claims that mandatory audit legislation lowers NIC. The $Pr[b_0 \leq -1.5685 \mid \beta_0 = 1.4935]$ is .0027; again, it is extremely unlikely that this empirical result would be obtained if the bureaucrats' assertions were correct.

The 22 municipalities' issues from pre-1969 and post-1973 experience seven increases in the number of bids submitted (four increases of one bid, two increases of two bids, and one increase of five bids) and 14 decreases in the number of bids submitted (six declines of one bid, two declines of two bids, four declines of three bids, one decline of five bids, and one decline of seven bids). Hence, prima facie evidence demonstrates that a lower number of bids was submitted to the same issuers after the transitional period which included implementation of mandatory audit legislation. However, since this increment in bids could be related to finance variables distinct from the presence of audit legislation, line 2 of table 5.3 presents the difference in the number of bids presented pre-1969 and post-1973 as the dependent variable and controls for the independent variables already described as well as NIC. The constant term bears an insignificant negative sign, suggesting that when finance variables are controlled, the number of bids submitted for the post-1973 period slightly exceeded the number submitted pre-1969. Given that a significant negative sign should be observed if the bureaucrats are 95 percent confident in their claims, the $Pr[b_0 \geq -.42 \mid \beta_0 = -2.59]$ is only .10. Again, the suggestion by bureaucrats that the effect of mandatory audit legislation will be to increase the number of bids submitted is not supported.

Line 3 of table 5.3 controls for the same independent variables, including the difference in number of bids submitted and the difference in NIC, while examining the dependent variable of bond rating. The constant term bears a positive sign suggesting that the bond rating was higher post-1973 relative to pre-1969 (remember, the smaller ratings are higher, i.e., more favorable). When the equation is tested using probit analysis to provide for the possible ordinal nature of bond ratings, (see note, table 5.3) the constant term is positive and significant at a .005 level. However, it should be noted that there is no independent variable controlling for shifts in the average bond rating for the municipal market over the time period examined.

The paired samples of Florida issues offer no support for the legislative rationale discussed in section 1 regarding a claimed significant improvement in interest cost or the number of bids submitted per issue. In fact, it appears that NIC has increased with the advent of mandatory audit legislation and is significant at the .05 level in its relation to the legislation event. These findings are consistent with those reported in sections 3 and 4. There does appear to be a significant improvement (when probit analysis is utilized) in bond ratings which are unadjusted for market level rating shifts. However, the implication of bureaucrats' claims that audit legislation leads to higher ratings which in turn lead to lower NIC is not supported.

To validate the findings reported for Florida, time series analysis of Tennessee audit legislation and the state's bond ratings and time series analysis of Michigan audit legislation and the state's NIC are performed.

## Tennessee

Prior to 1976, mandated audits in the State of Tennessee were limited to counties (Chapter 616, Tennessee Public Acts of 1974, amending Section 4-336 of the Tennessee Code

Annotated). The Tennessee Public Acts of 1977 (Chapter 221) mandating audits for municipalities was passed May 4, 1977.

Bond rating data were collected for all Tennessee municipal bonds (and a control sample of all South Carolina municipal bonds), which were reported by *Moody's Bond Record* for June 1976, May 1977, and January 1978. A paired sample per municipality was formed for the relevant event periods, i.e., each municipality rated on June 1976 was paired with the same municipality rated on May 1977 and on January 1978. The differences in means for the paired samples of all issues outstanding in June 1976 and May 1977 were measured and t-test statistics were computed.[18] This same test was applied to the paired samples of all issues outstanding in June 1976 and January 1978 as well as May 1977 and January 1978. The extended period allows for lags in bond rating adjustments by municipal bond rating firms. The paired sample test results are reported in table 5.4.

The positive mean differences indicate that the bond rating has improved over all three periods under examination, since the issue ratings are numerically higher for the earlier issues, hence qualitatively lower in rating (this is due to the scale of measurement with one representing the highest bond rating). The standard deviation and standard error per period are comparable for each of the subperiods and provide a measure of dispersion for the data under examination. The correlation between the first reported bond rating and the later bond rating is reported to be positive for each period; this is necessary for pairing to be effective. It appears that the pairing technique to reduce extraneous influences on bond rating is useful to this analysis. The related 2-tail probability for the correlation coefficient between the two observations suggests an improvement is made to the t-statistic by pairing[19] and that the covariance of the two ratings will compensate for the reduced degrees of freedom.

The paired sample results reported in table 5.4 indicate a significant improvement in Tennessee bond ratings for all three time periods. However, since bond ratings may have an interval or an ordinal scale of measurement, as opposed to a ratio scale, the results were validated by utilizing the Wilcoxon's signed rank test of difference score symmetry about zero, a nonparametric statistical test. The May 1977 to January 1978 period resulted in a positive rank sum of 17,205, a standardized minimum of -11.795, a 0.0001 probability of not exceeding the standardized minimum if the hypothesis of identical populations is true, and out of 185 ratings, a total of 174 ties were observed. The interpretation of these findings is a 0.0001 2-tailed probability of erring in rejecting the hypothesis of identical populations; therefore, as in the paired sample t-test, a significant change in bond rating is observed. The use of nonparametric statistical analysis does not alter the findings.[20]

It should be noted that there is no control for shifts in the overall level of bond ratings from 1976 to 1978 for either the t-test or Wilcoxon analysis. Therefore, a control sample from the State of South Carolina was drawn for the same time period. There has been no legislative activity in the state with regard to municipal audits or accounting practices (per correspondence with the Legislative Audit Council of South Carolina--a management analysis and program evaluation organization), yet the state's bond ratings improved over the Tennessee legislation time span. This control suggests that a large part of the rating improvement in Tennessee bonds may be due to general market shifts. In an attempt to determine whether the apparent upgrading of bond ratings is reflected in net interest cost when adjusted for the Bond Buyer's 20-Bond Index (NIC-BB) for Tennessee issues, another test was performed. The Tennessee hospital facilities issues for 1976 (15 issues) and 1977 (20 issues)--the same type of issue investigated in section 3--were compared by applying a t-test to NIC-BB for all such issues; 1976 relative to 1977 yielded a t-value of $-2.58_{22}$, significant at .017. This suggests that the amount by which NIC exceeds the index is significantly higher for 1977. This NIC result is consistent with NIC findings reported in sections 3 and 4.

Michigan

In 1968, Michigan mandated audits through Act 2 of the Public Acts of 1968. The *Michigan Municipal Review* reports municipal bond sales in Michigan, and data were obtained for 1967, 1968, and 1969. Municipalities issuing bonds in each of the three years were identified. The issue closest to 1968 was selected per municipality for years 1967 and 1969.

Paired samples per municipality were formed for bond issues in 1967 and 1969 (choosing the latest issue in 1967) and for 1967 and 1968 (choosing the earliest issue in 1968 for each municipality). Again, the use of paired samples should help to control for extraneous influences. Both time periods are examined since it is difficult to assess the exact timing of the legislation's effect, i.e., expectations should adjust market interest cost by 1969 but could affect the market in early 1968.

Table 5.5 reports the multiple regression results for Michigan paired samples relative to the 1967-69 period and the 1967-68 period. The first line reports the average difference in net interest cost (NIC) between paired issues for the sixteen Michigan municipalities having issues in both 1967 and 1969. The independent variables include the difference in the Bond-Buyer's 20-Bond Index, the difference in the maturity in years of the paired bond issues, the difference in the average life of the paired bond issues, and the difference in the issue size of the 1967 and 1969 bond issues. Because independent variables have been controlled, the constant term of the regression reflects the relationship of the mandatory legislation expectation and implementation period and NIC.

The negative significant constant term suggests that

NIC was higher in 1969 than 1967. This finding directly contradicts bureaucrats' claims that mandatory audit legislation lowers NIC. The $Pr[b_0 \leq -1.197 \mid \beta_0 = .476]$ is .0005; it would be extremely rare to observe this negative coefficient if a significant improvement in NIC occurred when legislation came into effect.

The second line of table 5.5 presents the same test for 1967 relative to 1968 with a sample of 31 Michigan municipalities making issues in both years. The constant term is significantly negative. This finding also contradicts bureaucrats' claims that mandatory audits lower borrowing costs. The $Pr[b_0 \leq -.307 \mid \beta_0 = .255]$ is .0005; again, this observation would be extremely rare.

The Tennessee findings regarding the bond rating correspond to Florida findings, but both analyses suffer from a lack of control for market level rating movements. The South Carolina control sample suggests that a market upgrading in ratings occurred during the Tennessee legislation time span.

The stronger evidence relating to NIC controlled for changes in the municipal market index presented for Florida, Tennessee, and Michigan (independent variables in addition to the index are controlled in the Florida and Michigan analysis) suggests the absence of any market reward for audit-related legislation. In fact, the Florida and Michigan results suggest that significantly higher NIC is observed for municipalities following the passage of the audit regulation. The NIC findings are consistent with the results reported in sections 3 and 4.

## 6. Summary and Conclusions

Proposed federal legislation to extend the securities laws to municipalities has been promoted with the stated rationale that there will be increased competitive bidding and improved bond ratings, resulting in lower interest rates. Since the rationale suggested for state legislation typically involves similar claims that favorable market effects will result, this study utilizes the variation of state legislation to provide empirical evidence on the likely effect of federal regulation of municipal disclosure.

The evidence presented in sections 3 through 5 consistently supports no effect or a negative effect of mandatory audit legislation on interest cost. This suggests that the burden of proof is on supporters of federal legislation to justify further their proposals. Not only has the claimed lowering of interest costs not occurred, but a significantly higher interest cost relative to the market is observed for states with mandatory legislation (section 3) relative to those states without such legislation. Obviously, one cannot observe what the net interest cost would have been in the absence of state legislation; nonetheless, unless proponents of mandatory audit legislation can explain the concurrent observation of mandatory audit legislation and higher interest cost across states and through time, another rationale for the proposed federal legislation will have to be presented.

Similarly, no significant favorable effect on the number of bids submitted is observed in the time series analysis of Florida legislation. Nor are the number of bids for the two states with more comprehensive audit legislation examined in section 4 higher than the two states with less extensive legislation. There is again a lack of evidence for the legislative rationale.

The evidence pertaining to bond ratings does suggest that an improvement in bond rating occurred when legislation was passed in Florida and Tennessee. However, there is no control for a shift in the average bond rating for the municipal market over the Florida time period, and a control sample for the Tennessee time span provides evidence of a market shift to higher bond ratings. In an attempt to measure whether these apparent favorable rating changes were translated into lower interest cost as suggested in bureaucrats' claimed effect of mandatory audit legislation, evidence on interest cost adjusted for the effect of the municipal market index was considered; this evidence suggests that the Florida and Tennessee rating statistics may very well reflect total market differences between periods.

Throughout the paper, the probabilities of obtaining the reported empirical results, given the legislators' claims are correct (at a 95 percent confidence level), are quantified and consistently found to be extremely low. The reported .0005 probabilities suggest that the repeated observation of relationships contrary to bureaucrats' claims would be such rare events that the evidence is strong that the bureaucrats' assertions are invalid.

The implications of the findings suggest that the claimed favorable market effects of mandated audits have not been observed for states mandating legislation and should not be expected for federal legislation.

TABLE 5.1. Cross-Sectional Multiple Regression Results for Audit and Accounting Legislation Variables: 46 States*

| Net Interest Cost is the Dependent Variable | Mandatory Use of Private CPA = 1 Coefficient (F-Statistic) | Mandatory Audit Less Frequently Than Annually = 1 | 100% of Municipalities Including Counties are Audited = 1 | Both Private CPAs and State Auditors are Used = 1 | Mandatory Accounting System or State Guidelines = 1*** | Mandatory Use of State Auditor Only = 1 | No Auditing Legislation = 1*** |
|---|---|---|---|---|---|---|---|
| SAMPLE: Hospital Issues for 1975 and 1976 | .7479 (15.869)**** | .5231 (3.021)**** | -.3323 (3.886)**** | .9536 (13.886)**** | .0509 (.091) | | |
| 452 issues; information complete for 394 issues. | | .4926 (2.645)**** | -.2014 (1.688) | .2266 (1.414) | .0498 (.086) | -.7027 (13.970)**** | |
| | | | | | | | -.1353 (.253) |
| SAMPLE: Pollution Issues for 1975 and 1976 | .0095** (.005) | .1341 (.438) | .1310 (.856) | -.0697 (.120) | -.1618 (1.535) | | |
| 360 issues; information complete for 274 issues. | | .0849 (.177) | .1593 (1.413) | -.0773 (.245) | -.1645 (1.598) | .1520 (1.015) | |
| | | | | | | | -.3640 (3.823)**** |

*A frequency table by state of the number of issues and total dollars of issues utilized in this cross-sectional test is provided in the Appendix, Table B. It should be noted that the following four states are unrepresented in both samples investigated: Alaska, Hawaii, Rhode Island, and Vermont.

**It should be noted that variation of demographic control variables resulted in a -.0459 coefficient, but due to the insignificance of the variable (.105), this is likely to be a spurious sign change.

***The dummy variable 1 = Mandatory System
0 = Only Guidelines or no accounting legislation
resulted in a negative coefficient of -.2216 (.398), still lacking significance.

****F-Statistic is significant at a .01 level.

TABLE 5.2. Multiple Regression Results for the Four-State Sample[1] [F-Statistics in ()]

| Sample includes all General Obligation and Revenue Municipal Issues during 1976 for Illinois, Michigan, Washington, and Ohio as reported in The Bond Buyer (School Boards are excluded) | Constant | Net Interest Cost Coefficient (F-Statistic) | Number of Bids Submitted | Bond Buyer's 20-Bond Index | Issue Size | TYPE OF ISSUER 1 = State or County 0 = Other Municipalities | Average Bond Sales for 1974 - 1976 | Revenue Sharing | States with More Extensive Legislation = 1[2] | $R^2$ (Adjusted $R^2$) |
|---|---|---|---|---|---|---|---|---|---|---|
| DEPENDENT VARIABLE: | | | | | | | | | | |
| Net Interest Cost (N = 274 issues) | .6394 | | .0128 (.555) | .8287 (25.106) * | .0000 (.537) | -.1629 (2.316) ** | -.0000 (.011) | -.0000 (2.714)** | .1556 (1.331) | .3233 (.3055) |
| Number of Bids Submitted (N = 274 issues) | -1.2502 | .1631 (.555) | | .1450 (.055) | -.0000 (.234) | .5915 (2.395) ** | .0000 (8.808)* | -.0000 (1.325) | -.1708 (.125) | .2109 (.1901) |

* Significant at a .01 level.
** Significant at a .05 level.

[1]One variable not controlled is the differential state income taxation of municipal bonds which may affect the dependent variables: Illinois levies state income tax on its own and other states' bonds for individuals and corporations; Michigan levies state income tax only on other states' bonds for individuals and corporations; Ohio levies state income tax only on other states' bonds for individuals (not for corporations); and Washington does not levy state income taxes on any municipal bonds ("News Report", 1978).

[2]When this dummy variable is broken into 3 dummies
1 - Illinois
2 - Washington
3 - Ohio
The dummy variables' coefficient and F-Statistic were as follows for the two models:

| | NIC Dependent Variable | BIDS Dependent Variable |
|---|---|---|
| D1 = Illinois | 2.4774 (.537) | -8.3195 (.613) |
| D2 = Washington | .6550 (1.327) | -.7252 (.127) |
| D3 = Ohio | -.1255 (1.327) | .1389 (.127) |

It is clear that the lack of association holds in each state.

TABLE 5.3. Time Series Regression Results for Florida [t-statistics in ()]

| DEPENDENT VARIABLE Sample = All Municipalities Issuing Bonds In the Period from 1966 to 1968 and the Period from 1974 to 1976 N=22. | CONSTANT | Number of Bids Submitted Pre 1969 - Post 1973 Coefficient (t-statistic) | Bond Rating Pre 1969 - Post 1973 (Ordinal Scale With 1 = highest rating | Bond Index Pre 1969 - Post 1973 | Issue Size Pre 1969 - Post 1973 | Net Interest Cost Pre 1969 - Post 1973 | Change from General Obligation to Revenue Issue Pre 1969 - Post 1973 | Change from Revenue to General Obligation Issue Pre 1969 - Post 1973 | County = 1 Other Municipalities = 0 | $R^2$ (Adjusted $R^2$) |
|---|---|---|---|---|---|---|---|---|---|---|
| Difference in Net Interest Cost: Pre 1969 - Post 1973 | -1.5685* (-1.86) | -.0767 (-.45) | -.2280 (-.70) | .0096 (.03) | -.0000 (-.27) | | 1.1643 (1.08) | .1766 (.14) | 1.2381 (1.22) | .2414 (-.1380) |
| Difference in Number of Bids Submitted: Pre 1969 - Post 1973 | -.6155 (-.42) | | -.5777 (-1.17) | -.5940 (-1.45) | .0000 (.07) | -.1899 (-.45) | .5263 (.30) | 2.0534 (1.05) | 1.5137 (.93) | .2458 (-.1313) |
| Difference in Bond Rating:** Pre 1969 - Post 1973 | .6824 (.92) | -.1533 (-1.17) | | .0282 (.12) | -.0001* (-2.10) | -.1499 (-.70) | .4464 (.50) | .5726 (.55) | 1.3914* (1.78) | .4444 (.1666) |

*Significant at a .05 level.

**Since bond ratings can be thought of as conveying ordinal information with unequal intervals, this equation was run utilizing Probit Analysis, a maximum likelihood approach appropriate when testing an ordinal dependent variable. The resulting equation follows:

Difference in Bond Rating: Pre 1969 - Post 1973 = 3.007 + .1546 bids + .0180 index + .0001 issue size + .1419 NIC -.4199 G.O. to Revenue
(3.281) (1.458) (.100) (2.279) (.870) (-.591)
-.7281 Revenue to G.O. -1.1600 county
(-.889) (-1.703)

$R^2$estimated = .4846
% predicted correctly = .4091

The independent variables being measured are identical to those reported in the regression results, although brief labels are used here. The maximum likelihood estimate (MLE) and the ratio of MLE to the Standard Error (in parentheses) are reported. Although the signs of the issue size coefficient and several of the insignificant coefficients have changed, the constant term remains positive and is significant at a .005 level.

TABLE 5.4. Paired Sample T-Tests on Key Legislation Data for Tennessee Municipal Issues (and a Control Sample)

| | Bond Rating* June 1976 to May 1977 | Control** |
|---|---|---|
| (Difference) Mean | .227 | .034 |
| Standard Deviation | 1.105 | .279 |
| Standard Error | .081 | .021 |
| Correlation | .940 | .993 |
| 2-Tail Probability | .000 | .000 |
| T-Value | 2.80 | 1.61 |
| Degrees of Freedom | 184 | 177 |
| 2-Tail Probability | .006 | .109 |

| | Bond Rating* June 1976 to January 1978 | Control | Bond Rating* May 1977 to January 1978 | Control |
|---|---|---|---|---|
| (Difference) Mean | .427 | .096 | .200 | .0618 |
| Standard Deviation | 1.538 | .559 | 1.112 | .477 |
| Standard Error | .113 | .042 | .082 | .036 |
| Correlation | .883 | .973 | .939 | .980 |
| 2-Tail Probability | 0.000 | .000 | .000 | .000 |
| T-Value | 3.78 | 2.28 | 2.45 | 1.73 |
| Degrees of Freedom | 184 | 177 | 184 | 177 |
| 2-Tail Probability | .000 | .024 | .015 | .086 |

*1 = AAA, 2 = CON(AAA), 3 = AA, 4 = CON(AA), 5 = A-1, 6 = CON(A-1)
7 = A, 8 = CON(A), 9 = BAA-1, 10 = CON(BAA-1), 11 = BAA, 12 = CON(BAA)
13 = BA, 14 = CON(BA)

**A control sample over the same time span permits comparison of

| PRIOR AFTER | with | PRIOR AFTER |
|---|---|---|
| No "Treatment" Municipal Bonds (South Carolina) | | "Treatment" Municipal Bonds (Tennessee) |

and is essential in the absence of any other control for market level bond rating shifts.

TABLE 5.5. Time Series Regression Results for Michigan
[t-statistics in ()]

| Dependent Variable is the Difference in Net Interest Cost | Constant Coefficient (t-statistic) | Bond Buyer's 20-Bond Index | Maturity | Average Life | Issue Size | $R^2$ (Adjusted $R^2$) |
|---|---|---|---|---|---|---|
| SAMPLE = All Municipalities Issuing Bonds in 1967 and 1969 N=16 Difference in Net Interest Cost 1967 minus 1969. | 1967 minus 1969 | 1967 minus 1969 | 1967 minus 1969 | 1967 minus 1969 | 1967 minus 1969 | |
| | -1.1972 (-4.52) * | -.0043 (-.03) | .0322 (1.96) *** | -.0541 (-1.66) **** | .0001 (.56) | .3813 (.1563) |
| SAMPLE = All Municipalities Issuing Bonds in 1967 and 1968 N=31 Difference in Net Interest Cost 1967 minus 1968. | 1967 minus 1968 | 1967 minus 1968 | 1967 minus 1968 | 1967 minus 1968 | 1967 minus 1968 | |
| | -.3066 (-2.05) ** | .3020 (1.14) | .0149 (.97) | -.0033 (-.12) | -.0000 (-.13) | .1710 (.0435) |

* Significant at a .005 level.
** Significant at a .025 level.
*** Significant at a .05 level.
**** Significant at a .10 level.

# Appendix

TABLE 5A. Cross-Sectional Multiple Regression Results for Municipal Bonds Issued in 46 States[1] [F-Statistics in ()]

| Net Interest Cost is the Dependent Variable. Samples | Constant | Bond Buyer's 20-Bond Index Coefficient (F Statistic) | Issue Size (,000) | Revenue Versus General Obligation Bonds 1 = G.O. | State Debt Outstanding (000,000) | Total Debt Outstanding (000,000) | Revenue Sharing (000,000) | Average Bond Sales for 1974-1976 (,000) | Number of Displacements |
|---|---|---|---|---|---|---|---|---|---|
| Hospital Issues 1975 & 1976 452 issues; information complete for 394 issues. | -2.647 | 1.2699 (59.877)* | .0303 (41.370)* | | -.0002 (2.628) | | -.0000 (.217) | .0000 (1.748) | |
| | -2.870 | 1.2843 (60.530)* | .0305 (41.628)* | | | .0000 (.001) | -.0000 (.067) | | .0211 (1.458) |
| | -2.1562 | 1.2956 (62.029)* | .0315 (44.900)* | | -.0000 (1.125) | | -.0000 (.010) | .0000 (.147) | |
| | -2.5095 | 1.3202 (63.361)* | .0338 (52.488)* | | .0000 (.001) | | -.0000 (3.044)* | .0000 (.388) | |
| Pollution Issues 1975 & 1976 360 issues; information complete for 274 issues. | -1.8972 | 1.3847 (119.66)* | -.0012 (.089) | | -.0001 (1.537) | | .0000 (.685) | .0000 (.007) | |
| | -1.6552 | 1.3622 (119.12)* | -.0003 (.007) | | | -.0000 (.789) | -.0000 (1.059) | | -.0333 (5.374)* |
| | -1.8686 | 1.3762 (118.17)* | -.0014 (.116) | | -.0001 (1.982)** | | .0000 (.772) | .0000 (.196) | |
| | -1.734 | 1.3580 (120.894)* | -.0011 (.076) | | -.0001 (3.666)* | | .0000 (.419) | .0000 (.580) | |
| Hospital Issues 1975 & 1976 for which the revenue versus general obligation classification is known: 204 issues. (All 1976) | 3.3396 | .4822 (4.903)* | .0127 (5.346)* | -1.2837 (77.449)* | | | | .0000 (1.172) | |
| | 3.9400 | .4357 (4.099)* | .0138 (6.386)* | -1.2468 (72.421)* | | | | .0000 (.043) | |
| | 3.6475 | .4925 (4.830)* | .0198 (13.979)* | -1.1913 (63.778)* | | | | | |

(continued)

# TABLE 5A - Continued

| Net Interest Cost is the Dependent Variable.<br>Samples | Mandatory Use of Private CPA<br>1 = yes | Mandatory Use of State Auditor Only<br>1 = yes | Mandatory[2] Accounting System or State Guidelines<br>1 = yes | Dollars of Displacements (,000) | Revenue from Localities (,000,000) | Revenue From The State (,000,000) | Property Tax Revenue (,000,000) | Population (,000) | Personal Income (,000,000) |
|---|---|---|---|---|---|---|---|---|---|
| Hospital Issues 1975 & 1976 452 issues; information complete for 384 issues. | .7479<br>(15.869)* | | .0509<br>(.091) | | .0002<br>(1.387) | | | | |
| | .7531<br>(10.429)* | | .1041<br>(.239) | | | -.0001<br>(.152) | .0002<br>(.734) | .0000<br>(.180) | .0000<br>(.834) |
| | | -.7027<br>(13.970)* | .0498<br>(.086) | | .0001<br>(.724) | | | | |
| | | | | | .0002<br>(3.341)* | | | | |
| Pollution Issues 1975 & 1976 360 issues; information complete for 274 issues. | .0095<br>(.005) | | -.1618<br>(1.535) | | -.0000<br>(.054) | | | | |
| | -.0459<br>(.105) | | -.2647<br>(3.668) | | | .0003<br>(1.307) | .0001<br>(.069) | -.0000<br>(.008) | -.0000<br>(.515) |
| | | .1520<br>(1.015) | -.1645<br>(1.598) | | -.0001<br>(.177) | | | | |
| | | | | | -.0000<br>(.000) | | | | |
| Hospital Issues 1975 & 1976 for which the revenue versus general obligation classification is known: 204 issues. (All 1976) | .3678<br>(3.461)* | | .0857<br>(.255) | .0000<br>(2.166)** | | | | | |
| | | -.4981<br>(4.995)* | .1089<br>(.418) | .0000<br>(4.404)* | | | | | |

(continued)

# TABLE 5A - Continued

| Net Interest Cost is the Dependent Variable. Samples | Less frequently Audited than Annually 1 = yes | 100% of Municipalities Including counties Are Audited 1 = yes | Both Private CPAs and State Auditors are Used 1 = yes | No Auditing Legislation = 1[3] | $R^2$ (adjusted $R^2$) |
|---|---|---|---|---|---|
| Hospital Issues 1975 & 1976 452 issues; information complete for 384 issues. | .5231 (3.021)* | -.3323 (3.886)* | .9536 (13.886)* | | .2868 (.2663) |
| | .4989 (2.286)* | -1.978 (.909) | .9519 (10.524)* | | .2865 (.2602) |
| | .4926 (2.645)* | -.2014 (1.688) | .2266 (1.414) | | .2834 (.2627) |
| | | | | -.1353 (.253) | .2513 (.2377) |
| Pollution Issues 1975 & 1976 360 issues; information complete for 274 issues. | .1341 (.438) | .1310 (.856) | -.0697 (.120) | | .3300 (.3018) |
| | .1094 (.187) | .0375 (.058) | -.2956 (1.798) | | .3600 (.3254) |
| | .0849 (.177) | .1593 (1.413) | -.0773 (.245) | | .3325 (.3045) |
| | | | | -.3640 (3.823)* | .3301 (.3125) |
| Hospital Issues 1975 & 1976 for which the revenue versus general obligation classification is known: 204 issues. | .8073 (6.955)* | -.3731 (4.171)* | .6038 (5.771)* | | .4485 (.4199) |
| | .9567 (8.491)* | -.3152 (3.718)* | .2818 (2.264)** | | .4528 (.4244) |
| | | | | .0759 (.105) | .3820 (.3696) |

(continued)

TABLE 5A - Continued

* Significant at a .01 level.
** Significant at a .05 level.

[1]A frequency table by state of the number of issues and total dollars of issues utilized in this cross-sectional test is provided in the Appendix, Table B. It should be noted that the following four states are unrepresented in both samples investigated: Alaska, Hawaii, Rhode Island, and Vermont.

[2]The dummy variable 1 = Mandatory System, 0 = Only Guidelines or no accounting related legislation resulted in a negative coefficient of -.2216 (.398), still lacking significance.

[3]The simple correlation of Net Interest Cost minus Bond Buyer's Index (NIC - BB) and the absence of audit legislation is -.0475, while (NIC - BB) and the audit by a private CPA are correlated .1217 for Hospital issues; -.0879 and .0114 respectively are the simple correlations for Pollution issues.

TABLE 5B. Frequency Table by State of the Number of Issues and Total Dollars of Issues Utilized in the 46 States' Cross-Sectional Multiple Regression Analysis

Key to Format of Statistics by State:

Total # Hospital Issues (# dropped from analysis due to lack of NIC information)

Total $ Hospital Issues (Total $ (000 omitted) Hospital Issues dropped from analysis due to lack of NIC information).

Total # Pollution Issues (# dropped from analysis due to lack of NIC information)

Total $ Pollution Issues (Total $ (000 omitted) Pollution Issues dropped from analysis due to lack of NIC information).

| AL | AK | AZ | AR | CA | CO | CN | DE | FL | GA | HI |
|---|---|---|---|---|---|---|---|---|---|---|
| 16 (7)<br>148.38<br>(22.9) | | 7<br>121.62 | 1<br>10.6 | 13 (2)<br>105.58<br>(12.76) | 5 (1)<br>29.87<br>(3.15) | 3<br>41.77 | | 4 (2)<br>44.34<br>(30.84) | 7 (2)<br>33<br>(7.52) | |
| 30 (8)<br>235.31<br>(34.36) | | 3 (1)<br>31.80<br>(3.10) | 6 (1)<br>34.85<br>(2.6) | 8 (1)<br>34.67<br>(10.70) | | | 2<br>34.70 | 15 (4)<br>147.74<br>(13.86) | 12<br>112.0 | |

| ID | IL | IN | IO | KS | KY | LA | ME | MD | MA | MI |
|---|---|---|---|---|---|---|---|---|---|---|
| 6<br>19.38 | 33 (5)<br>519.71<br>(62.89) | 13 (1)<br>72.16<br>(6.00) | 9<br>99.31 | 13<br>128.28 | 3<br>4.79 | 8<br>92.18 | 1<br>8.90 | 4<br>40.26 | 7<br>71.92 | 25 (2)<br>307.46<br>(11.91) |
| | 12 (3)<br>171.30<br>(13.70) | 8<br>170.90 | 6 (1)<br>48.45<br>(.75) | 3 (1)<br>46.22<br>(1.72) | 11 (1)<br>113.61<br>(1.20) | 20 (7)<br>243.96<br>(46.10) | 7<br>61.85 | 5 (3)<br>46.20<br>(15.20) | 1 (1)<br>2.80<br>(2.80) | 12 (5)<br>171.10<br>(58.0) |

| MN | MS | MO | MT | NE | NV | NH | NJ | NM | NC | NY |
|---|---|---|---|---|---|---|---|---|---|---|
| 42 (3)<br>156.5<br>(1.79) | 5 (3)<br>4.72<br>(.62) | 6 (1)<br>60.32<br>(8.10) | 2<br>5.35 | 4<br>30.08 | | 7 (1)<br>53.44<br>(4.22) | 4<br>25.03 | 4<br>19.06 | 8<br>71.05 | 14 (2)<br>349.81<br>(2.43) |
| 3<br>46.80 | | 4<br>50.92 | 3<br>72.90 | | 2 (1)<br>11.10<br>(1.10) | | 16 (5)<br>185.53<br>(66.54) | 3<br>115.00 | 1 (1)<br>2.50<br>(2.50) | 12 (3)<br>96.86<br>(3.85) |

| ND | OH | OK | OR | PA | RI | SC | SD | TN | TX | UT |
|---|---|---|---|---|---|---|---|---|---|---|
| | 20 (3)<br>366.51<br>(22.40) | 16<br>68.84 | 1<br>9.00 | 46 (6)<br>888.19<br>(34.90) | | 5<br>21.30 | 2<br>47.30 | 28 (7)<br>91.03<br>(22.80) | 24 (5)<br>82.33<br>(10.00) | 3<br>30.55 |
| 4<br>(52.60) | 24 (13)<br>194.02<br>(50.97) | 4<br>42.42 | 8 (1)<br>77.08<br>(1.00) | 29 (6)<br>397.40<br>(84.20) | | 2<br>21.65 | | 10 (7)<br>69.88<br>(18.23) | 29 (4)<br>524.36<br>(26.10) | 1<br>50.00 |

| VT | VA | WA | WV | WI | WY |
|---|---|---|---|---|---|
| | 12 (3)<br>133.21<br>(20.10) | 6 (1)<br>60.92 | 5<br>111.32 | 5 (1)<br>69<br>(32.0) | 5 (1)<br>12.25<br>(2.0) |
| | 12 (1)<br>119.40<br>(13.00) | | 11 (1)<br>133.65<br>(4.80) | 14 (5)<br>98.36<br>(11.90) | 7(1)<br>100.12<br>(2.80) |

TABLE 5C. NIC Correlated with State Regulation of Municipal Audit Practices (13-point scale: 1 = most comprehensive legislation)*

| Variable (Sample = 1975 and 1976 Hospital Issues by 46 states: Table B) | Kendall Rank-Order Correlation Coefficient (One-tailed test significance) (Kendall's tau) | Spearman Rank-Order Correlation Coefficient (One-tailed test significance) |
|---|---|---|
| NIC | -.1256 (.001) | -.1693 (.001) |
| NIC minus Bond Buyer's 20 Bond Index | -.1257 (.001) | -.1707 (.001) |

INTERPRETATION:

The ranking statistics suggest that the less comprehensive the audit legislation -- assuming the thirteen classification ordinal ranking -- the less the NIC of an issuer and the less the differential in NIC and the Bond Buyer's 20 Bond Index (NIC - BB). This ranking considers the requirement of private audits on an annual basis for all municipalities to be the most comprehensive form of legislation, and the auditor (private vs. state) distinction is considered to be a more important attribute than the frequency of the audit, which in turn is more important than the percent of units audited, in determining the extent of legislation.

*1 = 100% Audit by Private CPA. (N = 14 states)
2 = All Cities Audited by Private CPA. All Counties Audited by State Audit Arm. (N = 4)
3 = All Cities Audited by Private CPA. No Audit of Counties. (N = 3)
4 = 100% Audit by State Audit Arm Annually. (N = 1)
5 = 100% Audit by Private CPA less frequent than annually. (N = 2)
6 = 100% Audit by State Audit Arm less frequent than annually. (N = 2)
7 = Cities & Boroughs over a given size and counties Audited by Private CPA. (N = 1)
8 = Cities over a given size or in a given class subject to be Audited by Private CPA. All Counties Audited by State Audit Arm. (N = 2)
9 = Cities over a given size and Counties Audited by State Audit Arm. (N = 3)
10 = All Counties Audited by Private CPA. (N = 6)
11 = All Counties: State Audit Arm available, but Private CPA encouraged. (N = 1)
12 = Counties and School Districts Audited by State Audit Arm. (N = 4)
13 = No Required Audit. (N = 3)
(Note: Often PA is considered as acceptable as CPA by State Legislation).
(Petersen et. al., 1977 provide much of the information utilized to formulate the state legislation classification scheme.)

## Notes

[1]Neary provides the only quantitative analysis of the effect of a municipal state government program of which I am aware. He reports that the North Carolina Local Government Commission "appears to have increased the efficiency of the local bond market in North Carolina and helped municipalities to obtain significant cost savings."

[2]Evidence of widespread municipal audit practices prior to state regulation is presented in Wallace.

[3]For example, the State of Illinois Auditor General's expenditures in the fiscal year ending 9/30/77 were $5,307,444. The cash receipts of the auditor general for the same year were $27,676.

[4]It has been suggested that state audit legislation may alter expectations about such legislation as state bond banks. This is one example of potential state legislation which has been claimed to have favorable effects on interest cost but, in fact, on a governmental unit level, could have unfavorable effects. For example, legislation proposed and defeated in Illinois to formulate a state bond bank and float municipal issues in groups could lead to cross-subsidization from several smaller municipalities to Chicago and result in a greater number of municipal units bearing higher interest costs.

[5]The secondary market for tax-exempt securities is conducted almost entirely over the counter without an organized central market exchange. As a consequence, individual transactions occur among dealers, brokers, and retail customers without a general dissemination of information on such details as price and volume traded. The most comprehensive source of data on this market is the *Blue List of Current Municipal Offerings*, a daily financial publication, and it suffers from numerous shortcomings, e.g., advertised dealer inventories represent only a fraction of actual inventories and the listed "ask" prices or yields are likely to differ from the market clearing

price (Kenny).

[6]To test the correspondence between the NIC measure and bond yields, the regression model reported in Hastie, utilizing municipal bond yield as the dependent variable, was run for a small sample of Florida municipal bonds with NIC as the dependent variable. The signs of the variables correspond and the $R^2$ values for Hastie's sample and the Florida sample are similar.

[7]This interest rate computation is also referred to as the true interest cost, the bond book basis, the internal rate of return, and, for municipal bonds, the Canadian interest cost method.

[8]Prior to 1972 only one issuer (the Los Angeles Department of Water and Power) sold bonds on a PW basis; in 1976 there were 17 different issuers utilizing PW. Some jurisdictions currently require NIC by law, and preference for NIC due to familiarity by underwriters is evidenced in practice (Center for Capital Market Research).

[9]Displacements are unsuccessful competitive offerings due to no bids being submitted, rejection of bids, or postponement of issues. The figure typically does not include offerings of less than $500,000. It should be noted that an offering with several displacements is counted once unless it has substantially increased the amount offered at a later time or a year's difference in offering date occurs.

[10]Revenue sharing is defined as the amounts paid to other governments as fiscal aid in the form of shared revenues and grants-in-aid, as reimbursements for performance of general government activities and for specific services for the paying government, or in lieu of taxes.

[11]This index is the result of averaging the market value expressed in terms of yield on bonds (general obligations only) of the following issues with Moody's Bond Rating shown parenthetically: California (Aaa), Georgia (Aaa), Illinois (Aaa), North Carolina (Aaa), Chicago (Aa), Columbus, OH (Aa), Denver (Aa), Florida (Aa), Hawaii (Aa),

Memphis (Aa), Washington (Aa), Baltimore (A1), Cleveland (A), Massachusetts (A1), Nassau Co., NY (A1), New Orleans (A), New York State (A), Pittsburgh (A), St. Louis (A), Boston (Baa). Specific issues are not used in compiling these averages. Basis prices used are those applicable to a bond having a maturity of about 20 years and selling at a price close to par. The average rating of the 20 bonds used in this index falls midway between the four top groups as classified by Moody's Investors Service.

[12]This is a pledge of revenue from a specified income-generating facility such as a toll road or an electric power utility (and, increasingly, from rentals of industrial plants). The issues are not ordinarily guaranteed, but typically a system of sinking funds and operating controls is set up to assure investors that the financial affairs of the facility will be maintained in good order and all commitments honored.

[13]This bond is backed by the full faith and credit of the issuer. The issuer has pledged himself to raise funds by whatever means are required, including a tax increase or sale of property, in order to honor its full faith and credit.

[14]It should be noted that claims of bureaucrats are not limited, i.e., the assertions suggest that 100 percent of the time lower NIC will be observed.

[15]This converts to the $Pr\left[\frac{b_0 - \beta_0}{SE_{b_0}} \geq \frac{.7479 - (-.3093)}{.188}\right] = Pr[t_{394-12} \geq 5.623]$.

[16]These legislative attributes were utilized in an auxiliary, ceteris paribus, test of the ordinal relationship between varied forms of legislation and NIC. As discussed earlier, regulation imposes costs on governmental units, and these costs are likely to be positively correlated with the extensiveness of the state legislation. If the net interest cost of municipalities is reflecting the cost

of regulation as hypothesized in section 3, the interest cost would be expected to be lower for states with less extensive audit legislation. Preliminary evidence that such a relationship exists--given acceptance of the ordinal ranking of the extent of legislation--and is significant at a .001 level is presented in appendix table 5.C.

[17]Recent actions by the City of Columbus to arrange an agreement with the Ohio Auditor General that independent CPAs' reports be accepted in place of auditor general activities cited this key problem of timeliness: "In addition, certain audit reports were of little value because of their untimely completion, sometimes being issued long after a subgrantee agency (the auditee) became extinct" (Dorrian, p. 51).

[18]Individual issue information controlled by means of regression analysis for Florida bonds was unavailable for the State of Tennessee; therefore a t-test analysis was performed.

[19]The T-value presented is computed by forming the paired difference variable $D = X_1 - X_2$, where $X_1$ is the bond rating before legislation and $X_2$ is the rating after. D is normally distributed with mean $\delta$. The sample mean and variance ($\bar{d}$ and $s_{\bar{d}}^2$) are computed, and then $t = \frac{\bar{d} - \delta}{s_{\bar{d}}}$

degrees of freedom = n-1 where n is the number of pairs, and

$$s_{\bar{d}} = \sqrt{\left(s_1^2 + s_2^2 - \frac{2\ \Sigma S_1\ X_2}{n-1}\right) / n}$$

where $(\Sigma\ X_{1i}\ X_{2i})/(n-1)$ is the covariance between $X_1$ and $X_2$.

[20]Out of the 185 ratings analyzed, there were 23 changes in ratings, i.e., 12 percent of the municipalities and each of these changes was an improvement. Hence, it is likely that use of an ordinal assumption-based statistical technique would yield similar results.

## References

Alexander Grant & Co. "Municipal Accounting and Reporting: Issues for Research." University of Texas at Austin Conference, Nov. 11-12, 1976.

*The Bond Buyer's Municipal Finance Statistics.* Research ed. Joan Lulkovich. New York: 1974, 1976-78.

Center for Capital Market Research. "Improving Bidding Rules to Reduce Interest Costs in the Competitive Sale of Municipal Bonds." University of Oregon in cooperation with Municipal Finance Officers Association of the United States and Canada. Eugene, Oregon, 1977.

*The Daily Bond Buyer*, vol. 243, no. 25321. New York: The Bond Buyer, Friday, March 10, 1978, p. 4/p. 876 cumulative.

Daniel, Wayne W. *Applied Nonparametric Statistics.* Boston: Houghton-Mifflin Company, 1978.

Davidson, S.; Green, D. O.; Hellerstein, W.; Madansky, A.; Weil, R. L. *Financial Reporting by State and Local Government Units.* Chicago: University of Chicago Press, 1977.

Dorrian, H. "Reliance on Audits Performed by Others." *Governmental Finance* (May 1977).

Hastie, K. L. "Determinants of Municipal Bond Yields." *Journal of Financial and Quantitative Analysis* (June 1972): 1729-48.

Jensen, M., and Meckling, W. "Theory of the Firm: Managerial Behavior, Agency Costs and Ownership Structure." *Journal of Financial Economics* (October 1976): 305-60.

Kenny, John J. "The Secondary Market in Municipal Bonds." In *State and Local Public Facility Needs and Financing*, vol. 2 (Washington: U.S. Government Printing Office, 1966).

Kidwell, D. S. "The Ex-Ante Cost of Call Provisions on State and Local Government Bonds." *Journal of Economics and Business* (Fall 1977): 73-78.

Klapper, B. "Tell and Sell: Wall Street is Forcing Cities to Disclose More When Floating Bonds. Underwriters Hold up Issues to Back New Guidelines; A Boom for the Investor. Same Rules for All Players?" *The Wall Street Journal*, June 30, 1977, pp. 1, 23.

Local Fiscal Assistance Amendments of 1976. Fiscal Assistance to State and Local Governments, Regulations Governing the Payment of Entitlements under Title I of the State and Local Fiscal Assistance Act of 1972, 31 Code of Federal Regulations, Subtitle B. Part 51 (Department of the Treasury, Office of Revenue Sharing, November, 1977).

Neary, Robert. "N. C. Local Government Commission Cuts Municipalities Borrowing Costs." *The Daily Bond Buyer*, August 30, 1972, p. 32, and Securities Industry Association, "Municipal Market Developments," (February 1976), p. 1.

"News Report." *The Journal of Accountancy* (January 1978): 20.

Peat, Marwick, Mitchell & Co. "Comparative Analysis of Audit Requirements." *Selling Municipal Securities--What You Need to Know*. Municipal Bond Seminar, February 19, 1976.

Petersen, J. E.; Cole, L. A.; and Petrillo, M. L. *Watching and Counting: A Survey of State Assistance to and Supervision of Local Debt and Financial Administration*. National Conference of State Legislatures and Municipal Finance Officers Association (October 1977).

Sommer, A. A., Jr. "Municipal Disclosure and Accountability Must Increase." *The Money Manager*, December 1, 1975, pp. 3, 5, 26, 27.

U.S. Department of Commerce. *State Government Finances in 1975*. August 1976, p. 43.

U.S. Department of Commerce. *State Government Finances in 1976*. August 1977, p. 15.

U.S. Senate, Securities Subcommittee of Committee on Banking,

Housing, and Urban Affairs. *Municipal Securities Full Disclosure Act of 1976: Hearings on S. 2969* (Remarks of Senator Thomas F. Eagleton). 94th Cong., 2d session (February 24, 1976), pp. 15-16.

*Wall Street Journal*, May 12, 1978, p. 14.

Wallace, Wanda A. "Required Disclosure and the Municipal Market: An Evaluation of the Need for Extension of the Securities Law to Municipalities." Working paper, Graduate School of Management, The University of Rochester (December 1978).

Watts, Ross. "Corporate Financial Statements, A Product of the Market and Political Processes." *Australian Journal of Management* (April 1977): 53-75.

"Williams Introduces Revised Bill." *The Journal of Accountancy* (January 1978): 3.

# A Comment on Wanda A. Wallace's "The Effect of State Accounting and Auditing Regulations on Municipal Borrowing Costs and Bond Ratings"

Paul Rosenfield

American Institute of Certified Public Accountants

Professor Wallace has gone the sponsors of this conference one better. They focus on government regulation of accounting; she focuses on government regulation of government accounting, that is, federal government regulation of the accounting of state and local government. Here, questions of sovereignty and states' rights further complicate the usual problems of regulation of the private sector. And in fact the federal government and, to a considerable extent, the accounting profession as well traditionally have kept hands off such state and local government accounting. Rule-making has been left to state and local government accountants, who use as a guide "Governmental Accounting, Auditing, and Financial Reporting" (GAAFR), a publication of the National Council on Governmental Accounting (NCGA). The Financial Accounting Standards Board (FASB) has not yet established standards in the area. The AICPA has issued an audit and accounting guide of its own, but it generally embraces the previously published GAAFR and the group generally cooperates with the NCGA.

## Timely Study

Professor Wallace's study is timely. Since the New

York City financial debacle and then Cleveland's problems, it has been said with some justification that the governmental area is where the action is in financial accounting. The following developments highlight some of that action.

1. Senator Williams announced (*The Wall Street Journal*, 2/6/79) plans to reintroduce federal legislation intended to regulate state and local governmental accounting and financial reporting, a simplified version of his previous bills on which Professor Wallace focuses.

2. The FASB plans to issue a statement of financial accounting concepts for nonbusiness organizations, including state and local governments. *The Wall Street Journal* (2/7/79) reported that the FASB and the NCGA have agreed to cooperate in setting standards in the area.

3. The NCGA just issued a revision of GAAFR, reflecting developments since it was first published in 1968.

4. The AICPA's *Journal of Accountancy* devoted virtually all of its March 1979 issue to state and local government accounting and information, with articles discussing what the standards should be and who should set them.

5. The AICPA's Committee on State and Local Governmental Accounting is sponsoring an experiment in which cities across the country will be asked to apply novel accounting principles designed to simplify their financial statements and to revise the information to make it more useful to citizens, investors, and others.

6. Public accounting firms have sponsored studies and offered innovative services related to state and local government accounting.

## Fair Target

Professor Wallace has addressed a fair target. The sponsors of such legislation have made assertions about the benefits it will bring to the subjects of regulation--the issuers of the financial information. Claims that federally mandated audits with uniform standards will bring lower interest costs and more bids on bond issues have been written into the legislation, as Professor Wallace states. During hearings held in 1976, Senator Williams asserted that similar state legislation had resulted in lower borrowing costs to taxpayers and that in the absence of nationwide legislation, there would be less total municipal borrowing and at higher interest rates.

The sponsors of the legislation evidently were responding to the political realities of the situation. They apparently felt they could not propose legislation and tell a group as influential as state and local governmental units that it would be bad for their financial health. Furthermore, issuers have not shown the gratitude that might be expected. Their testimony at the hearings suggests that they believe federal legislation a bane rather than a boon.

Professor Wallace's continual reference to federal officials as "bureaucrats" reflects a healthy skepticism of the benefits of increased federal regulation. Her skepticism indicates perhaps a perception that the law of the hammer--a little boy with a hammer suddenly discovers that everything needs hammering--also might apply to federal regulation. And she certainly is justified in suspecting that federal legislation might not result in lower interest and more bond bids. If the circumstances of New York City and Cleveland are even suggestive of circumstances elsewhere, the opposite result seems more reasonable--that sounder information would discourage rather than encourage investment in state and local government obligations. Independent audits of previously unaudited financial statements of cities and states could as likely be expected to reveal a mess as to reveal gilt-edged security.

## Strong Case

Professor Wallace's paper presents a strong prima

facie case that the introduction of state legislation mandating audits resulted in higher interest costs and fewer bids. I am not an expert in empirical research of this type, but I cannot fault her methods or conclusion. Anyone wishing to promote federal legislation mandating audits of state and local governmental financial statements based on predictions of lower interest and more bids should from now on feel obliged to discredit her research methods, replicate her research with different findings, or demonstrate that federal legislation would have effects different from those of state legislation.

There is a danger, however, that her findings will be ignored rather than confronted. This means we accountants must not only be vigilant in testing assertions of non-accountants but also in communicating our findings to them convincingly. Perhaps Professor Wallace should put her findings in bureaucratese rather than academese and testify at public hearings on this year's bill if they are held.

## Keep Perspective

I think that in spite of the persuasiveness of Professor Wallace's conclusions, we should keep the research in perspective. After all, she is only attacking *one* of the reasons given in support of the legislation, and a reason that was not necessarily the most important in the minds of the sponsors.

She rightly places the burden of proof back on the supporters of the legislation, but the particular burden she places on them is too heavy and is unjustified. She says that they must "argue that a net marginal benefit accrues from federal legislation that does not or could not result from state legislation with respect to the claimed market effect." Thus, Professor Wallace would require the proponents to justify the legislation solely on the basis of benefits to the *issuers* of securities.

Maybe such legislation should not be enacted. But

there are other reasons that could be advanced in its favor, and some have been put forward by its proponents and even in the bills themselves. Professor Wallace gives only passing mention of one such reason. She says that the stated rationale of bill S2339 "includes the protection of investors. . . ." That is only part of a phrase stated repeatedly in the bill: "in the public interest and for the protection of investors."

The origin of the legislation was the federal assistance voted New York City in 1975. Congress wanted to be sure the need would not be repeated there or elsewhere. They were not looking for protection *for* the issuers; they wanted protection *from* the issuers, protection for the investors and the public purse that had suffered at the hands of issuers who threatened to default. Since poor accounting and reporting were believed to have contributed to deceiving investors, the conclusion that the federal hands-off policy should be ended was understandable.

Unfortunately, whether federal legislation would be a net benefit to the *users* of financial statements of state and local governmental units is a complex question not susceptible to the relatively simple empirical testing available for interest rates and bond bids.

Even the interest question is more complex than Professor Wallace implies: mandatory audits could have longer term effects that might not show up over the relatively short periods covered by her tests. If the audits reveal, for example, previously unknown poor record-keeping, poor accounting control, false reporting, mismanagement, negligence, fraud, the use of long-term borrowing for operating purposes, or insolvency--in other words, if they describe the present conditions of more than one U.S. city--confidence in the bonds involved naturally would decline, bids would dry up, and interest rates would climb. But revealing those conditions could set the stage for their correction, for fiscal responsibility that could eventually put the market for municipal bonds on firmer footing than ever. We would then not be inclined to look back nostalgically to what one witness at the public hearings called "the dream world" when bonds were bought on the faith that governments could always tax enough to pay off--in the days before Howard Jarvis and Proposition 13.

Other advantages of such legislation that have been advanced are improved and standardized accounting, auditing, and financial reporting and greater access to the antifraud provisions of the Securities Acts by persons defrauded.

The advantages and disadvantages of federal legislation to attain those goals are matters of judgment about relative costs and benefits and about the common good, which is the essence of the political process. While we should use all our tools to test testable propositions, we should recognize that complex questions such as the merits of this legislation are decided on the basis of a number of considerations, some of which do not lend themselves completely to objective analysis.

In conclusion, I compliment Professor Wallace on her choice of subject and thorough treatment of it. I encourage her and others to continue to ferret out uncertain assertions and predictions and provide a solid base of fact on which important decisions can be soundly made, such as whether to support federal regulation of state and local governmental accounting. Then, any resulting legislation will be seen by the public as a good bill and not a bill of goods.

# A Comment on Wanda A. Wallace's "The Effect of State Accounting and Auditing Regulations on Municipal Borrowing Costs and Bond Ratings"

Katherine Schipper

Carnegie-Mellon University

Professor Wallace's paper can be interpreted on at least two not unrelated levels. A normative level involves the question of whether the federal government should require municipalities to be audited. A positive or statistical descriptive level provides evidence on certain effects of state legislation requiring municipalities to be audited. I shall discuss the paper on this second level, beginning with Wallace's qualitative consideration of the likely effects of required audits and concluding with the empirical portion of the paper.

## Expected Effects of Audit Legislation

Wallace considers the effects of state legislation requiring municipal audits on the cost to municipalities of borrowing money. One view--and this is the one she wishes to debunk--is that required audits will lower interest costs and perhaps raise bond ratings, because, presumably, municipalities that are good credit risks will be more readily identified based on audited rather than unaudited statements. An alternative is Wallace's point that good credit risks can identify themselves regardless of audit legislation because they are free to contract with auditing firms. My own conclusion is that in equilibrium cost-minimizing local municipal managers already will have contracted for the optimal amount of auditing. If so, we would expect audit legislation to be irrelevant to borrowing cost. The only change is that certain municipalities will have to pay for audits they don't want.

Wallace discusses credit risk at some length. Risky municipal bonds, she says, are risky (i.e., they pay more than the risk-free rate) both because it costs resources to monitor municipal managers to ensure against fraud and because the municipality may have inadequate resources to pay its creditors. But, she continues, since auditing is inefficient relative to other monitoring mechanisms such as bond covenants, we can disregard this source of cost. Default costs, on the other hand, are increased by audit legislation to the extent that municipalities must alter their accounting systems and pay for undesired audits (thus consuming resources). If monitoring costs are largely unaltered, Wallace's specification of interest cost indicates that any *change* in interest cost is due mostly to the increase in default costs. I don't know how big audit fees and accounting system costs are relative to the assets of municipalities, but I would guess that they are small. In fact, I believe that any municipality whose default risk is appreciably increased by having to pay for an audit is probably so close to bankruptcy from other causes that its borrowing cost will be quite high anyway.

If audit legislation is essentially irrelevant to borrowing costs, I would expect an estimated coefficient of zero on the presence or absence of audit legislation in a well-specified model of municipal borrowing costs. If the default costs and monitoring costs discussed by Wallace have the form and effect she specifies, I would expect this coefficient to be positive but surely not very large.

If, on the other hand, audits appreciably reduce monitoring costs, we might expect a reduction in borrowing costs, based again on the relation Wallace specifies. Such an effect might occur if municipal officials were not minimizing borrowing costs by optimal audit contracts, in the absence of legislation. Then state officials would be making taxpayers better off by requiring audits that reduce borrowing costs.

Note that either of these contrasting hypotheses requires that one set of elected agents acts on behalf of taxpayers in arranging for audits while the other set does not. It may be difficult to explain why local officials would contract for the optimal amount of auditing, while state officials insist on (and succeed in) raising taxpayer costs by requiring more than the optimal level of auditing. It is equally difficult to explain why local officials would persist in non-optimal auditing behavior, while state officials would act optimally. Either hypothesis requires that elected officials act differently depending on their level (state or local) and that one group persistently acts in a way that makes taxpayers worse off.

In this paper, Wallace gives no consideration to these conflicting hypotheses and makes no progress toward a theory which predicts which set (if either) of elected officials is acting optimally with regard to auditing. We may, therefore, feel more comfortable if we begin by ignoring one side of the problem, assuming an equilibrium in which local elected officials have acted rationally to minimize borrowing costs. We then assume the amount of auditing existing before state legislation is optimal. Keeping in mind that this assumption (and its implication that audit legislation is largely irrelevant to borrowing costs) may be invalid (i.e., not supported by data), we can proceed to the empirical portion of the paper.

## Empirical Results

Wallace conducts two kinds of tests: for cross-sectional differences in borrowing costs for 46 states for two years and tests for over-time differences in the same state. I will treat these in turn. (One additional preliminary remark is in order. Lest we be unable to proceed at all, I will grant at the outset the validity of Wallace's measure of interest cost even though it does not take into account the time value of money.)

Tests of 46 States

From appendix table 5.A we see that four OLS regressions are reported for hospital bonds and pollution bonds. The dependent variable is always a measure of interest cost, but the set of independent variables is different for each equation. The independent variables of greatest interest are the presence of audit legislation in regression number 4 and the presence of various attributes of auditing (regressions 1-3). Assuming that regression 4 is well specified, we can infer that the absence of audit legislation has no effect on hospital bond cost different from zero at any reasonable significance level, but this same absence lowers pollution bond costs by about a third of a percentage point. Unless these results are spurious (i.e., due to statistical peculiarities of the sample or the model), pollution and hospital bonds interest costs are different with respect to audits. Given the hypothesis of the paper, I can see no ready explanation for this difference.

The other three regressions provide the basis for tests of a hypothesis that is not suggested in the paper. This hypothesis is that, given required audits, the attributes of the requirement should affect borrowing costs. Three attributes are considered: who audits, who is audited, and how frequent are the audits. Although Wallace predicts nothing about these, I would like to comment on them. If the regressions are well specified, we can think of dummy variables as ways of allowing for different classes of observations, while the constant is common to all classes of observations. (The fact that so many of the constants in table 5.A are negative is superficial evidence of misspecification.) Then the coefficient on "mandatory use of private CPA" can be thought of as the incremental borrowing costs associated with this class of observations, over and above the cost, contained in the constant, common to *all* classes. We can, therefore, compute the incremental borrowing cost of belonging to certain classes simply by adding the coefficients attached to those classes. Ignoring specification problems, we can draw the following conclusion from regression 1 in table 5.A: if we wish to decrease our hospital borrowing cost by .9 percent, relative to the no-audit case, we should require that state auditors audit 100 percent of municipalities, annually. Allowing both private CPA's and state auditors to be used reduces this improvement to .77 percent. Mandating only private CPA's increases hospital bond costs relative to the no-audit case (394-item sample) by .75 percent but has no impact on pollution bond costs.

Taking the results in table 5.A at face value, we must conclude that the absence of audit legislation has no appreciable effect on hospital bond costs, but this absence decreases pollution bond costs. At the same time quite comprehensive audit legislation, requiring state auditors exclusively, lowers borrowing costs. Clearly, these results are inconsistent both among themselves and with Wallace's hypothesis. They indicate that the audit attribute measures are proxying for something else or that the regressions are somehow misspecified, or both.

When specific risk (as measured by revenue vs. general obligation) is used to separate hospital bonds into two classes, the general obligation bonds as a class have lower interest cost by 1.2 percent. I suspect this designation is a proxy for some economic variable that changed over time, that in 1975 bonds of mostly one type (revenue or general obligation) were issued and in 1976 mostly bonds of the other kind. Since the effects of changes over time are otherwise omitted variables, we cannot draw any other conclusions about this possibility. But because there is at least prima facie evidence in support of the notion that some variable which changed over time has some explanatory power, it might be interesting to run the two years separately and compare the results.

Finally, a word about the observations themselves. With several hundred observations over 46 states (and some number of cities within states), several bond issues can be associated with the same city or state. What this means is that some independent variables do not vary for certain subsets of the data. If all cities within a state are mutually dependent on relevant variables, then we have 46 independent observations. If all bonds issued by the same city are dependent along relevant variables, then we have independent observations equal, at most, to the number of cities. This presence of dependent observations may help account for some of the empirical results, if the following conditions are met: (1) characteristics of bonds depend on the state or city in which they are issued; (2) high interest costs due to various economic events at the state level have prompted mandatory audits by private CPAs. Then the audit legislation will be (spuriously) associated with high interest cost for the sample as a whole.

## Tests Over Time

Bonds in three states were observed before and after audits were required to see if interest cost, bond ratings, or number of bids submitted changed. The number of bids submitted for Florida, the only state for which bids were studied, appears to be unrelated to the variables considered by Wallace (table 5.3). The other two variables, bond ratings and interest cost, deserve more consideration.

The change in bond rating was converted to a dependent variable by taking the difference between a pre-audit-legislation bond's rating and a post-audit-legislation bond's rating. But, as Wallace points out, bond ratings are ordinal, so it is not reasonable to do arithmetic operations (such as subtraction) on them. For differencing to have any meaning, the "distances" between categories must be defined by fixed and equal units. The "difference in bond rating" variable, therefore, has no properties on which a statistical analysis can be based.

In all the over-time regressions, the constant is interpreted by Wallace as capturing the change over time in bids or interest cost, assuming that the over-time change is due to audit requirements. This approach is reasonable whenever we have accounted for all other relevant variables which may have changed over the time period in question. This condition is not met in Wallace's paper, since in general, the presence of a negative or very small adjusted $R^2$ indicates that we have not controlled for many of these changes. Therefore, we can only conclude that *something* occurred (or changed) in the time interval under consideration; we cannot identify the source of the change as audit legislation.

## Tests of Coefficients

One test that appears repeatedly concerns the "confidence regions" of the estimated coefficients. As described by Wallace, this test computes the probability of obtaining a particular estimated coefficient, given that audit legislation lowers borrowing costs. What this test in fact does is to quantify the null hypothesis of lowered costs in terms of the *estimated* coefficient. Consider the first appearance of the test as an example. The null hypothesis as Wallace presents it is empirically represented by a number which is 1.645 times the standard error of the estimated coefficient, where Wallace chooses 1.645 because it represents the .95 level for a one-sided t-test, with degrees of freedom greater than 120. But this is inappropriate, because the null hypothesis as stated in the paper is not that the true coefficient is 1.645 times the standard error of the estimated coefficient. The null hypothesis is merely that the true coefficient is negative. This is a statement about confidence regions and is implicitly Bayesian. We can, therefore, say that the probability is .998 that the parameter lies between 1.33 and .167, given a diffuse prior, an estimated parameter of .7479, a standard error of .188, and degrees of freedom larger than 120.

## Some Suggestions

One alternative way to approach the question "Do state laws requiring municipal audits reduce borrowing costs?" is to begin by assuming the kind of competitive equilibrium discussed in section 1. In this equilibrium, all municipal units for which it is optimal (in the sense of reduced borrowing costs) to be audited have already contracted for audits. Then state legislation merely requires that a more-than-optimal amount of auditing will be done. The empirical questions then become: (1) how much worse off does this make the municipalities, and (2) where would we expect this effect to appear? The answer to the first is probably "not much" and the answer to the second is probably "in slightly higher administrative expense, to be reflected in slightly higher property taxes or slightly lower levels of service." In particular, we would not, under these assumptions, expect any measurable effect on borrowing costs.

In the context of this alternative approach, one might want to consider several changes in the empirical tests.

1. Attempt to obtain independent bond issues, even if many observations must be sacrificed. Alternatively, explicitly allow for dependence.

2. Eliminate bond ratings as a dependent variable entirely. Presumably these are relevant only if they affect interest cost, so the logical way to consider them is as independent variables.

3. Ascertain if certain audit attributes are proxying for economic variables and take account of these when "holding other things constant."

4. Insofar as possible, use some sort of yield as a measure of interest cost, unless, of course, this would

result in an unreasonably small number of observations.

## Conclusion

The issue of effects of state (or federal) mandates of municipal audits is interesting both in itself and as part of the larger issue of centralized vs. decentralized government and regulation. As the author points out, however, there is not a great deal of theory to guide the empiricist in this area. Nevertheless, structuring the empirical question in simple intuitive terms and relying on straightforward statistical tests will lead to insights which could be obtained in more or less strictly empirical studies.

# A Reply

Wanda A. Wallace

University of Rochester

The "audit revelation" effect proposed by Paul Rosenfield seems unlikely to occur *with* legislation, since--as suggested in section 2 of my paper--"evidence of widespread municipal audit practices *prior* to state regulation" exists.

I would hypothesize that many other "possible" effects of regulation will crumble as quickly as the market effect and revelation assertion in the face of empirical evidence. The evidence, to date, makes one question the validity of legislators' entire analysis.

Katherine Schipper's hypothesis that, in an equilibrium, cost-minimizing municipal managers will already have contracted for the optimal amount of auditing is consistent with widespread voluntary audits prior to legislation; however, her implication that audit legislation would therefore be irrelevant to borrowing cost is *dissipated* by (1) the effect on municipalities not desiring audits in cost/benefit terms, (2) the possibility of borrowing cost minimization diverging from utility maximization at the municipal level, (3) the regulation costs (the magnitude of such costs has been widely discussed at this conference), and (4) the constrained decision-making which results from increased state (or federal) control. The concurrent signal of increased probability of additional state legislation and the consequent loss of taxing power on the municipal unit level would be expected to affect borrowing cost. Hence, a conclusion *cannot* be drawn as to the effect of audit legislation on a purely theoretical basis; it is an empirical question. The point of this research effort is to test the common assertion that audit legislation has a favorable market effect.

This paper provides *initial* evidence on empirical relationships in the municipal sector; these results, as do the discussants' comments, raise several interesting research questions that warrant future investigation. However, to reconfirm the insights gained from this research effort, I will respond quickly to the technical issues raised by Professor Schipper.

(1) The constant term of the regression is positive in the hospital sample controlling for bond classification, and the research result is consistent with the larger sample--both indicating no significant favorable association between net interest cost and audit legislation.

(2) The claim of inconsistency of results is due to comparison of hospital bond implications to pollution bond results. The paper is not intended to explain the difference *between* the sample results, only the *consistency within* the samples in terms of NOT INDICATING ANY SIGNIFICANT FAVORABLE EFFECT ON THE MARKET.

(3) The separate year regression results for the 46-state sample were compared as a basis for presenting the larger sample results; hence changes in the included variables over time are not the determinants of the regression results. Similarly, since the hospital model controlling for bond class includes only 1976 issues, a shift in the type of bonds between years is irrelevant.

(4) The dependent observation criticism is in error. The assumption that "all bonds issued by the same city are dependent along relevant variables" is inapplicable to the study's regressions, which involve independent variables geared to the general market, the state, and *issue* attributes. The dependent variable, net interest cost, is also a *per issue* attribute. The use of repeated observations

simply adds precision to estimates and, in fact, is a common econometric technique with respect to tests for linearity and inclusion of dummy variables. In no sense is it correct to claim a reduced sample size of 46.

(5) An analysis of means and standard deviations of demographic variables classified on the 13-point scale reported in appendix table 5.C was performed in the initial stage of the research effort to avoid the obvious "coincidence" of audit legislation and demographic characteristics like tax burden per capita.

(6) There is no significant difference in the mean net interest cost of Illinois, Washington, Ohio, and Michigan; hence the criminal impetus to legislation would not appear to be a distinguishing factor of Illinois.

(7) The tests of coefficients, as discussed in the manuscript, give the benefit of a doubt to legislators by only requiring 95 percent confidence that the legislative effect be favorable, in light of results that find unfavorable or *insignificant* effects. The null is not an insignificant negative coefficient. There is a clear directional prediction by bureaucrats which asserts that 100 percent of the time lower net interest costs will be observed.

(8) Bond ratings are of interest due to real effects. For example, if bonds fall to noninvestment grade, transaction costs are incurred in selling such bonds out of portfolios, and the potential market for particular bonds shrinks due to such institutional requirements.

In conclusion, the evidence presented suggests that the burden of proof is on supporters of federal legislation to justify further their proposals.

6

# Synthesis

Nicholas Dopuch

University of Chicago

The synthesizer, according to the dictionary, should combine individual parts into a complex whole. Unfortunately, the papers presented at this conference were not limited to any single issue concerning regulation. My task would have been easier, for example, had the conference been organized around the obvious question of whether accounting should even be regulated, with all the arguments and evidence for and against regulating markets in general and the accounting information market in particular. Or, given that accounting is and probably will continue to be regulated, the conference could have stressed the issue of appropriate institutional framework for carrying out the objectives of accounting regulation. In recent years this has centered on the extent to which accounting should be regulated by a public or private agency such as the FASB. Or finally, there is the question of operational criteria, including studies on costs and benefits of alternative disclosure rules, to guide policy makers in their choices of accounting methods.

Although a focus on any one of these issues would have made a synthesis easier, it would have been impractical to limit a conference such as this to any single issue, if for no other reason than that various subtopics of regulation are not completely independent. To illustrate, I doubt I personally could come to a conclusion either in favor of or against regulation of markets without recognizing the operational problems encountered in making optimal social choices, regardless of whether we opt for private or public regulatory agencies.

The papers here fall along the entire spectrum of regulation issues, and perhaps it will be most useful to organize my synthesis of them in terms of the three issues noted above: the regulation of accounting, the appropriate institutional framework for such regulation, and the operational criteria for specific regulations.

## Should Accounting be Regulated?[1]

This question may seem somewhat rhetorical since the SEC Acts of 1933 and 1934 give the agency authority to regulate accounting measurements and disclosures, perhaps even to the point of issuing generally accepted accounting principles. Recall, however, that prior to the passage of the SEC Acts, decisions regarding the production and dissimination of financial information were made by private agents in what we might describe as a "free market setting." Arguments for moving to a regulated market setting for accounting are based on two types of alleged market failures. The first concerns public goods. An attribute of a public good is that it is difficult to limit the property rights of such goods only to those who pay for their acquisitions. One commonly used example is national defense. Anyone living within national borders will benefit from the defense of the nation and in a sense can freeload off those who pay for its creation and maintenance. Stated differently, the consumption or enjoyment of national defense services by one citizen does not reduce its supply to another. And if it is not otherwise possible to exclude nonpurchasers of a good from enjoying its benefits, a rational agent will not pay for these benefits.

Information is sometimes regarded as a public good,

since the receipt of information by one person need not destroy its usefulness to another. As an illustration, one person's reading of a newspaper does not reduce the information content of that paper. If timing of information is not an issue, a person might be willing to wait for another to discard the paper, thus freeloading on the first person's purchase. Indeed, we see this going on in libraries every day.

Financial information about firms may be a public good also since the use of that information to assess the probability distribution of future returns of securities by one person does not reduce its ability to serve the same function for other individuals. If this is true, then we no longer are justified in relying on regular arguments about the efficiency of competitive markets to lead to optimal allocations of society's resources to the production and dissimination of information.

I have no intention of getting into a debate about whether financial information is a public good. Too much probably has been made about this whole issue. Moreover, even if a commodity does have the characteristics of a public good, this does not rule out the possibility that market systems still can govern its production and dissimination. The public good factor merely changes the nature of the types of market systems which might be efficient.

A second type of market failure offered in support of the regulation of accounting is the existence of externalities or discriminatory conditions regarding the production and perhaps availability of information. A major problem arising in a market system for financial information stems from the fact that firms' managements possess monopolistic advantages concerning the information they could produce about their firms' activities. Outsiders simply cannot compete effectively with management in producing information about firms' activities. As a result we do not observe a competitive market on the supply side of financial information.

This particular type of market failure seems to be the major one relied on to justify the SEC's disclosure laws and its mandated audits. That is, in the absence of competitive sources of financial information, managements may attempt to withhold (or be selective as to who receives) information which would be detrimental to the firm's interests, even though such information is desired by outsiders. Hence, the need for disclosure laws. Similarly since management controls the source(s) of information provided to outsiders, audits are imposed in order to provide assurance of the veracity of that information.

These classes of market failures are the traditional ones we find in the economic literature in discussions of when (whether) government intervention into markets is justified. Note that each refers to a broad class of market failures. As such, however, they are not inconsistent with the arguments raised by Elliott and Schuetze in the first part of their paper, which also deals with the issue of whether accounting should be regulated. These authors offer six specific criteria which might be used in evaluating government regulations. However some of these are subsumed in the above class of market failure arguments. For example, their criteria numbers 2 and 3 stated on p. 109 refer to the prevention of real or probable social damage and the furthering of the public interest. The first is subsumed under the externality argument and the second under the public goods arguments. Their fourth and fifth criteria are subsumed in the general assumption that free market settings lead to more efficient allocations of society's resources in the absence of market failures. Criteria 1 and 6 do not relate to market operations but to legal issues with which, as they recognize, regulations were not supposed to deal in the first place.

Now the existence of market failures, whether general or specific, do not constitute both necessary and sufficient conditions for government regulations. In effect market failures merely indicate that an information market may not be able to function in the same manner as traditional competitive markets which are characterized by competing parties supplying and demanding a particular good or service. However, other types of market arrangements could be efficient in such allocations. At a theoretical level these are developed in part by Gonedes and Dopuch[2] based on some earlier work of Gonedes. At a more informal level, arguments along these lines are advanced by Kripke, whose central theme is that there are sufficient economic incentives for managers, exchanges, underwriters, and other groups to enter into negotiations about what information should be disclosed about firms' activities. In reading his paper, though, I was not sure whether he was advocating the demise of the SEC or merely a curbing of its future regulatory powers.

Recall that prior to the SEC acts, informal systems like the ones advocated by Kripke did exist in the U.S. and even exist today in the U.K.[3] as a substitute to government control over the information markets. However, some convincing arguments for regulation must have been advanced in the early 1930s to support the passage of the SEC Acts. The question today is whether the same arguments hold or whether we now can move to a freer market setting for information.

Like Kripke, George Benston also offers intuitively appealing alternatives to regulation, but neither provides formal proofs or direct empirical evidence that informal arrangements between firms, underwriting houses, and other "powerful" groups *dominate* a regulatory solution to the determination of optimal allocations of resources. This dominance issue is a difficult one to resolve, and I do not know of anyone who has provided conclusive empirical evidence in favor of one or the other alternative.

In the end, the acceptance of arguments in favor either of regulation or of free-market settings often depends more on our personal biases and experience rather than on the direct evidence at hand. I think this shows up particularly in Sandy Burton's paper. As a chief accountant of the SEC, he did not have to question the legitimacy of its charge; rather his responsibility was to define the operational tasks which would allow him to carry out his responsibility toward meeting that regulatory agency's objectives. But in the process he clearly revealed a commitment to the SEC's general objective of serving capital markets and in particular the common investor through regulations.

And even after leaving his post he still holds that commitment. In his paper he states that while a free-market setting was sufficient at one time--presumably before 1933--economic incentives were changing in response to changes in the environment in such a way that innovation in reporting and disclosure gave way to developing means of protection against liabilities. This tended to encourage the status quo rather than change.

These are reflections on historical events which I assume can be backed up with facts. But like most accounting historians, Burton's reading of what was going on before 1933 reflects a tendency to refer to those events which support his position and to ignore those which do not. George Benston examined the testimony before Congress prior to the passage of the SEC Acts and found little empirical evidence presented in support of the abuses that were supposed to have existed with a free-market mechanism for accounting information.

To summarize so far, I regard the Kripke paper and portions of the Burton and the Elliott/Schuetze papers as attempts to deal with the general problem of whether the accounting information market should be regulated. While Kripke believes market forces can overcome whatever market failures might exist, the others are more equivocal about which approach provides the best solution to the problem. Since it is difficult (impossible?) to design an empirical study which can provide direct evidence on whether regulations or market arrangements would be more efficient, given a particular time frame, current economic institutions, and the like, we tend instead to rely on less direct evidence to guide our personal choices. For example, we have studies that attempt to ascertain whether the SEC Acts had any impact on the equilibrium prices of securities--the results are inconclusive to all except the respective authors of the studies. Somewhat related are attempts to measure the impact of particular regulations on the equilibrium prices of the individual firms affected by them, such as the economic consequences of the FASB's opinions on oil and gas accounting and foreign currency rate transactions. Finally, as in the Buchholz and Wallace papers, here we all attempt to measure direct costs and benefits of certain existing regulations.

## Private Versus Public Regulatory Agencies

The issue of whether information markets should be regulated by private or public agencies has received much attention in recent years but little formal analysis. The question goes back at least as far as the enactment of the SEC Acts.

The Security Acts not only imposed disclosures rules on firms but also seemed to provide authority to the commission to issue generally accepted accounting principles. The first commissioners, however, did not use this authority and tried instead to encourage accountants to accept responsibility for GAAP. This resulted in the first private agency on accounting methods, the Committee on Accounting Procedures, which issued its first bulletins in the late 1930s and continued to do so until it was replaced by the APB.

The CAP had no formal authority to impose its opinions on firms, so it tended to concentrate on issuing guidelines as to which accounting principle was desirable under certain assumed conditions. Apparently, accountants, managers and investors were content with this situation until the 1950s. For various reasons, which no one has successfully articulated, this state of affairs came under heavy criticism in the late 1950s and culminated in the replacement of the CAP by the APB. The APB had more authority to enforce its opinions on firms than did the CAP in the sense that auditors had to qualify their reports if firms' accounting methods deviated from any APB opinion. This authority was made more explicit when the FASB replaced the APB in the early 1970s, since it became difficult for firms to have their reports accepted by the SEC if their accounting methods deviated from any FASB or APB opinion (given ASR #150).

The issue today is whether the present situation should continue or whether the SEC should move to take over the FASB's role. Unlike its shaky existence in the 1930s, the SEC seems now to have sufficient congressional support to supersede the FASB. No doubt, members of the AICPA view their self interests better served by the FASB since they have a stronger representation with that board than with the commission. But academics need not be bound by the same self-interest, and it is not apparent to me that the FASB has a relative advantage over the commission in carrying out the goals of the SEC Acts.

If the goal of the FASB is to provide information to investors (the user-primacy viewpoint), it nonetheless is expected to consider various other competing interests in the process of issuing any particular accounting opinion. These interests include auditors, managers, investors, government agencies, and other suppliers and users of financial information. If these interests must be considered and balanced, why should we assume that a group of individuals (whose selection still is largely controlled by an accounting institution) is best suited to represent these competing interests? We could ask whether the FASB membership today is in fact representative enough of such interests to balance them capably in arriving at an opinion. But this raises yet other questions about the proper voting mechanisms to achieve such a representation on the board. If we carry the analysis far enough, we may be forced to conclude that an agency like the SEC is more likely to achieve these ends than the FASB.

Of course, the accounting profession is not the only one having a private regulatory agency which it attempts to maintain. The medical and the legal professions offer the same arguments in favor of private vs. public regulatory mechanisms. I would even guess that there are members of each group who believe the private-agency approach is effective in their own profession (e.g., accounting) but not so in another (such as medicine).

The papers by Elliott and Schuetze and by Burton address this issue. Elliott and Schuetze recognize that because there is insufficient evidence on the costs and benefits of regulation, there "will be limits on the precision of comparisons between public-private sector regulation." They go so far as to present some indirect evidence of their own, however, in their comparative analysis of the quality of accounting and auditing standards in the U.S. vis-à-vis 14 other countries. They classify the countries by whether they operate under private or public agency control over accounting and auditing standards. The results show the U.S. to have the highest quality of both sets of standards; yet the U.S. is a country which has a unique combination of private and public agency control, so their evidence is consistent with Burton's main theme.

Somewhat surprising, in light of his previous position, is that Burton does not argue in favor of a complete switch to a public agency approach to the regulation of accounting. Instead, he presents a case for the continued existence of both our private agency--the FASB--and our public agency--the SEC. The latter's primary function in the area of GAAP is to serve as an irritant which Burton feels moves the former closer toward society's goals. We certainly can agree that the SEC has been an irritant in the past, especially during the years of his position as chief accountant. But I do not accept the conclusion that the changes motivated by the activities of the SEC automatically moved us closer to society's goals. A good illustration here is the replacement cost ruling. A considerable amount of society's resources was consumed in initial attempts to determine what estimates of replacement costs would be acceptable to the SEC. After a period of naiveté the SEC finally came around to the position that estimates based upon specific price indices were just as reliable as estimates based upon the more expensive direct method of estimation. It is interesting that the FASB's exposure draft of the impact of price level changes goes further by allowing firms to use either general or specific price indices. The former is about the cheapest method of price level accounting which a firm could employ. This suggests that accountants still are not convinced that replacement cost estimates are superior to general price level adjustments. In fact, I know of no empirical study that has yet demonstrated any usefulness either of the SEC's disclosures of replacement costs by firms or of GPLA adjustments.

The point is that very little is available to us either in the way of formal proofs or empirical evidence which could justify our present two-way system, or lead us to choose public over private regulatory agencies or vice versa. The arguments usually are presented within the context of the accounting profession, whereas the problem may require a much more general approach.

## Costs and Benefits of Specific Regulations

The last two papers I will refer to involve attempts to measure the costs and benefits of specific regulations. In one, Buchholz provides an estimate of the total costs incurred by a firm in complying with all of the government regulations imposed upon it. In addition to the problems involved in measuring (relating) incurred costs to compliance with regulations, which have been discussed already, there is the more general issue of what definition(s) of costs should be adopted in such studies.

Buchholz attempted to measure the out-of-pocket costs incurred in compliance and then reported these in terms of categories of regulations. Unfortunately, we were given only absolute amounts rather than some relative measures of significance. In an earlier version of his paper, Buchholz reported compliance costs as percentages of sales and income. My initial impression then was that the percentages of costs incurred by his case-study firm were rather insignificant in a relative sense. But that may be due in part to the fact that out-of-pocket costs are not reflective of the total costs of compliance. A large portion of the costs incurred may be opportunity costs a firm faces because of decisions forced by reporting requirements. The spirit behind government reporting regulations supposedly is that such decisions will have a positive benefit to society. But do they? Consider the area of illegal corporate payments. There are significant opportunity costs incurred by firms which no longer are able to compete by making payments which are legal in some jurisdictions but not in the U.S. Various types of decision effects of regulations may constitute a more fruitful focus of cost-benefit analysis than the out-of-pocket costs of compliance.

Somewhat related is the possibility that in accumulating data for government agencies, firms suddenly discover beneficial uses of that same data for their own decisions. The value of these internal uses of government-demanded data should be netted out against the costs of compliance, although I wonder to what extent such measures are feasible.

In the final paper, Wallace attempted to measure the impact of required municipal audits on the interest costs incurred by municipalities. The discussants provided specific comments useful in evaluating her study, so I need not repeat their remarks. What I would like to consider instead is the general problem encountered with this and similar attempts to measure the benefits, if any, of disclosure and measurement rules in accounting.

Most attempts to assess the impact of accounting regulations have involved an assessment of the effect of such rules on the prices of firms' securities. Because of data problems, Wallace had to work with a surrogate measure of price effects, namely changes in interest costs which could be associated with the imposition of the rule (i.e., changes in interest costs would be reflected in changes in prices of bonds if these were observable). Regardless of the price measure used, the fundamental problem encountered in these studies is simply that it is difficult to develop formally theories about what relationship should exist between an accounting or auditing regulation and the equilibrium prices of securities. Instead what we often observe are ex post facto attempts to rationalize whatever results are obtained.

At a more general level, take first the case of imposed audits. What should we hypothesize about price effects if certain classes of firms suddenly are forced to incur the costs of private audits? In a study of mandatory audits of banks, several sources of hypotheses were reviewed. First, there was a theory about the benefits of auditing in general. Another was a theory of equilibrium which would explain why some firms and institutions voluntarily have audits and others do not. A third involved assumed relationships between explicit audits and substitute mechanisms for audits. It is well known that much "auditing" is performed on banks by bank examiners so that a full-fledged private audit might be superfluous. Finally, it was hypothesized that any association between required bank audits and changes in their equilibrium prices of securities would depend upon what decisions might be influenced by audits. That is, imposed audits might change future decisions--e.g., cease questionable investments--so that unexpected returns are observed.

Unfortunately the evidence presented in that study was consistent with several of these hypotheses, but sufficient data were not available to discriminate between them. This is a common problem, and it exists as well in the so-called information content studies wherein attempts are made to assess the effects of alternative accounting methods. A recent and well-published example is the controversy over accounting for oil and gas drilling costs. Given the nature of the accounting issue, the efficient market advocates might have predicted that whatever accounting rule was selected, there should not be any effect on equilibrium prices of firms' securities. Yet in three "information content" studies on the issue, the same general patterns of price effects were observed--negative unexpected returns for all firms but especially for the full-costing group. In each case, however, a different interpretation was offered, so policy makers actually could take their pick of any explanation that suited their biases. My impression now is simply that our methodology for assessing costs and benefits of regulations tends to exceed our ability to develop theories which can predict either their magnitude or their direction.

## Notes

[1]This section borrows from a coauthored paper: see N. Gonedes, N. Dopuch, and S. Penman, "Disclosure Rules, Information Production, and Capital Market Equilibrium," *Journal of Accounting Research* (Spring 1976).

[2]See Nicholas J. Gonedes and Nicholas Dopuch, "Capital Market Equilibrium, Information Production, and Selecting Accounting Techniques: Theoretical Framework and Review of Empirical Report," *Studies on Financial Accounting Objectives, 1974.* Supplement to *Journal of Accounting Research*, sections 2-5 and the references therein.

[3]For a comparative analysis of the approaches of the U.K. and the U.S. to this problem, see George Benston, "Public (U.S.) Compared to Private (U.K.) Regulation of Corporate Financial Disclosure," *The Accounting Review* (July 1976): 483-98.